# It's Only a Movie

Outspoken, opinionated, and never lost for words, Mark Kermode has carved out a career in print, radio and television based entirely on the belief that *The Exorcist* is the greatest movie ever made, and that the *Pirates of the Caribbean* films should be buried in a very deep hole where they can never bother anyone ever again.

# It's Only a Movie

A Cinematic Autobiography
'Inspired by Real Events'

Mark Kermode

Published by Random House Books 2010
6 8 10 9 7 5



This book is substantially a work of non-fiction based on the life, experiences and recollections of the author. In some limited cases, names of people, places, dates, sequences or the detail of events have been changed solely to protect the privacy of others. The author has stated to the publishers that, except in such minor respects, the contents of this book are true.



First published in Great Britain in 2010 by
Random House Books
Random House, 20 Vauxhall Bridge Road,
London SW1V 2SA

www.rbooks.co.uk

Addresses for companies within The Random House Group Limited can be found at:
www.randomhouse.co.uk/offices.htm

The Random House Group Limited Reg. No. 954009

A CIP catalogue record for this book
is available from the British Library

ISBN 9781847946027

The Random House Group Limited supports The Forest Stewardship Council (FSC), the leading international forest certification organisation. All our titles that are printed on Greenpeace approved FSC certified paper carry the FSC logo. Our paper procurement policy can be found at www.rbooks.co.uk/environment

Roger Ebert's review of *Blue Velvet*, which is mentioned on pp.85-6, first appeared in the *Chicago Sun Times* on 19 September 1986

Designed and typeset by
Darren Bennett

Printed and bound in Great Britain by
CPI Mackays, Chatham ME5 8TD

# Contents

'Oh I used to be disgusted, now I try to be amused ...'

Elvis Costello,
'(The Angels Wanna Wear My) Red Shoes'

This book is
dedicated to the memory of
Arnold P. Hinchliffe
and Perry Keenlyside

# PROLOGUE

We were somewhere near Lookout Mountain, on the outskirts of LA, when Werner Herzog's trousers exploded.

It was a small explosion, admittedly, as if a firecracker had gone off in his pocket. But it was an explosion nonetheless, and in an area where unexpected bangs are to be treated with suspicion, if not outright alarm.

Herzog had been shot – that much was clear – and was even now bleeding quietly into his boxer shorts as a tiny plume of smoke drifted photogenically from his pelvic region and into the evening air of LA. And as we stood there, the bold Bavarian with a bullet in his groin and the befuddled British film critic with ridiculous hair from Barnet, I wondered exactly the same thing that anyone else would have wondered in similar circumstances …

'If this were a TV Movie of the Week, who would play me?'

I'd like the answer to be Richard Gere, although physically the front-runner is clearly Jesse Birdsall, on whose behalf

I have been merrily accepting compliments about my sterling work in 'that Spanish soap series' for years. Apparently Birdsall and I are all but physically indistinguishable to the public at large, and I've simply given up trying to tell people that I'm not him (I've even signed autographs 'with best wishes from Jesse' to those who won't take no for an answer). Sometimes I wonder whether this is a two-way street, and whether Mr Birdsall has ever been thumped for writing a rotten review of *Blue Velvet* or punched on the arm for dubbing Keira Knightley 'Ikea Knightley' in honour of her on-screen teakiness. If so, I apologise. And Jesse, if you're reading this, everyone really *loved* you in *Eldorado* and there's a genuine sense of outrage out there that the series was cancelled. Believe me, I know – I've experienced the love first-hand.

But looks aren't everything (did 'Sir' Anthony Hopkins look anything like Nixon? Was Kevin Spacey a dead ringer for Bobby Darin?) and since we're in the realms of fantasy here I think I should get to choose whoever I like to play me.

And I choose Jason Isaacs.

Hello to Jason Isaacs.

In case you don't know (in which case shame on you) Jason Isaacs is just about my favourite actor in the whole gosh-darned world. He's done everything from gritty TV dramas to rom-coms, war flicks, fantasy films and sci-fi blockbusters. To some of you he'll be best known as the fiendish Lucius Malfoy from the Harry Potter films, but to me he is (in the words of David Bowie) chameleon, comedian, Corinthian and caricature.

More importantly, he is also the person whom I most wanted to be as a child. You see, Jason and I were at school together, in the same class, although we never really spoke or even acknowledged each other's existence. I thought he was incredibly cool and aloof, being one of the first people at school to own a skateboard (a Fibreflex with Gullwing trucks and lime green Kryptonic wheels) and the very first to swear out loud in an English class ('Who made the bloody sandwiches?'). But it turns out that the real reason Jason never spoke to anyone was that he was just like me: isolated and alone, insecure and essentially out of place – albeit infinitely more handsome. If truth be told I think I had a sort of schoolboy crush on Jason Isaacs, and I've never really got over it. And if I get to choose who plays me in the movie of my life, then it's Jason all the way – he knows the background, he's done the research, and he would look really good with a quiff.

So, the lead role in *The Mark Kermode Story* (we'll need to come up with a better title – *Easy Writer* perhaps, or *The Man Who Watched The Man Who Shot Liberty Valance*) goes to Jason, with John Malkovich co-starring as Werner Herzog (same shaped head and hair, and I'm pretty sure Malkovich could 'do' Bavarian). Then, in the other assorted supporting roles I'll have Toby Jones as David Lynch (I've heard his impression, and it's really quite unusual), Samantha Morton as Linda Blair (because she's tough and smart and great in pretty much everything) and David Morrissey as Noddy Holder (he's got stature, plus he had good sideburns in *Stoned*, plus *plus* he was really funny in *Basic Instinct 2* for which I retain a foolish fondness). The role of my long-suffering partner in crime Linda Ruth Williams will be filled by four-time Academy Award nominee Julianne Moore who will have to work pretty damned hard to look unimpressed by all the zany scrapes into which Mr Isaacs will get himself. The Queen will play Dame Helen Mirren, obviously; Charles Hawtrey will play radio's very own Simon Mayo (his choice, not mine); Ian Hislop will play my great friend Nigel Floyd (not physically similar, but a perfect match in attitude and mannerisms); and Ken Russell will play himself (I've already asked him and he's said yes, as long as it's only in my head). Finally, Udo Kier will essay the key role of mad Ukrainian chauffeur 'Mr Nyet', having been cast entirely on the strength of that scene in *Flesh for Frankenstein* wherein he pulls the pulsating innards from a cadaver's chest, holds them out toward the audience (in 3-D!) and utters my favourite line from a movie ever: 'To know death, Otto, you have to fuck life ... *in ze gall bladder*!'

That's my dream cast. I know it sounds starry (getting Her Maj involved might prove tricky, particularly as I am a declared republican) but these days *everyone* is doing TV Movies of the Week. They've become completely respectable, as has the phrase with which they invariably open: 'inspired by real events'.

I *love* that phrase. 'Inspired by real events'. As opposed to what, exactly? 'Uninspired by real events'? Or 'inspired by *unreal* events'? Both seem equally applicable in my case, and both are on a philosophical par with Woody Allen's timeless maxim that 'Life doesn't imitate art, it imitates bad television'.

A key piece of 'bad television' which hangs like a cloud over this memoir is *The Karen Carpenter Story*, a spectacular piece of reductionist hackery in which the heroine's dawning anorexia is flagged up by a creeping close-up on leading lady Cynthia Gibb's face as she reads a review in *Billboard* magazine containing the phrase 'chubby sister'. One evening, several years ago, I found myself in a West End pub with the journalist and writer Jon Ronson, and after several pints of the old Johnny-Knock-Me-Down our conversation turned to that wince-inducing moment in *The Karen Carpenter Story*. Crucially, Jon had slightly misremembered the scene (another key element of this book will be misremembered movies) and in his mind, Cynthia/Karen had looked up from the paper and said perplexedly to herself: 'Chubby? Hmmm …'.

In the drunken haze that followed, Jon and I agreed to make a TV programme entitled *Chubby? Hmmm …* which would bring together all those terrible moments in 'real life' movies in which the famous subjects are seen doing *for the first time* the thing for which they would ultimately become famous – scenes like Kyle MacLachlan pretending to dream up the keyboard line from 'Light My Fire' in Oliver Stone's *The Doors* (tag line: 'No one Here Gets Out Awake') or that bit in *The Buddy Holly Story* where the boys realise that 'If you knew Cindy Lou …' didn't sound quite right.

Jon and I never made the programme, but the phrase 'Chubby? Hmmm …' has stayed with me ever since, and has become shorthand for all that is deeply rubbish about stories which purport to be 'inspired by real events'.

This book, which has about as much relationship to the 'truth' as *The Karen Carpenter Story*, is packed with 'Chubby? Hmmm …' moments, and I invite you now to shake your head, roll your eyes, and bang your fists against your head in horror whenever they arise. But arise they will, because that's the nature of the beast, and if it was good enough for Karen Carpenter and Buddy Holly, then frankly it's good enough for me.

What you're going to get in the following pages is a version of my life which has been written and directed by me, and on which I have acted as editor, cinematographer, consultant, composer and executive producer. The last few titles in that list are particularly important because they are the roles with which Richard Carpenter was credited on *The Karen Carpenter Story* but that still didn't stop him from reportedly disowning the movie several years later, claiming that several key scenes were bunkum, and declaring that he regretted being involved with the whole venture in the first place. I may well do the same thing – not because what I'm about to tell you is a bunch of lies (although it may be just that) but because my version of 'reality' has been so skewed by the conventions of narrative cinema that I am honestly unable to tell which part of any particular story I am telling is 'true' and which part is expedient invention cooked up to get the damn movie to *work*. In the vernacular of screenwriters, my life story is absolutely *full* of pink pages and it's impossible to tell the original script from all the rewrites and reshoots.

It doesn't help that I also have a shockingly bad memory, am given to exaggeration (if not outright fabrication), and generally regard almost everything as 'only a movie'. You know that scene in the docudrama *United 93* when someone has to explain to air traffic control that the inconceivable scenario unfolding before them is happening in the 'real world' rather than in some parallel fantasy universe? Well, that's how I feel most of the time.

Worse still, I have a tin ear for dialogue. I have often criticised Quentin Tarantino for being utterly unable to get inside the head of any character other than himself, with the result that *everyone* in a Tarantino film speaks like Quentin bloody Tarantino. Doesn't matter whether they're old or young, male or female, black or white, human or alien – *all* his characters sound like that nerdy guy from the independent video store down the street whose insights are entertaining for the first few weeks, but whose persistent yabbering finally sends you scurrying off to the anonymous ignorance of Blockbuster. The sole exception to this rule is *Jackie Brown*, the one Tarantino movie which is based on a literary source (Elmore Leonard's *Rum Punch*) whose writer seems to have *listened* to voices other than his own, and who thinks that a woman is more than just a guy without a dick. Significantly, *Jackie Brown* was a comparative box-office flop and its financial failure sent Quentin scurrying back to the infantile fan-boy claptrap of *Kill Bill* and its ilk. More's the pity.

Like all critics, however, I habitually slag others off for failing to do things which I clearly could not do myself. In the case of Quentin's solipsistic dialogue I am a worse offender than he has ever been, and you will notice that *everyone* in this book not only talks like me but, more often than not, like someone doing a *very bad impression of me*. I apologise for this in advance – particularly if you are one of the 'real' people into whose (fictional) mouths I have placed my second-rate B-movie dialogue. Please be assured that if it were in my power to make you sound more like *you* I would have done so.

But it isn't.

And I can't.

So I haven't.

Sorry.

And while we're in self-deprecating mode, let me take this opportunity to make it quite clear to *any* film-maker whose work I have criticised that no, I couldn't make a film, not even if my life depended on it. To twist the words of F. Scott Fitzgerald (something else I do quite a lot in this book) film-makers are different from you and me and, let's be honest, they do something that you or I could never *dream* of doing. Despite my reputation for lambasting movies with a passion which borders upon psychosis I remain genuinely *stunned* that anyone can ever get a film – *any film* – made at all. I've been on movie sets where I've witnessed the corpulent chaos of film-making first-hand and the sheer logistics of making sure everything doesn't go belly up on day one are mind-boggling. Someone once said that a movie in production is like a ship teetering on the brink of mutiny, and once the ship has set sail the director's job is not to conjure a groundbreaking work of art but simply to bring the whole thing safely into dock without the loss of a) lives and b) more importantly, *money*.

I remember novelist-turned-director Clive Barker describing his first day filming the ripping British horror movie *Hellraiser*, walking out on to the set to find everyone waiting for instructions on how to proceed. 'OK,' said Clive to the assembled masses, 'so … what do we do now?' At which point, he realised that he was the only person in the room who was *not* allowed to ask that question.

And it's not just Barker who has encountered such moments. Apparently Orson Welles' first day directing *Citizen Kane* was a disaster because the stage and radio graduate simply had *no* idea about the 'rules' of moviemaking. According to popular mythology, after a morning of fudging and fumbling, Welles was taken aside by battle-hardened cinematographer Gregg Toland who offered to explain to him how moviemaking worked. This he did by showing him a print of John Ford's die-hard Western *Stagecoach*, which he used to demonstrate such elementary principles as 'not crossing the line'; the cavalry are attacking from the left, therefore the Indians enter from the *right*, and so on. The next day Welles went back to work on the film that would effectively redefine the semantics of modern movie grammar, breaking rules as he saw fit (as, indeed, had Ford) to create what some consider to be the greatest movie ever made. But in order to *break* those rules, he first had to *learn them*, which he did with preternatural dexterity.

If Toland had explained those rules to you or me, and *we* had attempted to break them, *we* would have made *Howard the Duck*.

Like I said, film-makers are not like you and me.

Unless you *are* a film-maker.

In which case they are. Obviously.

So, to recap, what you're about to get is in effect the literary equivalent of *The Karen Carpenter Story*, as written by Quentin Tarantino's thick-eared sibling, and directed by a film critic who, by his own admission, wouldn't know how to direct traffic. It is 'inspired by real events' and therefore essentially untrue from start to finish. It is also executive-produced by its own subject, and in the manner of all 'authorised' biopics will also be self-serving, hagiographic, and deeply narcissistic.

How's that for a poster quote?

So, ladies and gentlemen, it remains only for me to remind you to switch of your mobile phones, take your knees out of the back of my chair, stop eating any noisy food, and basically shut the Sam Hill up as we dim the lights for …

'Our Feature Presentation'

# Chapter 1

## 'COME AWAY, OH HUMAN CHILD ...'

In my younger and more vulnerable years my father gave me some advice that I've been studiously ignoring ever since.

'Learn to speak properly,' he told me, 'and stop watching all those films.'

Having made a profession out of speaking improperly about films, I imagine that I must be a great disappointment to him. But hey, at least I didn't become a transvestite pop star which I frequently (and, it transpired, hollowly) threatened to do, so there was some cause for paternal rejoicing after all.

As early as I can remember, my life was defined by movies. I recall my childhood not as a succession of birthday parties, bruised knees and short-trousered playground scuffles but as a glorious parade of films – their posters, trailers and certificates; where I saw them; who I saw them with (usually no one); even which seat I was sitting in and how good the view was.

This last point is particularly important. From childhood to dotage I have always needed to see every *inch* of the screen and cannot bear even the smallest obscuring of the picture by heads, curtains or inadequately maintained projection lenses. When I see a movie, now matter how rotten it may be, I want to see it *the way it was meant to look* without interruptions, visual or aural, and on this issue I know no moderation. So, for example, if you ask me about *Silent Running*, which is probably my favourite sci-fi movie of all time, I can tell you that I first saw it in June 1972 in London's Baker Street with my school friend Mark Furst whose father (a famous conductor) took us for a treat on a Wednesday night. On arrival at the cinema, Mark and I surveyed the poster (of which I now own several signed copies) depicting Bruce Dern and a Drone robot planting a flower in an outer-space geodesic dome. We gawped at the poster, grinned at each other with glee, and did that early seventies playground hand-slap that was the forerunner of the now corporately institutionalised 'high five'. Inside, we sat on the left-hand side of the auditorium, about ten rows from the front with me on the aisle seat (another early obsession – I don't do 'trapped' seating) yet despite the vast Cinerama-style curved screen my view of the picture was troubled by the unreasonably big hair of the wide-lapelled gentleman in front of me. This would not do, and I had to lean right out into the aisle to remove the Mungo Jerry lookalike's presence from my line of sight – a position I remember maintaining for the duration of the movie. Now, whenever I think about *Silent Running* (which is quite often), I get a tweaking sensation in the back of my neck, as if my body were physically remembering the circumstances of seeing the film for the first time.

For the record, the supporting feature on the programme that night was a documentary about stuntmen which started with a ground-level shot of a man and woman running along some tarmac with fudgy greenery in the foreground which moved in and out of focus in that now nostalgic zoom lens fashion. I remember this *exactly* because it was during this shot that I did the physical maths to figure out *just* how far I had to lean in order to avoid Mr Jerry and his hair without falling out of the chair.

Oh, and the movie was really great, and made me cry.

Part of its tear-jerking charm was an unabashed and thoroughly unfashionable sentimentality, heightened by Peter Schickele's glistening score and a couple of heartbreakingly hippy-dippy future-folk songs earnestly warbled by Joan Baez. Decades later, I had the bewildering experience of sharing a small BBC studio with Joan Baez, who popped up on Radio Four's long-running arts programme *Kaleidoscope* in the mid-nineties to perform a couple of feather-throated acoustic numbers. I had arrived late to review some utterly forgettable film and, having no idea that Ms Baez would be there, was left in speechless palpitations by her radiant presence. As a teenager, I'd spent a *vast* amount of money ordering a Japanese import soundtrack album of *Silent Running*, the much-loved vinyl of which I had polished and treasured like a religious relic. And now here she was, in the *flesh* – the lungs, the lips, the larynx which had given birth to

'Rejoice in the Sun', the voice of God singing to me through the celluloid.

While we were on-air I struggled to contain my excitement, but the minute the show was finished and microphones were closed I virtually threw myself at her feet, to her astonishment and alarm.

'I'm really sorry, Ms Baez,' I blurted pathetically, 'but I just *have* to tell you that I absolutely love love love love *love* … *Silent Running*.'

She looked at me, blankly.

'Silent *what?*'

'Silent *Running*. You know … *Silent Running*. The seventies sci-fi film. Bruce Dern and the walking dustbins. Geodesic domes. Eco-warriors in space. '

A hint of recognition flitted briefly across her face.

'And *you*,' I continued. '*You* doing the theme song. You know, "Fields of children running wild, in the sun, tra la la la". Obviously it sounds stupid when I do it, but when *you* did it, it was *wonderful* …'

She screwed up her face a bit, and raised her eyebrows.

'Yeah,' she said, uncertainly. 'Yeah. I remember it. I think. *Silent Running*? Yeah, I got it …'

'Oh thank heavens … I was starting to think I was going mad.'

She paused.

'I remember the *song*,' she mused. 'Never saw the film.' She gave me a breezy smile. 'Any good?'

Such is the nature of songs and cinema; it's the ones you forget that everyone else remembers – and vice versa.

And, like Linda Blair in *Exorcist II: The Heretic*, I remember *everything* – or at least, I *think* I remember it ...

Let me explain.

It has often been argued that cinema has such a profound effect upon the viewer because it substantially mirrors the function of memory. When we look at the world we allegedly observe a linear narrative assembled with invisible old-fashioned Hollywood continuity editing rather than *nouvelle vague* European fast-forwards, flashbacks and jump cuts from one scene to the next. We are literally stuck in the moment, watching the uncut rushes, as it were, with life unspooling before us in real/reel time.

If this is indeed the case (and Buddhists who aspire to 'living in the now' would insist that it most definitely *is not*) we should be surprised that the montage of moving images which cinema has been serving up for over a century is not more baffling – a time-and-space-travelling mosaic in which our POV flits from one place and time to the next in an instant. Why does edited film, with its increasingly kinetic barrage of cubist visual information, seem so natural, so ordinary, so familiar? Billy Pilgrim, the hero of Kurt Vonnegut's novel *Slaughterhouse 5*, may have become famously 'unstuck in time' but the rest of us have no such luck. In our day jobs we are neither Time Lords nor gods blessed with omniscient all-seeing eyes. So how come we 'get' cinema at all?

One answer is that the Buddhists were right all along, and 'living in the now' actually takes several lifetimes of practice. Another (related) explanation may be that the act of watching movies somehow replicates the peculiar card-shuffling experience of memory – that we *remember* events in a manner strikingly similar to the way a movie constructs a story on celluloid. It's as if our memory was some kind of Freudian auteur, and each of us has their own jodhpur-clad Erich von Stroheim striding around in their frontal lobes, conjuring widescreen epics from the raw footage of our day-to-day experience. When we remember things, or when we *dream* about them, we are in effect sitting in our own private screening room, watching an egotistical director's cut of life as only we have known and lived it. As David Lynch tells us in *Twin Peaks: Fire Walk With Me*, 'We live inside a dream'. And we dream inside a movie.

This may sound like hooey to you (go talk to the Buddhists and see if they can do any better) but it makes perfect sense to *me* and since I am to all intents and purposes the auteur of this book and the director of this 'real life' Movie of the Week, you'd better get used to it. There'll be no test screenings nor audience feedback cards from here on in, OK? This is *my* movie and I get final cut – like Michael Cimino on *Heaven's Gate*, only with more jokes and less roller-skating. And in *my* film, memories and movies are all but indistinguishable. So when I say that something actually *happened*, it may well be that it only happened in the rancid, popcorn-filled drive-in cinema that is my head. But that doesn't mean it isn't 'real' – merely that, to me, it is *all* 'only a movie'.

The problem, as I have discovered, is that movies, like memories, are malleable and frequently exist in several different cuts. Just as Francis Ford Coppola can't stop fiddling with *Apocalypse Now* or Oliver Stone can always find another few hours of footage to jam into *JFK* we all seem to treat our personal back catalogue as a work in progress, to be restructured willy-nilly for each new performance. In my case, the situation is worsened by the fact that I appear to have a rogue editor running wild in my subconscious, randomly splicing scenes from one film into another with peculiarly anarchic results.

Let me give you an example.

When I was eleven, I saw a trailer for *Battle for the Planet of the Apes*, the last in the ongoing simian saga which would come to play an unhealthily large part in my psychological development. Indeed, I would argue that the seeds of the adolescent Marxist/Leninist leanings which I displayed in the mid-eighties were actually sown in the early seventies during a double bill of *Beneath the Planet of the Apes* and *Conquest of the Planet of the Apes* at the ABC Turnpike Lane. To the casual viewer, these films may seem to be dopey anthropomorphic fantasies with men in monkey-masks doing a sort of grown-up version of those PG Tips tea commercials in which chimpanzees in bowler hats attempt to move a piano up a flight of stairs ('Dad, do you know the piano's on my foot?' 'You hum it, son, I'll play it. Ha ha ha ha!'). Yet to the cognoscenti they are astutely sketched political parables, with *Beneath* offering a stern lecture upon the nuclear madness of 'Mutually Assured Destruction' (mutant humans worshipping the 'Father, Son and Holy Bomb') and *Conquest* littering its city-burning Spartacist rebellion with Black Power salutes and bold proto-leftie rights-for-all rhetoric.

Nowadays, I could pretty much recite the plots of all five *Apes* movies (plus the flawed 2001 Tim Burton 'update') and most of the spin-off TV show episodes at a moment's notice (don't push me, because I *will*). But back in 1974 I had never seen an *Apes* film, and I was utterly transfixed and baffled by the trailer for *Battle*. Two things I remember very clearly – the first was imploring my mum to take me to the Hendon Odeon to see *Battle* on a scorching hot summer's afternoon which she insisted would be much better spent at the lido in East Finchley. Regrettably, the film's A certificate required the accompaniment of a parent so there was no chance of her dropping me off at the cinema while taking my sister and brother for a refreshing dip. If I was going to the cinema, we were all going to the cinema – which (it was 'unanimously' decided) we *weren't*.

The second thing I remember with crystal clarity is a scene from that trailer in which a female ape, played by Kim Hunter under a mountain of prosthetic appliances, stared sadly into the middle distance and said with great poignancy, 'The poor man … he *tries* to love me.' This scene, with its strange transgenic longing, made a particularly strong impression on my prepubescent psyche, and even today I can hear that line delivered with a conviction which would shame Meryl Streep.

Imagine my disappointment therefore when, in the full flush of teenage independence, I finally got to see *Battle for the Planet of the Apes* on a rerun double bill at the Barnet Odeon and discovered that that scene *wasn't in it*. For a while I assumed that (as so often happens) it was an early out-take which had been used for publicity purposes but had hit the floor during the final editing of the film. A shame, but there you go. Yet I struggled to imagine *where* such a scene could have fitted into the film which I saw, and which contained precious little trace of the charged romantic entanglements implied in that trailer which I remembered so well.

Several years later, I found myself watching Bob Fosse's *Cabaret* and was shocked to hear Liza Minnelli deliver the line 'The poor man ... he *tries* to love me' in *exactly* the same manner as Kim Hunter, only with far less facial hair, obviously. I was utterly befuddled; what the hell was an out-take line from *Battle for the Planet of the Apes* doing being quoted in an Oscar-winning musical about naughty Nazis in the thirties?

The answer, of course, was that had I seen trailers for *Cabaret* and *Battle* back to back and my over-fried imagination had somehow spliced them together to create its very own mental movie mash-up in which a talkative ape spoke with the voice of Sally Bowles. The scene never existed in the 'real' world, but in the movie house of my memory it was playing five times a day to a packed house of me.

I am not alone in this kind of confusion. As recently as 2008 I managed to persuade Bill Forsyth (director of *Local Hero*, my second- or third-favourite movie of all time) to accompany me to Pennan, the tiny Scottish village where he had shot much of his magical, melancholy masterpiece. Forsyth is famously reticent about watching his own movies

(Woody Allen described the experience as being like a chef eating one of his own meals and tasting only 'too much basil') and generally spurns any opportunity to be nostalgic about his back catalogue. But after much cajoling he agreed to come to Pennan to film an item for BBC2's *The Culture Show* about the reopening of the village hall which had been destroyed by a mudslide during particularly harsh rainfall. The idea was that we would gather together people who remembered the production of *Local Hero*, and we'd put on a gala screening of the movie with Forsyth in attendance. The ceilidh band who appeared in the movie, the Acetones, also agreed to play a few tunes, and I insisted on being allowed to murder Mark Knopfler's haunting 'Theme from *Local Hero*' on bagpipes on the beach as the sun went down – an idea which was initially resisted for reasons which I never fully understood ...

Anyway, somehow the whole event came together and culminated in a dream-come-true evening in which I sat at the back of a packed hall in Pennan and watched the strange wonderment of *Local Hero* unfold with an increasingly emotional Forsyth by my side. Despite having watched it fifty or sixty times the movie never fails to move me, and as it played out on that starry autumn night I was once again enraptured by its dark and timeless spell. Some people think of it as charming, heart-warming fare but there's something much more moody and subversive which causes it to break my heart – a quality which Forsyth perfectly encapsulated when he described *Local Hero* as 'a cross between *Brigadoon* and *Apocalypse Now*'.

But as we sat there, with me wondering whether life could actually get any better than this, Bill suddenly leaned across and whispered in a not very sotto voce: 'This *isn't* the movie.'

'What?' I replied, baffled.

'This *isn't* the movie,' he said again. 'This is some TV version of the movie.'

I didn't understand what he meant. I looked up at the screen, wondering whether it was being projected in the wrong ratio (square, rather than oblong) but no; there was *Local Hero* in all its rectangular cinematic glory.

'What do you mean it's "some TV version"?' I asked.

'Well, there's loads of stuff *missing*,' said Bill.

'Stuff missing? What stuff?'

'Well like just then, when they stopped the car because it was too foggy to drive. There's a whole conversation that's been cut out – an entire scene.'

I thought about this for a moment. I'd been watching the movie very closely and I was pretty damn sure we hadn't skipped even a single word. Yet Bill was flustered, sure that something was wrong.

'Which scene do you mean?' I asked, adding gently that, 'I haven't noticed any cuts.'

Bill took a deep breath, as if readying himself to enact the missing scene right there and then.

Then he stopped. Deflated. Wrong-footed. Unsure.

'I think,' he said, as much to himself as to me, 'that I'm remembering the *script* rather than the film.'

He turned and smiled at me.

'I *think*,' he went on, 'that I cut the scene out myself. In the editing. I can't quite remember. I thought I'd left it in. But it was so long ago, and now I'm not sure.'

'Well I've seen this film *loads of times*,' I assured him, 'and honestly, what's up there on the screen is the film that's been out there in the world for the past twenty-five years.'

'Ahh yes,' said Bill sagely. '"The film that's been out there in the world." I'm not so familiar with that. I just know the film that's been inside my head.'

Exactly!

I wanted to hug him.

But I resisted, and sat quietly in my seat, dreaming of the film inside Bill Forsyth's head …

The film that has been playing inside *my* head for the last forty years is *Krakatoa: East of Java*, an old-fashioned action spectacular from 1969 which boasted *Thunderbirds*-style special effects, later enhanced by the stomach-rumbling power of 'Feelarama'. Today the film is perhaps best known for its geographically challenged title, for (as any fule kno) Krakatoa is actually due *west* of Java – duh! But for me, *Krakatoa: East of Java* retains a special place in my heart for containing the first scene I can actually *remember* seeing in a movie house – the Crescent, Douglas, Isle of Man. Oh, I *know* there was lots of stuff with ships and air balloons and exploding volcanoes – largely because most of those crowd-pleasing highlights were depicted on the poster, and very probably in the trailers. But I can't remember *watching* them – only being aware that I had seen them after the fact, and in the abstract.

Strangely, the only scene that I *can* actually remember

watching – that I can replay in what *Tropic Thunder*'s 'Simple Jack' calls 'mah head movies' – is a sequence which appears to have nothing to do with fiery mountains or thundering ships, the very elements which would doubtless have appealed to an enthralled six-year-old boy making an early foray into a picture palace.

Steven Spielberg once told me that he was crushingly disappointed when taken to see the movie *The Greatest Show on Earth* as a kid to discover that, despite the posters, it wasn't a 'real' circus at all – merely an image projected on to a flat screen behind a tatty velveteen curtain. Yet when that curtain drew back, and giant phantasmagorial moving pictures started dancing before his eyes, he was transfixed, not least by the spectacular train wreck which was the movie's hi-tech action highlight. I'm pretty certain that my reaction to *Krakatoa* would have been identical, but while Spielberg can still describe in detail the delicious terror of watching that train roll and plunge toward metal-grinding catastrophe, I can summon no such recollections of witnessing molten lava spew forth from a volcano while airships dangled perilously in mid-air. In fact, if you wait there a moment, I'll just pop over to YouTube, where someone has almost certainly uploaded the most memorable moments of *Krakatoa* (illegal, but useful) and see if they ring any bells. Won't be a moment ...

Righto, I'm back. You still there? Good. Sorry to have kept you waiting but it was worth it because, as I suspected, *all* the key scenes were indeed there (volcanoes, boats, waves, etc.) along with a trailer which reprised the most action-packed moments and I honestly can't remember seeing *any* of them before.

What I *do* remember, with the certainty of Noah deciding that umbrella stocks were going *up*, is this: a wounded, handsome man, is lying in his sickbed, unable to move (I think his leg has been damaged) but with his cavalier spirit clearly intact. In my mind he has a moustache, but that may well be wishful thinking; I have never been able to grow proper facial hair, and am therefore unreasonably impressed by anyone who can.

Anyway, the man is somehow incapacitated and is being tended to by a woman in a russet dress with reddish hair piled high upon her head. There is some kind of repressed playful tension between these two characters: he is roguish; she is demure; they are discreetly flirty. At some point she turns to walk away from him, moving from screen left to right, his head being at the far left of the picture, the camera at a low angle from the side of his bed. As she moves away, he reaches and slyly catches hold of the end of a piece of stringy lace which criss-crosses the back of her dress like a corset. She walks a couple of paces until the lace pulls tight, and then she turns to look back at him, with a knowing expression on her face. And then …

And then?

Who knows?

Does pulling the piece of lace (or string) make the dress fall off? I think not, certainly not in a U-certificate feature which had been passed as fun for all the family. In fact, surely pulling the lace would merely make it *more* secure, so that the woman's clothing would become even more impregnable than before? The scene could hardly be described as 'racy', even by the comparatively prudish standards of 1969. And yet it sticks in my mind in a manner which is so clearly primal and protean that I am almost embarrassed to have to write it down like this. I'm certain that anyone with a GCSE pass in elementary psychoanalysis could write a long and lurid essay on the significance of that moment in the evolution of my personality, doubtless concluding that I have grown into an S&M fetishist with a weakness for restraining straps and a side order of cross-dressing to go. But what's *more* significant than any evidence of traumatic erotic displacement is the fact that I'm not even certain that this scene was in the film at all. Like that whole Kim Hunter/Liza Minnelli mix-up, I may well be dealing cards from the bottom of my mental deck, merrily shuffling scenes from one film into another and then preserving them forever in the aspic of my unreliable memory. As I mentioned earlier, there's a psychotic editor on the loose in my head, creating their very own *Cinema Paradiso* – or, in my case, *Cinema Inferno*.

There's only one way to sift the fact from the fiction: I'm going to have to sit down and watch *Krakatoa: East of Java* again, for only the second time in forty years.

But not right now.

For now, let's move on to the other key moments of

merry hell which constitute my earliest movie-going memories.

When I was a child, film programmes changed not on Fridays (as is now the case) but on Sundays, which meant that even in a one-screen cinema it was possible to see two different films on a weekend – four, if you counted the supporting features. Growing up in Finchley Central, North London, I was in striking distance of several cinemas which represented the different distribution chains dominating the market in the early seventies. First and foremost there were the Odeons, two of which (Hendon and Temple Fortune) I could walk or cycle to within an hour. I could also catch a number 26 bus to both, but to do so would wipe out the pocket money which I was holding back for sweets, so I tended to go for the self-steam option. Further afield there were the ABC and Ionic cinemas in Golders Green, the Classic in Hendon (which oddly was nowhere near the Hendon Odeon), the Gaumont in North Finchley, and the Everyman in Hampstead. And then, of course, there was the Rex, latterly reborn as the Phoenix East Finchley, which remains the single most significant cinema in my development as a bona fide cinema obsessive. In moments of weakness I dream of dying and having my ashes scattered down the left-hand aisle of the Phoenix, marking the pathway from the door to the seat where I would sit religiously (ten rows from the front, aisle only, thank you very much) watching the late-night double bills which first introduced me to the work of David Lynch, David Cronenberg, George A. Romero, John Waters, Alejandro Jodorowsky, Ken Russell et al. It was here that I learned to be a film critic, but it was in the Odeons and ABCs that I gorged myself on the mainstream trash which I still love to this day.

For example, it was at the Odeon Hendon that I first saw *Brannigan* in which John Wayne played an artificially tonsured Yankee cop who comes to London to take on England's crooks 'Chicago-style'. The poster featured Wayne and his toupee brandishing a large gun in the foreground, while in the background a car leaped over a perilous gap between the tarmac jaws of the iconic Tower Bridge. It was also here that I saw *Juggernaut*, in which Shakespearean hellraiser Richard Harris downshifted as a bomb-disposal expert pitting his wits against the titular villain ('Oh you're a good man Juggernaut, but so am I!') who had laced an ocean liner with high explosives which threatened to blow Roy Kinnear right off the poop deck. And, most importantly, it was here that I first saw *Slade in Flame*, an unexpectedly grim gem starring everyone's favourite glam-rock stompers which I have since declared to be 'the *Citizen Kane* of British Pop Movies'.

This is no idle claim. Despite starting life as a goofy sub-Beatles knock-off, *Slade in Flame* really was surprisingly confrontational fare. Even the name was provocative, flickering with the promise of Britain's favourite pop act on fire with success, whilst ominously suggesting some sideburn-singeing, crash-and-burn conflagration. The official title may have been merely *Flame*, but that '*Slade in* ...' prefix was emblazoned on all the posters, and fizzled across the screen during the film's molten opening credits. Scenes of the band in white suits with projected infernos licking away at their lapels added to the sense of sacrifice, with Noddy, Dave, Jim and Don lit up on stage like some *Wicker Man*-style funeral pyre.

According to legend, *Slade in Flame* was originally envisaged as a sci-fi pastiche entitled *The Quite A Mess Experiment* ('Quatermass Experiment' – geddit?) which featured Noddy as the eccentric professor, and had Dave Hill killed by a triffid in the first fifteen minutes. Somehow this mutated into a more down-to-earth story about 'the reality, rather than the myth' of superstardom in the sixties and seventies. Director Richard Loncraine and screenwriter Andrew Birkin (brother of 'ooh-aahing' songstrel Jane) joined Slade on tour in America, using their adventures to fuel a down-and-dirty tale of bickering wannabe pop stars, snapped up by a soulless advertising magnate, and sold to the public as a pre-packaged product. ('I'm not a bloody fish finger,' complains Jim Lea in one memorably caustic moment).

Early drafts of the *Flame* script (bolstered by 'additional dialogue' from David Humphries) were sweary enough to earn an X-rating – a claim supported by John Pidgeon's savagely readable novelisation of which I still own a battered paperback copy (signed by the author!). To secure a wider audience (i.e. kids like *me*), the film-makers reined in the language, but kept the rough-and-toughness of the action. In its finished A-rated cut, *Flame* retained its vicious streak, with the scumbags of the music business jointly personified by greyhound-racing manager-cum-thug Mr Harding (Johnny Shannon, still sizzling from *Performance*) and slimy salesman

Mr Seymour (Tom Conti, in his first starring role). My favourite character was pub-circuit loser Jack Daniels, played by Alan Lake who had served prison time and who apparently researched his role with a liquid lunch which got him fired on his first day. After assurances that his spouse Diana Dors would police his sobriety for the rest of the shoot, Lake was reinstated and proceeded to earn his keep; a scene in which he is dragged semi-naked into a darkened street to have his toes smashed in with a shovel remains a wince-inducing highlight of *Flame*, closer to the hard-core nastiness of *Get Carter* than the food-fight fun of *Never Too Young to Rock*.

As for the band, they played the dark side of the rock 'n' roll dream with a commitment which bordered upon the kamikaze. Holder and Lea provided the dramatic core, scrapping and squabbling their way from pubs and clubs to studios and stages, with fleeting glimpses of friendship and affection giving way to shouting matches and petty spats (a typical onstage exchange: 'Will you *shut up*!'; 'At least I was *in tune*!'). Don Powell was the sympathetic dork, the learning of his lines made harder by a car crash which had left him with amnesia. Dave Hill, meanwhile, played Flame's knob of a guitarist Barry with a frighteningly relaxed naturalism, despite worrying that the movie might dispel the pop-star myth and thereby damage the band's reputation.

The fact that the pubescent pop-pickers reacted so negatively to *Slade in Flame* in the early seventies merely increased its stature in my eyes, and I have been dutifully extolling its virtues ever since. In the nineties, when I was working at Radio One, I toured art cinemas around the country lecturing on the 'Great British Pop Movie' and showing *Slade in Flame* to audiences who were universally amazed by its downbeat miserablism. More recently, Slade have become the focus of reverential critical attention in magazines like *Mojo*, and I was thrilled to be asked to knock off a thousand words on the subject of what was so great about *Flame* when a special edition DVD of the movie was released in 2007. Most rewardingly, writer and broadcaster John Harris told me that when he had interviewed Jim Lea, the bassist and songwriter said that he *knew* the band had been right to make *Flame* when 'that Kermode bloke kept going on about how great it was'. I was a greying forty-four-year-old when I heard that comment, but in my heart I was a lithe twelve-year-old, running up and down the aisles of the Hendon Odeon screaming 'Jim Lea knows my name! Jim Lea knows my name!'

*Slade in Flame* was an unpredictable gem, but back in those innocent days before the internet and easy access 'international journalism' it was still possible to be genuinely surprised by movies – for better or worse. Today, net-nerds upload reviews of films which aren't even finished yet (which serves studios right for relying on audience test screenings) and the box-office takings of every new release are splashed across the web before its opening weekend is through. Try as you might, in this culture of twenty-four-hour Infotainment it's increasingly hard to see a movie without some prior knowledge of its form, history and financial performance. Some may see this as an empowering process, enabling the consumer to refine their viewing choices and to know exactly what they're getting before shelling out for a ticket. But it also removes the element of risk which played such a positive role in my early filmgoing years.

Listen – if I'd known what a downbeat stodge of a movie the Charles Bronson Western *Breakheart Pass* was going to be in advance, I would never have stumbled upon the supporting film *Jeremy* which affected me so deeply that I simply couldn't concentrate on the main feature. The story of an awkward misfit's fumbling first relationship with a graceful ballet student, *Jeremy* was a melancholic forerunner of *Gregory's Girl*, a film which so perfectly captured the poignant anxieties of young love that you felt like you'd been personally wooed, seduced and then dumped by the movie. During the final reel, as Jeremy said a tearful airport goodbye to Susan whose parents had suddenly decided to move to another city (bastards!) I found my heart breaking into a thousand familiar pieces – this despite the fact that I had never *had*, let alone *lost*, a girlfriend in 'real life'. In many ways, Susan *was* my first girlfriend, and the eighty-six minutes we spent together in the Odeon that Sunday afternoon in 1975 have stayed with me to this day. 'Promise you won't forget me,' Susan cried as she prepared to board the plane, and I found myself replying out loud 'I won't!' A few embittered cynics in the audience snickered at my outburst, but I didn't care; I think Susan heard me. And she knew, she *knew* ...

Decades later, I was in a record store in London with Todd Haynes, director of *Velvet Goldmine*, *Far From Heaven*, and the adventurous Bob Dylan 'non-biopic' *I'm Not There*. We were filming a piece for *The Culture Show* which required a backdrop of vintage vinyl and inbetween set-ups we'd both started compulsively browsing through the random second-hand selection. By strange serendipity our eyes alighted at exactly the same moment on a dog-eared soundtrack LP for *Susan and Jeremy* (the alternative US title, apparently) the cover of which bore a photo of the girl I had loved and lost all those years ago. It was an ickily Proustian moment which made me shriek with surprise, a reaction made all the more powerful by the fact that Todd Haynes did exactly the same thing. As our hands reached out to grab and cradle the LP, we turned to each other in joyous disbelief, both babbling something along the lines of 'Oh my gosh I can't believe you love this movie *too*, I always thought it was just *me*!' If truth be told, I also felt a little pang of jealousy that Susan had been charming other men while I had devoted myself so singularly to her (overlooking a minor crush on the dark-haired girl out of *Lost in Space* which didn't count because you could only ever *flirt* with a TV show – *love* was for the big screen). In fact, it transpired that she had been unfaithful with the whole of the Cannes Film Festival where *Jeremy* had been a minor hit in 1973, which perhaps explains how this 16 mm indie oddity found its way on to the mainstream B-feature circuit in the first place. But such rivalries aside, a bond was formed between Todd and I at that moment which was in no way diminished by the fact that the LP cover turned out to be *empty*, the record itself having long been lost amongst a mountain of scratchy black vinyl. No matter; we agreed to purchase the empty sleeve anyway ('Er, 50p mate?') and then let Susan decide whose home to grace with her tattered snapshot presence. It would be indiscreet to say whether she chose Todd or me, but let me just say that she looks very happy to be where she is – sandwiched snugly between Joan Baez and the soundtrack to *Rollerball*. (Which reminds me – another reason I admired Jason Isaacs so much as a kid was that he made up a playground game of 'Rollerball' which involved being dragged along behind a pushbike on a skateboard and attempting to pick up a tennis ball before falling off and hurting yourself really badly while everyone stood round and solemnly hummed Bach's 'Toccata and Fugue in D minor'. It was brilliant!)

Of course, my love affair with Susan (and Jeremy) would never have happened if I had been one of those flibbertigibbets who only showed up for the main feature, and who could be found loitering in the foyer while the adverts and trailers were playing – often the most invigorating part of the programme. I well remember the earnest discussions which led cinema chains to agree not to show trailers for movies with adults-only certificates before child-friendly fare for fear of encouraging younger viewers to try to 'bunk' into AA and X-rated movies. In the days before such censorious enlightenment, however, trailers were a glorious free-for-all which gave audiences of all ages a tantalising taste of the most grown-up 'Coming Attractions'. I remember being taken to see the Magic Roundabout feature *Dougal and the Blue Cat* at an impressionable age and sitting through a terrifying trailer for *An Investigation of Murder* which consisted of a POV shot of a man getting on a bus and then apparently slaughtering anyone who saw his face – which was *everyone*. Time for bed, Zebedee! I also saw memorably disreputable trailers for *Enter the Dragon*, *The Godfather*, *The Last Detail* and (as I mentioned previously) *Cabaret*, all of which titillated my young imagination in ways which I shudder to recall. But the trailer which had the most profound effect upon my developing consciousness was, of course, a discreet teaser for the greatest movie ever made – *The Exorcist*.

Not surprisingly, I can remember *exactly* where I first saw this trailer – it was at the Classic cinema in Hendon, in Screen Two, before a performance of Woody Allen's *Sleeper* which I'd gone to see on the strength of its comically sci-fi inflected poster. I already knew something about *The Exorcist* because I'd seen a story on the BBC magazine programme *Nationwide* in which it was reported that American patrons had been swooning and vomiting at screenings, and being carried out on stretchers only to recover and rush back in to test their endurance once again. In a three-minute segment, Sue Lawley quickly recapped the film's plot (a young girl in modern-day Washington DC becomes demonically possessed), recounted tales of stateside hysteria, questioned the involvement of teenage actress Linda Blair, and wondered whether the film shouldn't be banned in the UK.

I was engrossed, not least by the whiff of physical endangerment that surrounded the film – the sense that this was something so scary that it might actually *damage* its audience, permanently. Certainly that was the line that evangelist Billy Graham was toeing when he declared that there was something evil trapped within the very celluloid of the movie, a demonic force which was unleashed each time the film passed through a projector. Soon, stories began to circulate of punters being driven mad by *The Exorcist*: of grown men throwing themselves at the screen; of pregnant women miscarrying; of sleepless nights and admissions to asylums. Most of it was clearly nonsense but that didn't matter a jot – by the time *The Exorcist* opened in England in March 1974, armies of nuns had been corralled to sprinkle holy water on to punters queuing to see the film and hand out leaflets giving them a number to call if they felt troubled by the devil in the sleepless nights that would inevitably follow.

All this madness was in the air when that trailer started to work its weird magic as I sat there innocently waiting for Woody Allen to make merry in the Classic Hendon. The trailer started innocuously, unannounced, with a view of a darkened street and car headlights moving slowly toward the camera. A strange noise hung in the foggy air, a noise which it transpires was made by soundman Ron Nagle and composer Jack Nitzsche running their fingers over the tops of wine glasses, a popular party trick put to skin-crawlingly eerie use. I vaguely recognised the street but had no idea why. As the headlights moved closer the vehicle was revealed to be a black and red cab which swung round to the left and stopped, its rear passenger door opening to let a man step out into the night, battered valise in his left hand, hat on head, his increasingly familiar silhouette illuminated by an unearthly light shining from the first-floor window of a colonial-style house. The effect was like watching an explosion in reverse – seeing a group of disparately shattered elements being drawn inexorably together, reconfiguring themselves into something horribly recognisable …

And then the voice began; quiet, low-toned, serious.

'Something almost beyond comprehension is happening to a young girl on this street, in *this* house …'

I didn't like the sound of this at all.

' …and a man has been sent to help her. This man is …'

Oh jeepers.

'…The Exorcist.'

At which point the picture froze into that iconic image that had been emblazoned on posters in Tube stations and bus stops all over the country – the black and yellow image of Max von Sydow standing outside the house on Prospect Street in Washington DC where the scariest thing *ever* was playing five times a day to shrieking, incandescent audiences.

I was absolutely terrified – afeared for my very life.

Of course, the trailer, like the poster, contained *nothing* that was overtly upsetting or shocking, merely the sight of an old man getting out of a car on a foggy urban street. How scary could *that* be? But somehow the utter absence of anything even remotely frightening merely made it all a million times *more* frightening. While traditional horror posters and ads would usually feature blood-curdling screams and terrified faces aplenty, the marketing campaign for *The Exorcist* seemed to imply that what was going on 'on this street, in this house' was so far beyond the bounds of acceptable screen terror that even to hint at its existence would be overstepping the mark. It was as if the film-makers were suggesting that the sight of this old bloke standing outside a house was the *only* thing they could show us without blowing our collective fuses. And in my case they were right.

I went home that night with a head full of hideous visions of demonic possession – I even remember waking up and checking to make sure that if I turned my head it wouldn't go *all the way around* like I had heard happened to the girl in the movie! Nor was I alone in this kind of madness. In the weeks and months after the opening of *The Exorcist* the entire country went on a bananas possession jag, with all manner of strange and antisocial behaviour being explained away with the phrase 'The Devil Made Me Do It!' In the wake of a story in the *Daily Telegraph* headlined 'Man jailed after *Exorcist* attack' the film's dangerous reputation was increased by a widely reported claim that sixteen-year-old John Power had *died* after seeing *The Exorcist* (it transpired that he had suffered an unrelated epileptic attack, but hey – print the myth). In October 1975, a full eighteen months after the initial furore, seventeen-year-old Nicholas Bell claimed in York Crown Court that his killing of a nine-year-old girl had been driven by the Devil who had entered him after a screening of *The Exorcist* (Bell later admitted that 'he made up the story about being possessed by the Devil in the hope that the police would let him go'). My favourite piece of cuckoo courtroom baloney came in the case of a woman accused of stealing a jacket and trousers from Top Shop who admitted the crime but claimed that she had become 'psychologically disturbed' after a viewing of *The Exorcist* – a viewing not by *her*, but by her *teenage daughter*, a sort of trauma by proxy which had turned her into a demonic shoplifter. Brilliant!

Of course the film-makers exploited such insane publicity to the hilt. Stories of a demonic curse had long haunted the production of *The Exorcist* with supposedly supernatural occurrences ranging from the death of actor Jack MacGowran (whose character Burke Dennings dies in the film – *spooky* …) to the burning down of the house-interior set one Sunday morning. The film's writer William Peter Blatty would regularly dismiss such rumours as 'utter foolishness' but when I made a documentary about *The Exorcist* for the BBC in 1998, Ellen Burstyn was still babbling happily about the deaths of nine people being somehow connected to the movie. Director William Friedkin also told me that he personally knew of a case in England in which a friend of one of the Royal princes, no less, had seen the movie and then run into the nearest church where he immolated himself upon the altar. I have never been able to find any record of such a case (and believe me, I have looked) and must conclude that it is just another of the bizarre urban myths which surrounded this most headline-friendly frightener.

As for me, it would be a full five years before I finally got to see *The Exorcist*, on a late-night double bill with Ken Russell's fiery classic *The Devils*. I remember sitting in my favoured aisle seat in the Phoenix in 1979, waiting for the movie to start, my entire body crackling with anxious electricity; I was so wired up I thought I might actually spontaneously combust. As the quiet opening credits began I remember looking around the cinema at the other punters in an attempt to reassure myself that we were all collectively going to be OK. 'Look, there's an old woman over there,' the voice in my head said calmly. 'She's probably quite frail and *she* doesn't look like she's bothered. You'll be *fine* ...'

That first viewing passed in an almost orgasmic whirl of fear, and remains one of the most genuinely transcendent experiences of my life. Rarely have I been more aware of being *alive* and *in the moment* than in the two hours that it took the movie to run through the projector that night. People talk endlessly about the damaging effects of horror movies but too little is heard about the life-affirming power of being scared out of your mind – and, in those very rare cases, out of your body. You ask me if I think there is more to this world than the grim 'realities' of ageing, disease and death, of mourning and loss, and I will refer you to that first viewing of *The Exorcist* during which my imagination took flight, my soul did somersaults, and the physical world melted away into nothingness around me. I don't *think* that there is a spiritual element to human life, I *know* it because I have experienced it first-hand, and I have horror movies to thank for that blessing.

Since then, I have seen *The Exorcist* about two hundred times (I stopped counting after the first hundred) and I can honestly say that there isn't a day goes by that I don't think about it, even if only for a moment. I know that sounds mad, and I fully appreciate just how boring I have become on the subject of 'that film', and how little sense my obsession with it makes to anyone else. I have written books about it (three editions of a 'BFI Modern Classic' which my friend Alan Jones has dubbed 'everything you never wanted to know about *The Exorcist* but were scared Mark was going to tell you anyway'), made radio and television documentaries about it (*The Ghosts of Prospect Street* and *The Fear of God*, the latter of which now adorns DVD copies of the film) and even been vaguely instrumental in prompting the creation of an extended cut released in 2000 subtitled 'The Version You've Never Seen', of which director William Friedkin said 'You'd better like it, because it's kinda your fault it happened.'

And, of course, I've stood outside that house on Prospect Street, stepping into the shadow of Max von Sydow, putting myself into the picture that haunted my childhood and which will surely follow me to my grave. Worse still, I have forced my entire family to make the pilgrimage to Georgetown just to parade up and down the precipitous steps which plummet from Prospect Street to M Street and which feature so prominently in the film – first my long-suffering wife Linda, then more recently my kids and my mother, who haven't even seen *The Exorcist*. Friedkin was once quoted as saying that on his gravestone would be engraved the words 'The guy who made *The Exorcist*'. He meant it self-deprecatingly but at least he actually *made* the damn movie, of which he should be proud. On *my* gravestone it'll just say 'The guy who bored his family and friends to death with *The Exorcist*'.

Of course *The Exorcist* is just the tip of the iceberg in terms of my obsession with horror movies. Writing in the *Guardian*, the journalist and broadcaster Mark Lawson once asked 'Did someone jump out of a cupboard and frighten [Kermode] at an impressionable age?' I can recall no such event (and nor can any other self-respecting horror fan I know) but from a very early age horror movies struck a chord deep within me. As a kid I remember sneaking downstairs after my parents had gone to bed to watch 'The Monday X Film' on ITV. To avoid detection I had to have the sound turned right down, but even without words the silent shapes and shadows of those old chillers made perfect sense to me. It was, indeed, my first real experience of discovering something that was uniquely *mine*, something that existed outside the domain of my parents' control and authority. And, of course, it was forbidden, secretive, taboo – and therefore irresistible.

When I think back to those furtive nights in front of the cathode ray, the titles that stand out are old Hammer flicks like *The Quatermass Xperiment* (aka *The Creeping Unknown*) and *The Curse of Frankenstein*, alongside the Vincent Price frightener *The Fly* which became my 'favourite movie of all time' for about a week. I clearly remember walking to school one windy morning and reciting the entire plot of *The Fly* to a goggle-eyed friend who got so creeped out by my animated description of insect heads transplanted onto human bodies (and vice versa) that he literally started to cry. And I vividly recall returning home one afternoon to find that my father had left *specific instructions* with my mother 'not to let the kids watch *Village of the Damned*' which was playing on BBC1 that evening. The next day was hell on earth for me because it seemed that every other kid at school had stayed up to watch this tale of alien children taking over a small English village, and no one could talk of anything else. There were even kids who had brought in the book (John Wyndham's *The Midwich Cuckoos*) just to relive some of the more terrifying moments in the playground. I was mortified – it was (to quote the underrated farting kids' fantasy flic *Thunderpants*) 'the worst day of my life – ever!'

It is surely no coincidence that I spent many subsequent years obsessing about *Village of the Damned*, tracking down articles about the film in old movie magazines, reading everything John Wyndham had ever written, from *The Kraken Wakes* to *Chocky* to *Jizzle* and more, and even surreptitiously attempting to persuade my parents to 'take us for a nice day out at Letchmore Heath' where I *knew* that many of the key scenes of *Village* had been filmed. When I came to write my PhD thesis about modern English and American horror fiction fifteen years later, I would devote a lengthy section to *The Midwich Cuckoos* and its place within the canon of 'paedophobic' literature. To this day, the very thought of *Village of the Damned* gives me an illicit tickle. Significantly I can't remember where I finally first saw it – only where I first *didn't* see it.

If there is a moral behind all this it is surely that attempting to repress something will only cause it to resurface elsewhere, bigger, stronger, and *nastier*. I am living proof of the inherent failure of censorship – if you tell me that I *can't* watch something, then my desire to see it *immediately* will be equal and opposite to the force of your refusal. You know, like that law you learned about in physics lessons; let's call it 'Newton's Law of Motion (Pictures)'. I'm honestly certain that if my father had never told my mother to tell me that I couldn't watch *Village of the Damned* I would have forgotten about it long ago. As it is, at the age of forty-six I still feel an irresistible urge to slam my old VHS copy of the movie into the machine *right now* – just because I *can*.

This electrifying awareness of the forbidden was clearly hard-wired into my psyche at an early age and frankly it has never gone away. Nor would I want it to. I have had *fantastic* times watching things I was told not to watch, and I pity those who have never known the delicious pleasure of good honest visual *guilt*. Look at Lars von Trier, whose recent movie *Antichrist* has been (wrongly) dubbed 'the most shocking movie ever'. Von Trier reportedly grew up in a fantastically liberal Danish household in which rules were frowned upon and look what it did for *him* – he is now a self-confessed neurotic depressive who is 'afraid of *everything* in life' and makes movies about people cutting their genitals off with scissors. As for me, I was told clearly from an early age that certain things were just plain *wrong*, and I am now a very happy horror-film fan who has derived hours of harmless pleasure from watching people pretend to disembowel each other with chainsaws.

And I sleep like a baby, since you ask.

Righto then, there's no point putting it off any longer. It's time to deal with the man and the woman and the mysterious piece of lace corsetry in *Krakatoa: East of Java*. Or maybe *not* in *Krakatoa: East of Java*. Let's see.

I've popped into HMV and bought a copy of the film on DVD – a snip at £5. Astonishing that such a valuable piece of my childhood can be purchased so easily, and so *cheaply*. Nothing seems to have value any more.

I slip the DVD into my laptop so that I can watch it while I write – another modern miracle. The film starts with a split-screen montage of a volcano exploding, and a hot-air balloon skittering through the skies which, as we have established, is pretty much all I remember about the movie other than that primal scene which probably isn't even there anyway. After that, the first fifteen minutes are taken up with plodding plot exposition; the loading of the ship, introducing the passengers, establishing their personal needs and quirks – the usual disaster-movie fare. At some point in all of this we meet a vibrantly attired Barbara Werle whom I vaguely recognise from a couple of Elvis movies. I pause *Krakatoa* and check the Internet Movie Database and there she is, hot from supporting roles in *Charro!*, *Harum Scarum* and *Tickle Me*, the last of which has the honour of being the very worst film The King ever made – which is really saying something. Ms Werle looks great, but she's blonde and her travelling companion is a clean-shaven Brian Keith, so it's clearly not going to be them getting their fingers caught in the corsetry. A far more likely pair of canoodling candidates are Maximilian Schell and Diane Baker who take top billing and fit the physical description of the film playing in my head – he is dark, brooding and bearded, she is auburn and mysterious. Yup, the more I look at the pair of them meeting on the gangplank the more I can imagine him being heroically injured and her nursing him back to health with the aid of a piece of string. Or lace. Whatever.

That is, of course, assuming that the scene is in the film – which it almost certainly isn't.

But guess what – it *is*, and a mere nineteen minutes into the action.

I wasn't making it up!

I am stunned.

Maybe this book isn't going to be a bunch of half-remembered falsehoods, fictions and outright lies as predicted.

I got the people wrong, however. And indeed almost everything else (so probably 'falsehoods, fictions and lies' after all). But there's just enough of an echo of the scene which I described earlier to suggest that the fantasy film playing in my head actually *was* 'inspired by real events'.

Here's what *really* happens.

During that early scene with Barbara Werle, her character Charley meets the manly Maximilian Schell on the gangplank and gives him her card, boasting that she is a popular singer available for 'Weddings, Social Occasions and Smokers' – whatever 'smokers' were (and even before I knew the answer to that question, they sounded saucy). It is also established that her partner Harry (Brian Keith) is a diving expert of some renown and is embarking upon this voyage in order to earn money through his legendary salvaging skills. She is flirty; he is grumpy; they are both broke. And thus, when they retire to their cabin below decks, they begin to bicker. We, meanwhile, find ourselves hiding in the closet (oo-er) in which Ms Werle promptly starts to hang her clothes, the camera peering out in an eerie pre-echo of Kyle

MacLachlan's peeping Tom from *Blue Velvet* while Harry playfully badmouths Charley's singing career.

'You were so lousy,' he says dismissively, throwing himself fully clothed on to his bed, 'you put your piano player to sleep!'

'Maybe,' she says with a minxy smile, slamming the closet doors shut. 'But I knew how to keep *you* awake, Harry.'

And suddenly, this putative disaster movie turns into a musical, replete with non-diegetic orchestral accompaniment as Charley grabs the end of the four-poster bed and starts to sing, swaying suggestively.

'I'm looking for an old-fashioned boy,' she trills, 'who's looking for ...'

The camera angle changes and *there it is*! There's the shot I remember; the shot with the man lying prostrate on his back, seemingly disabled (by sleep, or booze, rather than injury), his head to the left of frame, her body in the background, the camera skulking behind the bed, peering out from the skirting board.

'...an old-fashioned girl.'

As she sings this last line, Charley turns her bustle toward the bed and (let's not be coy) gently shakes a tail feather, looking over her shoulder as she does so, slightly lifting the hem of her jacket to accentuate the ribbon tied somewhere other than around the old oak tree.

Harry yawns theatrically, but I'm starting to doubt his disinterest.

'Just a nice old-fashioned girl like me.'

Stirred from feigned slumbers, Harry reaches out his hand (as I had remembered, only quicker, and with far less ambiguity) and pulls on the ribbon with practised dexterity; in a flash the ribbon comes undone and the camera follows the falling skirt swiftly to the floor, revealing ample light-blue petticoats beneath.

He yawns again, and then snorts like a braying horse.

Hmm. This is a lot racier – and a lot less 'symbolically suggestive' – than I had remembered, No wonder they upped the certificate from U to PG for the DVD.

Back to the action. Charley kneels to pick up the red dress and starts to walk away from bed, singing 'I want a boy who's happy that *I* ...'

On the word '*I*' she gives a suggestive dip and holds the discarded skirt up to her bosom, apparently hiding behind its crumpled pleats in a gesture that stretches the boundaries of coquettishness.

'...can blush, because I'm bashful and shy ...'

And with that she drop-kicks the skirt across the room toward the bed, its silky folds opening in mid-air like a giant crimson butterfly as it soars straight toward the camera which rests once again behind the man's bed.

From here on in, it's effectively a well-behaved striptease, with Werle shedding her jacket top, the arms of which she waves like hoofers' tassles before draping it upon Harry's tutting head. He moves to throw it away, but winds up using it as a pillow, while all the time continuing his Benny Hill-style parody of sleepiness – the man tired but tempted, the woman needy and naughty, a dynamic which seemed to be the norm for all nudge-wink 'family entertainment' in those days. The clothes continue to come off, but there's little chance of nakedness – after five minutes of theatrical undressing Ms Werle is still covered from head to foot in the most modest of undergarments which seem to exist in never-ending layers of mystery. If she walked out down the street like this today she'd still look overdressed.

Suddenly the sound of castanets fills the air and things take a decidedly Latino turn. *Hola!* Harry bangs his head on the bedstead – things are hotting up. He laughs. Charley sings some more. She caresses her corset and deftly drops her petticoat revealing pink garters with little blue bows on. Harry is undone. She drops the petticoat on to his chest and starts to slip one of the garters of her leg. Harry is clearly aroused. He lifts the petticoat toward his face – to do … *what?*

To put it over his head so he can go back to sleep.

Clearly he's impotent. Or gay. Or English.

It's time to bring out the big guns. Charley drapes herself around a four-poster pole, raises a knee, and pulls on a straw boater.

And *that* does it. Forget the corsets, the frocks, the petticoats, the garters, the ribbons, the laces, even the red shoes which I notice now she still has on. It's the straw boater that finally seals the deal for Harry.

And clearly for me. Because *now*, after all this song-and-dance hanky-panky, we finally get the *other* bit of the scene which I remember; the bit in which the woman walks away from the man, apparently done troubling him, at which point the man, who up till now has been so reticent to get involved, calls her back by reaching out and catching hold of the lace which trails behind her.

Only, that's not what happens. Not quite. Clearly I've transposed the bit with the lace from earlier in the scene when he was whipping off her skirt – with her consent, of course. By now, however, Harry has clearly gotten off his horse and drunk his milk and is in no mood for namby-pamby niceties. No Sirreee Bob. Now that his bloodlust has been inflamed by that damn straw boater it's time for manly action. So as Charley turns to walk away in something approaching an unsatisfied strop, Harry reaches out, grabs her by the wrist, and hauls her giggling with gaiety on to the bed where the happy couple are finally conjoined in three seconds of laughter-filled canoodling climaxing in him patting her once again on the bum.

Cut to the engine room, and a shot of huge pistons pounding in and out, up and down, in an orgy of mechanical thrusting and pumping.

Really.

I stop the DVD, and take stock.

All said, it's pretty depressing. There was I imagining that my young mind had somehow latched on to something profoundly Freudian and symbolic, something which would have suggested a deeper appreciation of the mysteries of the adult world than befitted a six-year-old boy, something which proved that even at an early age my eyes were looking *beyond* the screen to the story *behind* the picture.

The truth is far more mundane; at an early age I watched Barbara Werle stripping down to her corset and petticoat and showing off her garters and clearly I have never got over the impenetrable longings which that experience provoked.

This is emblematic of so much of my early life, and the sooner I face up to the fact that my entire adolescent world view was informed by the fairground thrills of exploitation cinema the better.

In my formative years, everything I knew about politics I had learned from *Planet of the Apes*.

Everything I knew about pop music I'd learned from *Slade in Flame*.

Everything I knew about heartbreak I'd learned from *Jeremy*.

Everything I knew about religion I'd learned from *The Exorcist*.

And, apparently, everything I knew about 'adult matters' I'd learned from *Krakatoa: East of Java*.

And you thought *you* were messed up.

## Chapter 2

## BRIGHT LIGHTS, BIG *CITY LIFE*

Just as watching movies defined my childhood, so writing about cinema became an early obsession. At around the age of nine or ten I brashly embarked upon an unauthorised novelisation of *2001: A Space Odyssey* (not realising that Arthur C. Clarke had beaten me to it), cramming my own messed-up memories of the entire movie into four badly typed pages for which I then constructed a 'hardback' cover using cardboard and Sellotape. I don't have a copy of that magnum opus any more but I remember that it didn't make much sense – although you could say the same of Kubrick's movie (but not, crucially, of Clarke's novel). From here I graduated to compiling 'books' of film reviews which I would then place casually upon bookshelves around the house in the forlorn belief that someone would start reading them without noticing that they were home-made. It wasn't until my teenage years, however, that my written work became available outside of my own home and, like so many wannabe journalists in the seventies and eighties, the first thing I ever wrote that actually got published was a schoolboy letter in the *New Musical Express*. Although it was nearly thirty years ago, I can still remember clearly the substance of the letter, which took the form of a short play (I was a pretentious arse even back then). This Beckettian gem, which was essentially a rip-off of the surreal ramblings of genius cartoonist Ray Lowry, took the form of an argument between two of the *NME*'s most flamboyant (and therefore greatest) writers: Paul Morley and Ian Penman. If memory serves, these two journalistic behemoths were portrayed as squabbling in fluent lavatorial *Goon Show* gibberish before the fey arrival of Japan frontman David Sylvian who announced simply 'I have no make-up' and then died. At which point, the entire *NME* cast turned up 'dressed as Monty Smith's stomach' to sing an enthusiastic roundelay of 'Show me the way up my own bum'.

And they say satire is dead.

The worst thing about this hideously smug and *faux* anarchic missive was the fact that I had clearly thought about it for a *long time* before sending it, hence my word-perfect recall almost three decades later. I can't remember a single line of Shakespeare, Milton, Keats or any of the other immortal poets and playwrights whose wonderful works I studied at O level, A level, and university. But can I remember *every* sodding word of a stupid letter I sent to the *NME* back in the late seventies? Of *course* I can. I've got a head so full of junk there's no space left for the good stuff to go.

Equally shameful is the amount of effort I expended attempting to appear utterly 'off the cuff' and hilariously flippant. Plus, the entire satirical aim of the piece was clearly *not* to mock the writers in question at all, but to appear somehow 'in' on the gag in a way which would make me appear to be 'one of them'. People ask me nowadays why I'm so vitriolic about anything which could be described as vaguely quirky or madcap and the honest truth is that I cannot forgive any sin in which I am so deeply steeped.

I signed that letter 'Henry P' which was an obscure reference to my favourite band of the time, Yachts, whose frontman Henry Priestman I idolised. By a peculiar twist of fate, that name stuck thanks to the mocking derision of my very close friend Simon Booth who *saw* the letter and *knew* at once that it was from me. Some time later I would move to Manchester, where nobody knew me, and where the university was awash with people called 'Mark'. So, for the first few weeks of the academic term people would politely ask my name, and I would reply 'Mark' and they would instantly forget because they already had fifty other 'Marks' backed up in their 'which one are you?' cranial databanks. Then, sometime around week three, Booth came up to visit me in Manchester and was overheard to refer to me as 'Henry' – of which there were few others. So the name stuck. And for the rest of my six years in Manchester I was known almost interchangeably as 'Mark' or 'Henry', or even occasionally 'Mark Henry' which sounded like some moonshine-drinking dungareed mountain-dweller from *The Waltons*. After a while I got used to it, and convinced myself that I had acquired the 'Henry' nickname after Jack Nance's generously bequiffed screen icon in the cult movie *Eraserhead* – more of which later.

Getting into Manchester University had proved something of a slog because I was not much cop at school and had unimpressive grades to prove it. In fact, on my first UCCA form (known now as UCAS, I believe) I got *five* flat rejections, being turned down by everyone including my 'sure-fire safety net' fifth choice which the good folk at careers advice assured me 'never rejected *anyone*'. I didn't just get *rejected* – they asked to see me *in person* before deciding that I was not the sort of chap they wanted cluttering up their esteemed seat of learning. This was an important life lesson, because it taught me that if someone isn't sure that they want me to do something, whatever it may be, then actually *meeting* me will merely confirm their worst fears. To this day I have *never* got *any* job for which I have had to be formally interviewed or do an audition.

Never.

*Ever*.

I think that says a lot about how charming I am in person.

Anyway, after a brief and foolhardy flirtation with the entrance examiners for Mansfield College, Oxford (who also told me to get lost, but in a very nice and affirmative way – I was apparently their 'top rejection') I applied again to Manchester and finally got in which was great because it was the only place I really wanted to go, having read all about it in the *NME*. On my first day there I trotted down to the Hacienda club (brainchild of Factory supremo Tony

Wilson) and obtained my beautiful yellow and silver constructivist-style designer credit-card membership ID. These cards are apparently now valuable collectors' items, and I would happily sell mine on eBay were it not for the fact that I cut it up to make plectrums after falling upon hard times during an intense 'rehearsal schedule' with my never-to-be-famous band Russians Eat Bambi. No, nobody else has ever heard of them either.

Like Hunter S. Thompson's San Francisco in the mid-sixties, Manchester in the mid-eighties was 'a very special time and place to be a part of ... whatever it meant'. Part of what being in Manchester 'meant' was getting caught up in the heady tide of hard-left student politics which swept along the Oxford Road and guaranteed that at any time of day or night your passage could be impeded by balaclava-clad protestors demanding equal rights for Latvian yoghurt farmers, angrily stamping on Nestlé chocolate bars, and threatening to burn down Barclays Bank. Along with its fashionably industrial music scene, Manchester was the UK's premier hotbed of sub-Trot NUS militancy – no wonder the *New Statesman* dubbed it the 'crucible [in which] a generation learned its politics and went on to become the heart of New Labour'. Today, people still talk of the role of the 'Manchester Mafia' within modern politics, since so many of those who were radical young turks in the eighties grew up to be rather less radical old farts in the nineties and noughties, helping to put Blair and Brown in power (hey, thanks for that!).

As for me, I was always going to be a sucker for revolutionary politics because I'd spent so much time watching *Conquest of the Planet of the Apes*. So, with my usual flair for moderation in all things I mutated during my time in Manchester from snot-nosed *NME*-reading angsty teenager to red-flag-waving bolshie bore with a subscription to *Fight Racism Fight Imperialism* and no sense of humour. I also developed an addiction to stern gender politics which made me both unfunny *and* unattractive – a real double whammy. Whilst many of my more well-adjusted peers were taking drugs, having sex, and experimenting with new and exciting forms of liver abuse, my student years were defined by a profound belief that a hard rain was indeed going to fall and this was no time to be *enjoying oneself*. In the words of *Withnail & I*'s prophetic guru Presuming Ed, we had spectacularly 'failed to paint it black' and there were going to be a lot of casualties …

In my defence, I'd like to say that you would have had to have been a fully paid-up piece of pond life *not* to have got the impression that something was profoundly *wrong* with Britain in the mid-eighties. The evidence of impending Bastille-storming upheaval was everywhere – and nowhere more so than in Manchester. When the Home Secretary Leon Brittan visited Manchester University's Students Union in 1985, thirty-two people were arrested (and others injured) as the police battled protestors blocking the entrance to the building. The resulting debacle made the national news and seemed to us to represent a throwing down of the gauntlet by Manchester Police's then chief constable, James Anderton, a man who was famously on first-name terms with the Almighty. Unaffectionately nicknamed 'God's Copper',

Anderton made headlines at the height of the AIDS panic with comments about people 'swirling about in a human cesspit of their own making' – comments which helped turn him into a near-mythical bogeyman for those of a liberal persuasion. Indeed, anyone drifting even idly toward the radical left needed only to take a cursory glance at Anderton's more outrageous outpourings to spur them on to man the barricades forthwith.

In my case, the 'barricades' were a series of anti-deportation campaigns which centred around Viraj Mendis, a Sri Lankan activist whom the government were attempting to repatriate despite well-supported claims that he would be persecuted for his political beliefs (he was a passionate advocate of the Tamil Tigers) if sent back to his country of origin. Viraj had a lot of support in Manchester, where he had lived for several years, and his campaign to stay in the UK grew in size, importance and popularity throughout the eighties, becoming the focus of numerous similar anti-deportation battles. In December 1986, things cranked up a gear when Viraj went into sanctuary in Hulme's Church of the Ascension after a deportation order was issued against him by the Home Office. He stayed there for 760 days, publicly defying the authorities who finally ordered the police to batter down the doors of the church and forcibly remove him in the early hours of 18 January 1989.

During the years of Viraj's 'voluntary' incarceration, his support team the Viraj Mendis Defence Campaign (VMDC, of which I was an active member) fought and *won* a number of other anti-deportation cases whilst simultaneously maintaining a twenty-four-hour vigil at the Church of the Ascension. Once a week, each of us would get to stay up all night in the dingy foyer of that church discussing the inevitable decline of capitalism (thus combining my two favourite obsessions – religion and politics) with Viraj's comrades in the Revolutionary Communist Group (not to be confused with their sworn rivals the Revolutionary Communist *Party*, or indeed the Judean People's Popular Front) and in my case writing rude and satirical songs about James Anderton.

Here, for the record, are the lyrics of my best efforts in this area:

James Anderton is big and strong
James Anderton is in this song
James Anderton, his friends call him 'Jim'
How truly wonderful to be like him
Oh please don't think I'm faking
But I'm swirling in a cesspit of my own making
For you
Do-be-do-be-do.

You probably had to be there.

One of the acceptable hobbies for a fledging comrade was the writing and publication of articles in newspapers, presumably because this would provide a future opportunity for 'subverting the mass media from within'. By happy coincidence I had been making inroads into journalism ever since my arrival in Manchester thanks to the open-door policy of *Mancunion*, an award-winning publication based on the second floor of the Students' Union. As far as I could tell the paper was pretty much obliged to support any and all budding student journos by printing their submitted copy, no matter how poor – an opportunity which I exploited to the hilt. It was in the pages of *Mancunion* that I made my 'proper' newspaper debut, a review of the funk-punk band the Higsons (hark, is that the sound of the system collapsing?) at the Hacienda. As before, this was yet another attempt at sub-*NME* scribery which I spiced up with interview quotes obtained by cornering frontman Charlie Higson backstage armed with a pen, a pad of paper, and the scarily convincing declaration that I was 'from the local music press, alright?' By a peculiar twist of fate, Charlie Higson would later go on to present the short-lived Channel 4 film show *Kiss Kiss Bang Bang*, making him a far more famous and successful film critic than me and thus the subject of my ongoing envy. He also starred in *The Fast Show* which, for my money, is one of the funniest TV programmes ever.

But I forgive him.

Hot from my 'page twenty-three, lower-left column' success with the Higsons review I filed an equally hot-headed account of Orange Juice's Hacienda show, by which time I began to feel that I had utterly conquered rock journalism. I still wrote with all the style and grace of an idiot fanboy who desperately wanted to be Lester Bangs but was more (as Kurt Vonnegut put it) Philboyd Studge. Yet I had learned two important lessons: firstly, that you should keep and file all your old press cuttings, because nobody else will;

and secondly, that in journalism you can be whoever you want to be as long as you have enough front. And no shame.

Of course, what I *really* wanted to be was a film critic (if I wasn't going to be a pop star, which I clearly wasn't and if the revolution wasn't happening *right now*, which it didn't seem to be), but there was no chance of that at *Mancunion*. Gig reviews were fine – you just paid to see the show then wrote about it the next morning. But film reviews had to be filed *in advance* and that meant gaining access to *private preview screenings*. Figuring out who organised these secretive screenings, and where and when they happened, was difficult enough, let alone getting your name on the mystical 'list' which was spoken of only in hushed whispers and overheard asides. You remember all that nonsense that Tom Cruise's character goes through in his attempts to get into the masked orgy in Stanley Kubrick's rubbish *Eyes Wide Shit* (sorry, *Shut*) – having to get a piano player drunk to prise the location out of him, then hiring a fancy dress get-up at midnight from some Slavic pimp-cum-costumier, then getting a taxi to drive for hours to the middle of nowhere before enduring hours of awful 'plink plonk *bong*' avant-garde atonal piano squonking and failing to get even a blowjob despite being able to produce the password '*Fidelio*!' when requested to do so by a man dressed as a chicken? You remember all that? Well, trying to get on to the Manchester film preview screening circuit was *worse* – and a lot less funny.

For a while, I thought you probably had to *kill* someone and eat their still-beating organs in some *Angel Heart*-type twisted satanic ritual before the wanton pleasures of the preview screening would be revealed to you. Later, I discovered that you just had to be 'invited' by someone 'in the know' – or to be 'sent' by a magazine, which in my case turned out to be *City Life*.

*City Life* was a small but thriving Manchester listings magazine which had been set up in 1983 as 'a cross between *Time Out* and *Private Eye*'. Over the years the magazine had become an admirable thorn in the side of James Anderton, thanks largely to the persistence of news editor Ed Glinert who seemed to have an inside track on the chief constable's bizarre beliefs. One story had it that a disgruntled copper had actually bugged his boss' office and was feeding stories to Glinert (who stoically refused to reveal his sources). Whatever the truth, *City Life* was a flag-waver in the war against Anderton, and that made working for it a worthy cause indeed.

Like *City Limits* in London, *City Life* was a workers co-op, which brought numerous benefits including (crucially) assistance from the Manchester Co-operative Development Agency, aka Mancoda. The co-op structure put in place a rigorously egalitarian framework within which everyone did *everything* and everyone was *equal* – at least in theory. In practice, the magazine was run by three quixotic editors: Glinert, Chris Paul and Andy 'Spin' Spinoza, all graduates of *Mancunion*, and all of whom would ultimately go on to excel in their various chosen professions.

Spinoza was particularly industrious, becoming the diary editor at the long-running *Manchester Evening News* before setting up the thriving Spin Media agency and establishing himself as the North-West's premier public-relations guru. Spin could make a news story out of *anything*. When I completed my PhD thesis in 1991, he got in touch to ask me if I had any 'interesting' plans for the future, now that I was officially a 'Doctor of Horror'. I told him that Linda and I were getting married in Liverpool that same week, after which we were going to travel around America for a fortnight, stopping off briefly at Georgetown in Washington DC so that I could finally see the '*Exorcist* steps'. Spin promptly filed a story for the *Evening News* which ran under the splash headline 'Dr Horror Plans Haunted Honeymoon'. I still have it framed on the mantelpiece, one of a very few genuinely treasured press cuttings. (Spin reckons I got off lightly, pointing out that when a fellow *City Lifer* got a PhD in Popular Culture, the *MEN* diary pages dubbed him 'Dr Disco'.)

'I edited *City Life* for six years,' Spin told the *Guardian* when interviewed about his lively career a few years ago, 'and never earned more than £75 a week. We lived off the thin of the land. But it wasn't about the money. It was about our independent voice. It was a fun, very creative environment. I interviewed everyone from Alan Bleasdale to Bernard Manning. And we gave the first chance to writers like Jon Ronson and Mark Kermode ...' Reading this made me strangely proud, because it suggested that no matter how piffling my role in *City Life* had been (and believe me it was *really piffling*) I had somehow passed into the annals of its illustrious history – a feat I never *dreamed* could become a reality.

I first joined the (outer) ranks of *City Life* when I answered an ad for an 'enthusiastic and outgoing' (ha!) wannabe journalist to sell advertising space in their forthcoming 'Student Special' edition. Back in the eighties, Manchester was home to 60,000 students (there are even more now) making it 'the densest student population in Europe' – a totally non-ironic phrase which I would repeat down the phone for weeks on end in the desperate attempt to sell some wretched ads. It turned out I was a completely useless salesman, and the amount of ad revenue which I personally managed to raise for that issue was way below par. But by the time the balance sheets were totted up I'd already got my feet under the table and was attending co-op meetings like my life depended on them – which, in a way, it did.

Co-op meetings were fun, if a bit mad. Politics were always high on the agenda, with the inevitable interface between lofty ideals and practical commerce provoking regular sparks. At one meeting we rowed for hours about whether to accept a lucrative full-page ad for Brian De Palma's new film *Body Double* which depicted a semi-clad (and apparently endangered) Melanie Griffith being leered at through half-opened blinds by a shadowy stalker. In the end, Spinoza and I won the day on right-on points, and the ad was voted in true co-op fashion to be 'unsuitable' – to the dismay of the ad team who were having a hard enough time financing the mag, and who shook their heads at the loss of such badly needed income.

Of course, the core *City Life* team were a volatile bunch given to vigorous squabbling for which the co-operative rule-book provided a firm and rigidly egalitarian structure.

I remember more than one meeting in which the agenda of issues for discussion (neatly typed and recorded for posterity) would read something like: 'ITEM ONE – The frankly unacceptable behaviour of Co-op member X, as proposed by Co-op member Y; ITEM TWO – The frankly unacceptable behaviour of Co-op member Y, as proposed by Co-op member X; ITEM THREE – The frankly unacceptable behaviour of Co-op members X *and* Y as proposed by *everybody else*.' The exact nature of the 'frankly unacceptable behaviour' would vary from week to week, but the key issues remained the same: creative people, crammed together in a small office like Coppola's colourful *Rumble Fish*, needing to blow off steam in the relatively safe environment of a really well-organised row.

Occasionally, the creativity tipped over into madness. Like all my memories of Manchester, everything that happened in the *City Life* offices seemed unbelievably important and prone to controversy – even the simple task of making a cup of tea. I remember my first experience of 'being mother' for the assembled masses, proudly scrabbling around the smelly kitchen in search of an old teapot in order to prepare a proper brew – after all, the people who worked here were 'real journalists' and frankly I was in awe of them. I diligently took orders for milk and sugar, and produced a tray of steaming teas that duly matched their exacting demands. Everyone was suitably grateful and polite except one *CL* stalwart who made a silent but commanding gesture for me to wait while he tasted the tea which I had brought. I stood, uncertain as to whether this was a joke. It wasn't. It was *deadly* serious. He lifted the cup to his lips, took a tiny slurp, swilled it around his mouth, considered for a moment, took *another* slurp, exercised his palette some more, and then slammed the teacup down on to the desk, a look of assertive rapture in his eyes. He stared at me, astonished.

'Number four!' he said grandly. 'Straight in at *number four*!'

I had no idea what he was talking about.

I looked at him. He looked at me.

Then he swung round in his chair and ripped down a piece of paper which had been Sellotaped to the wall of the office.

'Number four!' he said again. 'Ahead of Auty in '83, but just behind Spinoza *and* Spinoza again in '84, and *way* behind Hill, still untouchable at the top spot.'

'What?' I said, confused.

'Top Ten Teas!' he replied grandly, as if it were the most obvious thing on earth. 'You're straight in at number four, but Hill and Spinoza are still ahead. Spinoza *twice*!'

I looked at him, certain that he was having me on. But the list, which he was now studiously rewriting, spoke for itself. There, scribbled but precise, was an account of the top ten cups of tea that had been served in the *City Life* office, with names and dates dutifully recorded like a court record-keeper's log. And there was I, new on the list, going 'straight in at number four', thereby displacing the former numbers four to nine and knocking out number ten entirely.

*City Life* really did keep a list of 'Top Ten Teas'.

And this was *years* before Nick Hornby and *High Fidelity*.

And I was straight in at number four.

I *loved* working for *City Life*!

But inevitably, *City Life* didn't always love me – particularly when I crashed their delivery van.

The delivery run was one of the many tasks to which more lowly members of the co-op would aspire. Due to my student status, I was only ever a part-time worker and therefore a part-time co-op member, which meant that I got all the perks of working at the mag with little or none of the real responsibility – both practical and financial. I was, in effect, a makeweight, although it has since pleased me to insist that I was a core member of the *City Life* family. The truth is more mundane – I was a hanger-on, albeit an enthusiastic one.

I wasn't much good at anything, but I did have a clean driver's licence and I had never been declared legally bankrupt, which was not something that *everyone* at *City Life* could say. So, more often than not, I got the job of driving the *City Life* van over the moors to the printers in Batley, and then shipping the finished copies back to a string of distribution warehouses on the outskirts of Manchester overnight, before doing early-morning drops at local newsagents in the city centre. It was fantastically exciting stuff, turning up at remote depots at all hours in the morning and being referred to as 'Driver!' (rather than 'Student Wanker') wherever you went. The vehicles themselves came from Manchester Van Hire, and if you were lucky you got one with a radio and even (occasionally) a cassette player which would turn your journey into a sublime musical odyssey. I remember pulling out of the printers with a full load and pressing uphill on to the dual carriageway with the Comsat Angels' first album

*Waiting For A Miracle* warbling on the stereo and thinking I had never been happier in my entire life.

The problem was that driving all night with your hands wet on the wheel (in the immortal words of Golden Earring) wasn't great from a safety point of view, particularly if you'd spent the whole of the previous day industriously attempting to smash the state by standing on some dodgy student picket or other and playing South African liberation songs on the French horn and trombone. This is not a joke; I really *did* play in a quasi-revolutionary brass band who performed foghorn-like arrangements of ANC anthems to lift the spirits of protestors as they trudged through the streets of Manchester – a weekly occurrence in those heady days. We were very enthusiastic but also quite terrible. I remember very clearly turning up late to one particular march and as my mouthpiece-wielding compatriots and I ran to catch up with the crowd, a long-suffering policeman was heard very loudly to exclaim, 'Oh God, not the band … *please, not the band*!'

But marching and blowing can leave you all puffed out, and driving the van after a hard day's radical flugelhorning was always going to end in tears. So it was that early one morning, toward the end of the *City Life* run, I was coming off the M56 on to the series of slip roads which feed on to the Princess Parkway – a large dual carriageway leading straight into the centre of the city. There was neither traffic around nor any adverse weather conditions – surprisingly for the so-called rainy city. As I came off the motorway I banked left with the slip road, then curved right as it looped back on itself before snaking up toward the dual carriageway. It's a tricky stretch, ideally taken at around 30 mph but with a temptingly twisty appearance which seems to say 'Go on, you can do it, it'll be fun .... *Let's floor it*.' For the record, I never actually 'floored it' – I was always too chicken. But I would take asinine delight in accelerating slightly out of the first turn and into the second bend because the van would lean one way, then the other, in a manner which seemed far more dramatic than it actually was. Pathetic, I know, but hey I was young and foolish.

Nowadays I am old and stupid. So it goes.

Anyway, as I came into the second bend, something happened. For years I would assert that the load shifted in the back of the van – which indeed it *did*, toppling awkwardly from one side to the other and thereby briefly unbalancing the vehicle. Recently I have come to accept the more shameful possibility that I was actually checking my hair in the rear-view mirror and was temporarily caught off guard. Whatever – the result was the same; the van wobbled and I overcorrected with the steering wheel, causing it to slew. The back of the van swung out and the whole vehicle started careening gracefully toward the restraining barriers on the outside rim of the road. Although I wasn't actually going very fast, the rear end of the van had a fair amount of weight and thwacked into the barriers, striking the offside corner with a rubbery thud. Now, if you know anything about motorway barriers (which I didn't, but do *now*) you'll know that they are designed to be flexible, to *absorb* the shock in the event of being struck by a vanload of *City Lifes*. In my case, the barrier absorbed the shock extremely effectively but then, like some oversized guitar string being plucked, appeared to *twang* back against the van, swatting the rear corner away like a fly, and causing the *front* offside corner to perform an almost identical pluck-and-recoil manoeuvre. Baffled, but still moving forward, I hit the brakes which simply put the van into a skid and sent it lurching *back* across the carriageway toward the opposing barriers, upon contact with which it conducted another vehicular hokey-kokey, putting its front end in, its back end out, in-out in-out shake-it-all-about-and-turn-around, while in the cabin I went all knees bent, arms stretched, ra ra ra!

By the time the van came to rest in the middle of the slip road, I had managed (very effectively) to knock seven bells out of *all four* of its corners, prompting the question upon my return to the *City Life* office, 'Which direction were you actually travelling in when you hit the barrier(s)?' From the look of it, the van had been at the centre of a complicated four-way pincer movement in which the entire motorway had risen up from north, south, east and west and struck the unsuspecting vehicle from all sides at the *same time*. It was pretty impressive.

In the wake of the van incident it was decided that I could probably do less damage behind a desk, and since I'd been promised some writing assignments when I first came on board, it seemed the right time to let me loose in the pages of the magazine. The first major piece I filed was an interview with Douglas Adams, who was in town to promote the newly published scripts for his *Hitchhiker's Guide to the Galaxy* radio series. I was a huge *Hitchhiker's* fan and grilled him with the intensity of a sci-fi stalker, which he seemed to find at once flattering, annoying, and unsettling. As for my prose style, I had graduated from writing like a tea boy at the offices of the *NME* to Minister in Charge of Paper Clips at the Department of Pedantic Dullardry. I saw this as a huge improvement, and indeed 'pedantic dullardry' remains a touchstone of my journalistic endeavours to this day.

The first film I reviewed for *City Life* (and therefore my first ever properly *published* film review) was of Dan O'Bannon's workaday horror spoof *The Return of the Living Dead*. A cheeky riff on the legacy of Romero's *Night of the Living Dead*, this splattery romp was played broadly for laughs; in the US, *Return* was released with the self-parodic tag line 'They're back from the grave – and they're ready to party' whilst in Germany it was retitled *Verdammt, die Zombies kommen* which roughly translates as 'Oh crap, the zombies are coming!'

The film was flawed, but the gruey special effects were fun, including reanimated bisected dog corpses and various undead dismembered limbs. Apparently, *Texas Chain Saw Massacre* director Tobe Hooper had at one point been planning to film it in blood-splattered 3-D, a format which had experienced a fleeting return to fashion in the mid-eighties with the spaghetti western *Comin' at Ya!*, followed by the schlocker sequels *Jaws 3-D*, *Amityville 3-D* and (most famously) *Friday the 13th Part III in 3-D*. Today, were are all being told that '3-D is the future!' once again, thanks to a string of flashy kids' digimations (*Monsters vs Aliens 3-D*,

*Bolt 3-D*, *Toy Story 3-D*, *Ice Age 3-D*, *Cloudy with A Chance of Meatballs 3-D*), scrungy horror throwbacks (*My Bloody Valentine 3-D*, *Scar 3-D*), pop-concert films (*U2 3-D*, *Hannah Montana 3-D*, *The Jonas Brothers 3-D*) and big-budget fantasy adventures (Cameron's *Avatar*, Spielberg's *Tintin*, etc.). The truth, which should be apparent to anyone with a vaguely cynical soul, is that 3-D will always be the *past*, and is only being rammed down our throats as something excitingly 'new' right now because it is much harder to pirate 3-D films than good old flat ones. Big Hollywood studios want you to believe in 3-D because they want to carry on believing in their own bank accounts. It has nothing to do with 'the future' of cinema, merely the future of film finance.

As for *The Return of the Living Dead*, the real joy for me was the fact that I was seen as some kind of expert in this area because I had actually *heard* of Dan O'Bannon (who is now probably best known as the co-writer of *Alien*) and was familiar with Romero's back catalogue, which I had devoured during late nights at the Phoenix. Moreover, I recognised scream-queen Linnea Quigley, who was rapidly becoming a cult star thanks to low-rent slashers like *Savage Streets* and *Silent Night, Deadly Night*. In short, I 'got' the movie – and therefore I 'got' the gig.

Since my *Return* review attracted no abusive letters or legal suits and didn't actively bring the magazine into disrepute, it was considered that I had basically done a good job. A month or so later I was invited to attend a preview screening of Romero's *Day of the Dead* (the *official* sequel to *Night of the Living Dead* and *Dawn of the Dead* whose thunder *Return* had sneakily striven to steal) and felt as though I'd been given the keys to the city. Despite the fact that I'd had precious little published I now viewed myself as a fully-fledged film critic, ready to swap pithy cinematic epithets with anyone and everyone. I was sure of my opinions, certain of my judgement, and immutable in my prejudices, both personal and political.

I thought I was the next Barry Norman-in-waiting.

In fact, I was a mouthy know-nothing upstart.

Over the years, very little has changed.

In the TV Movie of My Life, the Manchester years would be represented by those cod dreamy flashback sequences in which you can't tell whether what you're seeing is real or imagined but you're pretty certain that everyone's wearing a wig. What I remember most is the sheer *intensity* of it all – the fact that *everything* seemed like a matter of life and death. The most emotively fraught battles were in the area of gender politics, with American author Andrea Dworkin's tub-thumping tome *Pornography: Men Possessing Women* being required reading for concerned gender warriors everywhere.

Dworkin hung like a dark shadow over the sexual-political landscape of the eighties, a terrifying voice of doom who explained in thunderous Moses-like tones that everything I'd ever suspected about being a worthless piece of crap was essentially true. If you've never read *Pornography: Men*

*Possessing Women* and you like a good scare then believe me you're in for a treat – it is one of the most upsetting books ever written, and will leave you wanting to kill either yourself or others. It is ferociously argued and hectoringly delivered – Leon Trotsky was a lightweight compared to Dworkin. Its central thesis (as the title pithily suggests) is that pornography is not only rape but also the perfect expression of man's wide-ranging subjugation of women over the centuries – a weapon of war, an act of violence, a tool of slavery. Over several hundred incendiary pages, Dworkin conjures a history of prostitution, child abuse, torture, imprisonment and mass murder, and relates – not to say *attributes* – it all directly to the glossy pages of *Hustler* magazine and the writings of the Marquis de Sade. By the time she gets to the end of the book she is describing her own soul as having become almost possessed by the demonic presence of porn, and being haunted at night by Gothic apparitions of vile and violent sexuality.

Substantial credence was lent to Dworkin's polemic in the early eighties by her association with Linda Lovelace, the former star of the seventies porno-chic blockbuster *Deep Throat* who had since conducted a dramatic volte-face and become a militant poster girl for the anti-porn lobby. Claiming that her husband/manager Chuck Traynor had beaten, threatened, and otherwise violently coerced her into prostitution and porn, Lovelace published hair-raising accounts of her ordeals which Dworkin was now helping to publicise. Together with fellow campaigner Catharine MacKinnon, Dworkin even took the battle against porn to the courts, arguing that it violated the civil rights of women, with Lovelace as one of their star witnesses.

Many argued that Lovelace's claims were turncoat baloney – that she had been vociferously enthusiastic about making *Deep Throat* at the time, and that her subsequent renunciations were self-serving and insincere. But as someone who actually *met* Chuck Traynor (albeit decades later), let me say that he seemed every bit as unloveable as his former wife had suggested. When making the Channel 4 documentary *The Real Linda Lovelace* in 2002, I interviewed Chuck in a hotel room in Gainesville, Florida, having taken the precaution of asking our burly soundman Duncan to sit between Traynor and me in case he tried to thump me – this being a perfectly understandable response when someone asks if you did indeed arrange for your wife to be gang-raped in a Miami hotel room before ordering her at gunpoint to have on-camera sex with a dog, as Lovelace had famously claimed.

In the event Chuck's response was far scarier – he never batted an eyelid, never flinched, nor blanched, nor recoiled, nor nothing. He didn't even deny that much – certainly not that he knocked his wife around, which he seemed to think was perfectly normal. When confronted with the worst of Lovelace's allegations, Traynor simply looked at me with 'aw shucks' amusement, as if the charges against him simply weren't that remarkable.

A few months after our interview, Traynor dropped dead, to the dismay of some of Lovelace's friends and relatives who declared their sadness that they had been denied the chance to kill him themselves. As for Dworkin (who I also interviewed for that documentary, and who turned out to be really nice and not at all frightening) she surely shed no tears for Chuck who had been living proof of her thesis about the very worst aspects of masculinity. Yet whereas Dworkin believed passionately that porn represented an assault upon women, I came to the conclusion that the truth of Lovelace's life was both more complex and mundane – she wasn't the victim of porn per se, but of domestic violence. She married a man who beat her up, battered and prostituted her for the best part of two years, and who ironically only stopped doing so when the success of *Deep Throat* unexpectedly made her a star. Indeed, there were those close to her who insisted that without the celebrity which that movie bestowed, Lovelace could easily have ended up as 'just another dead hooker in a hotel room'.

If there is a moral to Lovelace's unhappy story, it seems to me to be that porn – which is neither inherently good nor bad – needs to be regulated (rather than outlawed) at the point of *creation* rather than just the point of distribution. That is something that can only happen if the industry remains legalised and open – perhaps even respectable. Having always been innately suspicious of censorship (growing up as a horror fan will do that to you) it seems self-evident to me that banning porn won't make it go away, it'll just make it harder to police. Nor will it stop men beating up women.

It's worth pointing out that in her 2005 book *The Erotic Thriller in Contemporary Cinema*, my partner Linda Ruth

Williams argued that many soft-core exploitation videos with titles such as *Carnal Crimes* and *Night Rhythms* were actually less politically problematic than their more 'acceptable' Hollywood counterparts such as *Basic Instinct* – and often more interesting. My small role in this book was to transcribe the hours of interviews which Linda had conducted with everyone from A-list Hollywood directors to hard-core sleaze-mongers and frankly the latter often came across as more open-minded on the subject of gender equality. Linda's conclusion (which I have since stolen and passed off as my own – as with so much of her work) was that films which *look* leerily misogynist on the outside can often be deceptively subversive, while the most pernicious gender stereotyping thrives unchecked in respectable mainstream fare.

This mirrors my experience of horror movies, the gawdy trappings of which often hide a level of radical intelligence which critics of the genre simply can't (or won't) see. But despite my early confidence about the value of gore, in the early eighties I couldn't see through Dworkin's arguments about 'damaging' depictions of women, and as a result devoted many hours to toe-curlingly earnest 'Men Against Sexism' meetings which were every bit as breast-beatingly awful as they sound. We didn't do very much except sit around and despise ourselves, to which end we were aided and abetted by screenings of feel-bad movies like *Not a Love Story: A Film About Pornography* and readings from Dworkin and her ilk. But even in the midst of all our abject angst, we believed fiercely and inarguably that what we were doing was *right* ...

One of the great things about knowing that you're right is that it removes inconvenient self-doubt. My mother, who was a GP, once told me that the more she learned about medicine the more she realised just how *little* we really understand about the human body. This is not an uncommon conclusion – in almost every field of expertise, the actual extent of someone's knowledge and understanding can be gauged by the degree to which they are willing to accept that they actually know *nothing*. While expertise has been characterised as the art of knowing more and more about less and less, true learning (it seems to me) is all about understanding and appreciating just how much you will *never know*. For example, at the age of forty-six, I am just starting to realise how *vast* and *unbridgeable* are the gaps in my knowledge of the history of cinema, a medium which has only been around for just over a century. Even if I dedicated every waking moment of the next twenty years to studying the art of silent cinema, the growth of Indian cinema, the canon of Japanese cinema, and the bewildering marketing expanse of the 'Pacific Rim', I'd *still* be only scratching the surface. I recently read that, at a conservative estimate, something like twenty per cent of the films ever made no longer exist, thanks to the tendency of celluloid to disintegrate over time. Yet even with one fifth of *all* movies wiped out by the helpful degradations of time, there's still no hope of me ever being able to declare myself 'across' the history of movies which stretches like Cinerama beyond the comforting borders of the horizon. Like my mother, the older I get, the less I know I *know*.

Yet at the age of twenty-three, with a couple of dodgy horror movies under my belt and a copy of Dworkin's book in my coat pocket, I knew that I knew *everything*. And it was with this utter sense of blinkered self-certainty that I walked out of David Lynch's *Blue Velvet* – a film which I now recognise to be one of the greatest movies of the eighties – and straight into somebody's fist.

How did this happen? Let's start at the beginning …

I had seen David Lynch's debut feature *Eraserhead* as a teenager at the Phoenix, where it played on a regular Friday late-night double bill with George A. Romero's *The Crazies*. The film was described by Lynch as 'a dream of dark and troubling things' and became the quintessential midnight movie hit in the US before slowly spreading its diseased spell around the globe. A surreal nightmare about a terrified man who finds himself in sole charge of a monstrous child, *Eraserhead* boasted extraordinary monochrome visuals, a hair-raising performance from Jack Nance ('Henry', as previously noted), and a disorientatingly powerful soundtrack cooked up by Lynch and his long-time aural collaborator Alan Splet. In an early review, the trade mag *Variety* described it as 'a sickening bad-taste exercise' – which sounded like a recommendation to me.

*Eraserhead* took ages to make; Lynch reportedly started work on it back in May 1972 and didn't lock the final cut until early 1977. During the course of the film's protracted gestation and birth, the director wrestled with marriage, divorce and fatherhood, supported himself with a paper round, and fuelled his soul with sugary caffeine drinks from the local Bob's Big Boy Diner. During one hiatus, he completed the short film *The Amputee*, images from which would later be echoed in his daughter Jennifer's feature *Boxing Helena*. Indeed Jennifer, who was born with club feet, has been quoted as saying that *Eraserhead* 'without a doubt ... was inspired by my conception and birth, because David in no uncertain terms did not want a family. It was not his idea to get married, nor was it his idea to have children. But ... it happened.'

Exactly what *Eraserhead* is about remains a mystery. Lynch himself has proven consistently unwilling to explain the film, becoming particularly evasive on the subject of the creation of the 'baby' (some reports suggest that it is an animated bovine foetus). The director has, on occasion, claimed that it 'could have been found'. All we can be certain of is that the film's primary register is nightmarish and symbolic – it is not to be taken *literally*.

Obviously.

The first time I saw *Eraserhead* was with my friend Nick Cooper, a schoolmate and jazz pianist whom I would enlist to play drums in an earnest post-punk sixth-form school band called the Basics. When I first met Nick he had a disastrous flyaway haircut and wore flares – an unforgivable crime. After three weeks in the Basics he had a killer crew cut and was sporting skintight Sta-Prest trousers and cool-as-nuts Harrington jackets of varying colours. It was an amazing transformation, for which I would like to take full credit. The truth, however, is that Nick's straight-legged butterfly emerged from the chrysalis of his eighteen-inch flapping cocoon after he and I went to see *The Wanderers* at the Barnet Odeon. The film, which was set in the Bronx in 1963, had such a profound effect on both of us that after the screening we opened up the palms of our hands with a rusty penknife and became blood brothers there and then. Nick promptly went home and sorted out his fashion mojo, and remains to this day one of the best-dressed men I have ever met. God bless Philip Kaufman.

Dress sense aside, Nick's judgement on movies was not always on the money. Admittedly he was so scared by *The Exorcist* (which we both saw for the first time together at the Phoenix) that he had to come back to my house and sleep on the floor, for which he will always retain a special place in my affections. And he'd been pretty open to most of the early Cronenberg canon, including *Shivers* and *Rabid*, both of which were fairly freaky films full of creepy latex mutations and twisted sexuality. The latter starred porn queen Marilyn Chambers in one of her few 'straight' dramatic roles as a woman who becomes infected by a phallic parasite which lives in her armpit and bites people during sex. Chambers had teamed up with Cronenberg at the suggestion of producer Ivan Reitman and had worked on the movie under the watchful gaze of our old friend Chuck Traynor, who was by then her manager/husband, and whom Cronenberg significantly described as 'not my favourite kind of guy …'

Anyway, Nick coped with the sexual monsters of *Rabid* OK, but when it came to *Eraserhead* and its journey into the dark heart of man's most deep-set Freudian nightmares, he just didn't get it *at all*.

It was easy to tell when Nick wasn't 'getting' a movie because his left leg would bounce up and down in a state of hyper-caffeinated agitation. The more his left knee trembled, the worse his experience of the film. It was like watching someone review a movie in real time, but from the waist down – even if his mouth said nothing, his fidgeting calf muscles spoke volumes. The leg trembling began about fifteen minutes into *Eraserhead*, at around the time that Henry first returns home with the mutant baby whose existence is never explained beyond a general sense of creeping guilt about *everything*.

As Henry laid the baby on the table, Nick muttered loudly, 'Well *that* would never happen.' At first, I thought he was making some sort of profound surrealist joke, and laughed – it was like looking at a painting of melting watches by Salvador Dali and declaring that 'they'll never be very effective timekeepers'. But Nick wasn't joking. He was seriously doubting that someone would find themselves in the position of having fathered a bizarre alien baby, and then being required to tend to its needs in a small room which contained little other than a bed and a radiator in which lived a hamster-cheeked woman who sang to you at night whilst squishing extraterrestrial sperm beneath the heel of her tap shoes. It just *wouldn't happen*.

My only comparable experience of this sort of overly literal film criticism came when I took my sister Annie to see Lucio Fulci's entertainingly revolting *City of the Living Dead* at the ABC in Edgware. She was training to be a doctor, and during one particularly gruey scene in which a demonically possessed young woman vomited up her internal organs, Annie turned to me and whispered, 'Well *that's* not scary – they're all in the *wrong order*.' Apparently the offal spewing from the poor actress' mouth was not biologically accurate and was therefore failing to send a shiver down my sister's hospital-hardened spine.

As for Nick, he expressed his belief that *Eraserhead* 'just wouldn't happen' in increasingly irritated tones, his pulsating left leg throbbing to the rhythm of his growing impatience, causing an entire row of chairs to quiver and quake like jelly on a plate. It was like watching the movie in Sensurround.

A year or so ago, whilst broadcasting on BBC 5 Live, I described Nick's declaration that 'that wouldn't happen' as being the stupidest thing I had ever heard anyone say in a cinema. Nick promptly texted me to take full credit for the comment and to assert that he still stood squarely behind his original assessment. This is one of the reasons that I like Nick so much: not only was he the person with whom I had the electrifying experience of watching *The Exorcist* for the first time, not only was he living proof that a good haircut and a Harrington could turn you from zero to hero overnight – over and above all these things, he was as forthrightly mad and assertive in his opinions of *everything* as I was. This was a man who, when everyone else was sporting sunny 'Nuclear Nein Danke!' stickers had 'Peace Through NATO!' proudly emblazoned upon his windshield. Politically we were worlds apart. But personally we really *were* blood brothers.

Anyway, back to Manchester. My respect for David Lynch had grown with *The Elephant Man*, which I took as proof that

Nick had been *wrong wrong wrong* about *Eraserhead* (after all, John Merrick really *did* happen) and I'd even had a bash at embracing the dismal *Dune*, which I remember largely for containing a scene in which Sting comes out of an interstellar steam shower with nothing but a pair of silver wings on his knackers. I could go back to the movie to check whether this scene really *happened* or whether I'm just making it up but frankly I can't be bothered – considering Sting's recent adventures with a lute and his outpourings about tantric sex (not to mention the rotten music he's made since 'Roxanne') I think he deserves to come in for a little un-fact-checked stick. Oh, and for the record, I thought he was crap in *Quadrophenia* too. Ace Face my arse!

But *Blue Velvet* was a problem. Firstly, I'd made the mistake of reading a load of press coverage about the movie long before I saw it, something I have since learned to avoid. According to the reports, Lynch's latest wallowed in the degradation of women, and featured a central character (Dorothy, played by Isabella Rossellini) who actively colluded in her physical abuse by a psychopathic misogynist kidnapper (Frank, played by Dennis Hopper,who famously told Lynch 'I *am* Frank.'). Reports of a prone Dorothy instructing Kyle MacLachlan's preppy Jeffrey to 'hit me' after she had been raped by a drug-crazed Frank presented a picture of an indefensible male fantasy – particularly to a know-it-all adolescent politico who couldn't see past the end of Andrea Dworkin's nose.

So there I was in the Cornerhouse cinema, a head full of dogma, watching *Blue Velvet*, my overly politicised psyche growing more frazzled by the minute. We'd got through Dennis Hopper throwing Isabella Rossellini on the floor and screaming 'Baby wants to faaaaaaaaack' while inhaling some non-specific gaseous substance, watched through the slats of a closet door by a furtive Kyle MacLachlan who was indeed then instructed to 'Hit me! Harder!' It was a bizarre and shocking scene, disorientating and grotesque yet simultaneously orchestrated and absurd, but since I had *known* that it was coming I was kind of prepared for the worst. What I *wasn't* ready for was the sight and sound of Dean Stockwell lip-synching to Roy Orbison's 'In Dreams' while cradling a cabin light in his hand like the old lozenge microphones which crooners would caress, a performance which Dennis Hopper's over-agitated Frank would memorably describe as 'Suave! Goddam you are one suave *fucker*!' Now, being a fan of fifties' and sixties' bubblegum pop I *really* liked 'In Dreams', and my response to this unforeseen audio-visual stimulation was not unlike that scene in *A Clockwork Orange* in which Alex is forced to watch horrible acts playing out on-screen to the accompaniment of his beloved Ludwig van Beethoven. 'It's not right!' screams Alex, and at that moment I knew *exactly* how he felt. Without even thinking what I was doing I sprang out of my seat and headed up the aisle, unsure as to exactly *which* of the movie's many offences (the violation of women or the violation of *pop* music?) had really pushed my buttons. All I knew was that this was a 'bad' film. And I was going to say so.

Which I did, first vociferously in the bar, and then later in print, in the pages of *City Life*. Oh, don't get me wrong,

I didn't get the prestigious 'first review' of the film – just a tiny listings round-up during the later phase of its release. But I badmouthed it in print, rubbishing Lynch's puerile grasp of complex sexual politics and charging him with several politically incorrect offences against right-thinking right-on sensibilities. I really couldn't imagine a situation in which it was justifiable (let alone *helpful*) to come up with a story in which a woman becomes sexually enslaved by a psycho only to discover that his violent madness is perversely in tune with her own latent masochism – making *his* madness somehow *her fault*. As usual, I was *right*, Lynch was *wrong*, and that was all there was to say on the matter. Like I said earlier, it's amazing just how confident you can be when you really don't know what you're talking about.

On the other hand, American critic Roger Ebert *did* know what he was talking about, and he really took against *Blue Velvet* too. His one-star review, however, was erudite and well argued (unlike mine) and beautifully expressed his negative reactions to the film. 'A film this painfully wounding', wrote Ebert with his usual honesty and candour, 'has to be given special consideration. And yet those very scenes of stark sexual despair are the tip-off to what's wrong with the movie. They're so strong that they deserve to be in a movie that's sincere, honest and true. But *Blue Velvet* surrounds them with a story that's marred by sophomoric satire and cheap shots.' He proceeded to berate Lynch for flip-flopping between ice-cold sexual horror and cheesy satirical Americana, arguing that 'the movie is pulled so violently in opposite directions that it pulls itself apart' and demanding,

'What's worse? Slapping somebody around or standing back and finding the whole thing funny?'

Ebert's insights were right on the money, and I wish I had had the skill and self-awareness to say something half as interesting. Crucially, Ebert recognised and acknowledged that his *problem* with *Blue Velvet* lay in its power, a power which the critic felt almost angry at the director for squandering and mocking. If the film had just been rubbish, Ebert surely wouldn't have taken against it so staunchly – it would have just been another flawed two- or three-star movie featuring a few distracting set pieces, but little to get upset about. Yet the fact that the scenes of Rossellini's assault, masochism, and later public degradation hit Ebert so hard, and indeed seemed to contain some kind of awful human truth, made the fatuous context of their presentation all the more intolerable. It was precisely the things that Lynch had got *right* that fired Ebert to berate him for what was *wrong* with *Blue Velvet*. It was a terrific example of a critic taking responsibility for his own reactions to a film.

My review had *none* of that – none of the critical insight, none of the self-awareness, none of the literary grace ... none of the *doubt*. In truth, Ebert and I had had a very similar reaction to *Blue Velvet*, being horrified not so much by the ultra-grim scenes of sexual violence but by the surreal and presumably parodic insanity which surrounded them. Ebert (who had penned his own sexually violent and parodically insane script for *Beyond the Valley of the Dolls* years earlier) understood this, and his review manfully owned up to something I had no way of comprehending, let alone *admitting*. If, as F. Scott Fitzgerald claimed, intelligence is the ability to hold two contradictory ideas in your head at the same time, then I was the very definition of Stupid.

A few months later, me and my stupidity were drinking in the Cornerhouse bar when some oiky art-student type approached me and said, 'You're the guy who wrote that review of *Blue Velvet* in *City Life*, aren't you?' Dazzled by my own local fame, and wowed by my ever-widening sphere of critical influence, I turned proudly toward him and declared, 'Yes, that was me …' firmly expecting a warm handshake, the offer of a pint, and ten minutes of stimulatingly self-congratulatory conversation.

What I actually got was this: he hit me.

Now, when I say 'hit' I may be exaggerating the actual force and vigour of our brief but unmistakeable moment of physical contact. To those accustomed to the world of fisticuffs and street brawls, it would probably count as no more than a slap, a light brush, even a mere push. But to me, who had never been in a fight in my entire life, it was a palpable punch, accompanied by the guttural muttering of the word 'Wanker!' just to make sure there was no confusion as to his disagreement with my views.

I stepped back (or 'was knocked helplessly to the bar' depending on who's directing this 'true story') and before I had time to respond (oh come on – what was an utter weed like me honestly going to do?) he was gone.

The memory of this altercation did not, however, depart so quickly and played upon my mind for months to come – although surely not in the way that my unexpected adversary had intended. On the contrary, I took his fleeting recourse to physical contact to be definitive *proof* that I had been *right right right* about *Blue Velvet* all along. After all, if the movie's supporters couldn't fight their corner verbally, then there was clearly no merit in their cause. Violence begins at the point where reason and discourse end, and I have yet to see evidence that any disagreements may be satisfactorily solved through a punch-up.

Putative pugilists take note – thumping me will merely make me even more obnoxiously smug.

Allowing me to beat *myself* up however (psychologically speaking) can be devastatingly effective. And as the emboldening memory of that punch started to fade, I fell victim to the sneaking suspicion that I had been *wrong wrong wrong* about *Blue Velvet*, a thought which gnawed at my conscience like a guilty secret. What troubled me was the fact that I really couldn't explain *why* the film had provoked such an explosive reaction. Oh, I could *justify* it with a whole load of off-the-peg blather about unhelpful interventions in the ongoing sex war which Dworkin and her cohorts had made seem *very real indeed*. But beneath all the rhetoric I knew that wasn't really the problem at all. The *problem* was that the movie had got to me – got under my skin – and was now eating away at my psychological wiring like some Cronenbergian superbug.

Looking back now I can see my uncomfortable and contradictory reactions to *Blue Velvet* as a crucial part of my critical development, demonstrating that responses to movies are never simple or clear-cut. It's one thing to admit that all criticism is subjective, but quite another to accept that each individual subject is usually far too confused to understand their own personal responses, let alone anyone else's. Those mired in the hoary old traditions of 'effects theory' will blithely tell you that audiences respond to movies en masse – that the mythical über-viewer 'identifies' with *this* character or 'shares the experience' of *that* situation. For decades, such certainty underpinned the actions of the British Board of Film Classification, enabling former chief censor James Ferman to cut and ban movies whose precisely pernicious effect on audiences he claimed to understand. Yet the truth is far more unruly – people respond to movies in ways which are so violently (self-) contradictory that pretending to be able to police their 'effects' is at best foolhardy, at worst farcical. As Kyle MacLachlan's character says to Laura Dern's increasingly cracked schoolgirl Sandy in *Blue Velvet*, 'It's a strange world, isn't it?'

Oh lordy, yes it is.

So as the months went by, and *Blue Velvet* failed to fade from my memory, the realisation of my own profound fallibility grew by the day. William Friedkin once told me that he believed the power of *The Exorcist* lay in the fact that 'people take from that movie what they bring to it'. The same is true of *Blue Velvet* and, in a peculiar way, of *Deep Throat*, which was variously hailed as a 'celebration of personal freedom' and decried as 'a violation of human rights' – sometimes by the very same people.

By coincidence, the Cornerhouse cinema, where I first saw *Blue Velvet*, used to be a porno cinema, enticingly named the Glamour, where furtive punters would gather to quietly choke the chicken in the days before video made masturbating to moving pictures an entirely homespun recreation. The films that played at the Glamour weren't 'hard core', although a kaleidoscopically edited version of *Deep Throat* did show up there on occasion under its 'sex club' members-only licence. Years later I would learn that an unusually large number of Cornerhouse patrons had to be thrown out for wanking their way through Abel Ferrara's thoroughly unsexy *Bad Lieutenant*, a phenomenon the manager of the cinema told me she 'struggled to comprehend'. Perhaps, like the haunted houses of so many ghost stories, the building itself retained a memory of its disreputable past, and decent art-house patrons were somehow possessed by the demonic spirits of the raincoat brigade, desperate to find relief wherever it reared its ugly head.

Or perhaps people are just weird.

Whatever the truth, it's impossible not to conclude that human responses to the audio-visual stimulations of cinema are unfathomable in the extreme. Was walking out of *Blue Velvet* any more sensible than attempting to crack one off in *Bad Lieutenant*? Was watching *Deep Throat*, as Linda Lovelace later claimed, 'an act of rape' rather than (as she had previously claimed) a 'blow for liberty'? Was the Glamour cinema's ascension from lowly porn palace to church of cinematic art-house chic an indication of the triumph of 'culture' over 'crap', or just business as usual?

By the time I got up the nerve to watch *Blue Velvet* a second time, I was far more resigned to the certainty of uncertainty.

I had started to understand that it was possible to be enthralled and agitated by enthusiastically expressed views (both personal and political) while still fundamentally disagreeing with them – or at least, remaining *sceptical* about them. Most importantly, I had learned that if you take *any* fixed set of preconceptions into a movie theatre, then the better the movie the *more likely* you are to have those preconceptions confirmed. You can love bad movies, and you can hate good movies. But brilliant movies are often the ones that you love and hate *at the same time*. That's what makes them brilliant.

Or so it seemed as I sat in that second screening of *Blue Velvet*, surrendering to the awful beauty of its phantasmagoria ('In dreams, I walk with you' sings Roy Orbison) and being engulfed by a wave of shame and rapture, repugnance and delight which my naïve political correctness could no longer seek to deny. While the scenes of sexual degradation and despair remained almost unendurably harsh, an amazing transformation had occurred during those other moments which Roger Ebert had dismissed as 'cheap shots'. Having finally surrendered to the horror of *Blue Velvet*, I found myself unexpectedly touched and moved by the very elements that had formerly repelled me. The real revelation was my reaction to a much-quoted scene in which Laura Dern's Sandy recounts her vision of ethereal robins, a scene which Ebert doutbtless had in mind when citing the 'sophomoric satire' and 'campy in-jokes' of *Blue Velvet*.

'I had a dream,' Sandy tells MacLachlan's straight-faced Jeffrey as Angelo Badalamenti's suspended score surges in quietly choral tones. 'In fact, it was on the night that I met you. In the dream, there was our world. And the world was dark because there weren't any robins. And the robins represented *love*. And for the longest time there was just this *darkness*. And all of a sudden thousands of robins were set free and they flew down and brought this *blinding light* of love. And it seemed like that love would be the only thing that would make any difference. *And it did!* So I guess that means there is trouble till the robins come …'

Seeing that speech written down it looks like the goofiest garbage any actress ever had to deliver, and indeed the first time I saw *Blue Velvet* I interpreted it as nothing more than smart-alec satire. But the second time, having succumbed to the film's dark spell, I took it literally … *and I bought it*! My heart swelled, my soul surged, my eyes teared up, and I was gone, gone like a turkey in the corn. By the time Dean Stockwell grabbed that cabin light and started lip-synching 'A candy-coloured clown they call the sandman, tiptoes to my room every night …' I was buzzing like a horsefly. Audiences watching William Castle's 1959 shocker *The Tingler* and experiencing the bum-shaking thrills of 'Percepto' (buzzers hidden in selected seats, folks) couldn't have been more vibrantly thrilled!

Years later I interviewed Lynch for *The Culture Show* and felt duty-bound to tell him how much I had hated *Blue Velvet* first time round, and how I'd stormed out and written a review that said it was garbage. I meant it as a compliment, although thinking about it now it may have seemed unnecessarily confrontational. Certainly there was a moment in my rambling eulogy when Lynch looked genuinely concerned as to where I was going with all this. But, bless him, he stuck with me and by the time I got to the bit about going to see the film a *second* time and realising that it was a masterpiece after all he seemed to be on board. That's how it looked to me, anyway.

What I was *trying* to say was that this really is 'a strange world', and somehow my polarised love/hate responses to *Blue Velvet* perfectly proved that point. Lynch seemed to agree, particularly when our conversation drifted into a discussion of *Lost Highway* which had received some of its best reviews in Paris from critics who had been shown the reels in the *wrong order*. It was amazing, we agreed, how the human mind could impose order upon chaos, seeing patterns where there are none, finding meaning in meaninglessness – and vice versa.

Tangentially, I had a strangely similar experience with Marc Evans' psychological thriller *Trauma*, which I saw in the company of Radio One's long-standing film critic James King. The film largely takes place within the mind of its (deranged?) protagonist, played by Colin Firth, and boasts an elliptical structure which mirrors the temporal dysphasia of his inner turmoil. Except, of course, it doesn't; the reels just got mixed up in the projection booth the first time I saw it. I remember with horrible clarity how James complained afterwards that the film 'made no sense' and how I berated him for his simplistic demand for a 'linear narrative structure'. I remember, too, the sense of skin-crawling embarrassment I got when receiving a text message from the producer explaining that the film had been projected the wrong way round, and asking if I would watch it again in the right order. Worse still was the fact that, after that *second* screening, I remained convinced that I had enjoyed the movie more the first time.

To Lynch, who genuinely believes that 'we live inside a dream', this all made perfect sense. And somehow, through the absurdity of my reactions to his work, and to Evans' film, and to all the movies that I now claim to love and cherish, we seemed to have found common philosophical ground. Plus, Lynch had complimented me on my choice of tie which I took to be the highest accolade since he was a man who used to like ties so much he would wear *three* at once. Now he wears none.

Over the years I've interviewed Lynch on several occasions, for *Q Magazine*, for BBC radio and TV, and most recently on stage at the BFI Southbank (formerly the National Film Theatre) in London. During that encounter, I talked to him about the 'sweetness and innocence' of *Blue Velvet* – the same film that had sent me storming from Manchester's former premier porno cinema in a huff of politicised anger all those years ago. Back then the film had seemed irredeemably corrupt, the jarring juxtaposition of brutal psychological realism and corny insincere Americana epitomising the maxim that 'postmodernism means never having to say you're sorry'. Now here I was waxing lyrical about its utter *lack* of irony, particularly Sandy's dream of the robins.

'The thing I absolutely love about that scene,' I told a benevolently smiling Lynch, 'is that when Laura Dern describes her dream, she's *not* doing it in a goofy way, but in a *real* way. This has been written about often as ironic, but to me it seems completely sincere and not ironic at all. You do really *mean* it, don't you?'

'Oh yes,' agreed Lynch, in his clipped 'Jimmy Stewart from Mars' chirrup. 'We all have this thing where we want to be very cool and when you see something like this, really kind of embarrassing, the tendency is to laugh, so that you are saying out loud that "This is embarrassing and not cool!" and you're hip to the scene. This kind of thing happens. But we also always know that when we're alone with this person that we're falling in *love* with, we *do* say goofy things, but we don't have a problem with it. It's so *beau-ti-ful*. And the other person's so forgiving of these beautiful, loving, goofy things. So there's a lot of this swimming in this scene. At the same time, there's something to that scene, a *truth* to it, in my book.'

Love. Beauty. Truth. All the things Ebert (and I) had thought were missing from *Blue Velvet*.

Yet there they were all along – staring us right in the face.

By the time I left Manchester at the end of the eighties, I wasn't sure *what* I believed in any more. I had discovered that my judgements about movies were irredeemably flawed; I had learned that doctrine rarely coincided with desire; and I had come to accept that freedom of speech meant allowing people to say the things you *don't want to hear*.

On the night before I shipped out to London, I trekked to Salford Quays on my own to watch a late-night screening of Clive Barker's lively horror romp *Hellraiser*, now widely regarded as the best British horror film of the decade. And as I sat there watching Clare Higgins lusting after the freshly flayed corpse of her reanimated boyfriend and wincing at the sight of giant fish hooks tearing strangulated faces apart, I realised that very little had changed since the days when I took refuge from the horrors of school life in triple-bill X-rated all-nighters at the Phoenix East Finchley.

When everything else was uncertain, gore cinema never let me down.

Pass me that chainsaw.

# Chapter 3

## 'COME BACK TO CAMDEN'

'London is dead, London is dead, London is dead ...'

So said Morrissey, but only after he'd severed his Salford Lads Club alliances and headed for the beautiful South, finding musical solace in the (metaphorical) arms of Boz Boorer whom I personally credit with putting his ailing career back on the road to glam-stomping longevity. And if Morrissey could run off to the smoke and be a Polecat then I was pretty sure that I could too. After all, we had the same hair.

So, after bailing out of Manchester, *City Life*, Men Against Sexism et al., I found myself back in my hometown, tired of politics and hungry for work. Although my written output at *City Life* had been less than prolific, I *had* remembered to keep copies of *everything* I had *ever* had printed, and so at least I now had a 'portfolio'. The exact form of this portfolio was peculiar – having been a devout fan of both The Clash and

William Burroughs as a kid, I had become besotted with the cut-up aesthetic (which now masquerades as the video 'mash-up') and decided that my work would be best presented in a manner which reflected this avant-garde appreciation. So, armed with a crisp £5 note and a collection of *City Life*s I proceeded to a West End newsagent wherein I photocopied a selection of my finest reviews and studiously 'ripped and remixed' them to conjure a creative collage of work which was then photocopied *again* to give it a rebellious post-punk agitprop feel. Written down this looks pretty stupid, particularly in an age when photocopying itself is seen as slightly less exciting that the purchase of a new ballpoint pen. But this was 1988, and back then I was really 'pushing the envelope'.

Really.

Here was what I knew: every John, Jack and Mary wanted to work for a hip listings magazine, and to get paid for writing about watching films. Since the job itself wasn't exactly rocket science, you had to have *something* to mark yourself out from the crowd. My 'something' was that ridiculous piece of thrice-photocopied paper – that, and the fact that I actually showed up *in person* and simply refused to take no for an answer. I figured that if I was persistent enough, in the end it would be easier for them to give me work than to have to keep turning me away. And in the end, I was right.

The first office upon whose hallowed doors I solemnly banged like Martin Luther nailing his Ninety-Five Theses to the church door was that of *City Limits*. For political reasons,

I *really* wanted to work for the nominally co-operative *City Limits*, but there was simply no room at the inn – for which I remain retrospectively grateful.

My next stop was the *New Musical Express* which by that time had moved from its funky bohemian offices on Carnaby Street to the altogether more corporate surroundings of IPC Towers on the South Bank. Whereas legend once had it that any old wino could roll in off the street to have a pee in the stairwell and end up reviewing the new album by ELP, now you had to get past a doorman and negotiate a lift to the fourth or fifth floor where you would be met by a 'receptionist' who would 'buzz' whoever it was you were hoping to meet while you waited in the foyer. Remember that scene from *King of Comedy* where Rupert Pupkin sits like a plank in the foyer of Jerry Langford's TV show while endless others are ushered silently past him? It was like that – except I was no De Niro. In the end, I wound up handing my post-punk photocopy over to the receptionist and leaving with promises to 'call back' – never an effective technique.

Only slightly disheartened I proceeded forthwith to the Southampton Street offices of *Time Out* in Covent Garden. As I mentioned previously, *City Life* had styled itself as a 'cross between *Time Out* and *Private Eye*' and we had been sending each other complimentary copies of our respective magazines for several years. In fact, some of the freelance contributors who wrote for *Time Out* topped up their income by filing for regional mags such as ours, and thus I had been blithely subbing copy by Nigel Floyd (who was a stalwart of the *Time Out* film section) without ever having set eyes on him since my arrival at *City Life*. Despite the lack of personal contact, I believed that I had some connection with *Time Out* and therefore felt emboldened to stride into reception and announce my arrival as if everyone should automatically know exactly who I was.

'Hello,' I said to the impishly handsome young man behind the desk (who later turned out to be *Time Out*'s much-mourned Gay London editor Michael Griffiths, gracefully multitasking in the mornings). 'I am Mark Kermode from Manchester's prestigious *City Life* magazine, and I should like to see your film editors, Brian Case and/or Geoff Andrew, both of whom know of me and my work, obviously, and are very probably expecting me.'

Which they weren't.

Michael smiled politely, picked up a phone, dialled a number, got no answer, tried again, got no answer again, put the phone down, smiled again, whispered 'Excuse me,' then leaned over into the back of the oddly warren-like but allegedly 'open plan' office and screeched '*Geeoooooffff!*'

There was a scurrying from the back of the office, which looked uncannily like the set of Terry Gilliam's *Brazil* due to the fact that the ceiling area was bedecked with vast exposed heating pipes which seemed set to blow at any moment. Then a head popped round a pillar, friendly but slightly rattled, looked at Michael who nodded toward me, looked at me, completely blank (understandably), then back at Michael.

'What?'

'Him.'

'Who?'

'*Him*. There. He's here to see you. From Manchester.'

'Who is?'

'*He is*. That bloke there. You know him, apparently.'

Geoff came out from behind the pillar, looked at me again, clearly racking his brain to remember where on earth he might have met me before, but (reasonably enough) coming up with nothing.

'I was just on my way out to lunch ...' he began, but before he could get any further I leaped into the fray.

'Hi!' I said, grabbing Geoff's hand with what I considered to be confidence-inspiring force. (I have a thing about firm handshakes – I think they're important and, crucially, unisex. I can't be doing with all this French-style cheek-kissing nonsense – no wonder their county keeps getting invaded – and I see it as a sign of respect that I shake hands with women and men equally. A handshake doesn't have to be crushingly tight or 'manly' to be 'firm' – merely forthright. Disappointingly, the *worst* handshake in the world belongs to one of my greatest heroes, Woody Allen, whose dangling half-hearted grip is like grasping a bag of wet, limp lettuce.)

'I'm Mark Kermode, from Manchester's *City Life* magazine,' I announced again with confidence turned up to eleven. 'We've never actually *met*, what with me being in Manchester and you being here in London and everything, but we *have* spoken on the phone [no we hadn't] and we've been in occasional correspondence obviously [not really true either] and you said that if I was ever in London I should pop in [nope, none of the above]. So, here I am.'

Geoff smiled politely, looked at Michael, who shrugged,

looked back at me, and opened his mouth to say something. Probably 'Go away.' Only politely. But again I got in first.

'Anyway, as you probably know I've actually *moved* to London [how would he know this?] and I thought I'd come and see you *first* [an utter, outright lie, as you know] about the possibility of doing some work for you. For *Time Out*. For the Film Section.'

Silence. Dead space. Press on.

'I've brought some cuttings so you can have a look at my work, although you probably know it from the magazine [we have now passed into the realms of fantasy], but I thought that I should bring it anyway. You know, out of politeness.'

I thrust the photocopied sheet into his hand. He took it, and looked at it, albeit briefly.

I hadn't been thrown out. This was going *brilliantly*!

'Well, thanks very much,' he said with admirable composure. 'The thing is, we don't really *need* any more film reviewers at the moment. We've got a full Film Section here in the office, and a solid roster of regular freelancers …'

'Like Nigel Floyd!' I interjected. 'Of course, I know him well [total untruth]. He's been writing for *City Life* for years, as you know [worth a try], and I've been subbing his copy. He's great [true! At last!].'

There was a brief pause.

'You sub?' said Geoff, his interest marginally piqued.

'Oh yes, I do *everything*. Subbing. Listings, driving the van. Or *crashing* the van ha ha ha – only joking. But what I *really* want to do is *write* and — '

It was Geoff's turn to cut in.

'You've done listings?'

'Oh yes. But I really want to *write* ...'

'But you *can* do listings. You have experience?'

'Yes I have experience in listings. And writing.'

'But listings?'

'Yes, listings. And writing.'

'But *listings*?'

With my highly trained super-perception journalist skills I had started to detect a subtle undercurrent in our conversation which may not have been obvious to the untrained ear. Through some uncanny sixth sense I began to divine that Geoff may have an interest in someone with skills in the area of '*listings*'. Without realising it, he had unwittingly allowed me an entry into the otherwise impenetrable fortress of the *Time Out* Film Section which I would now subtly exploit to my own advantage.

'Do you,' I ventured nonchalantly, 'need someone to do ... listings?'

'No,' said Geoff.

Bugger.

'At least, not right now.'

Un-bugger. A bit.

'But I might need someone in a couple of weeks' time.'

Aha ...!

'We've got some holidays coming up and we might need some cover ... in listings. And if you could do *listings* then there might be the possibility – only the *possibility* mind you – that I might perhaps conceivably be able to pass a little bit of ...'

'Writing?'

'Yes … "writing"… alongside the listings … your way.'

I decided to play it cool.

'*I'll do it!*' I shrieked. 'When do I start?'

Geoff looked slightly taken aback.

'Well, like I said, it's only a possibility. And we may be covered after all … I'm not sure. I'll have to check. Leave your phone number with reception and I'll give you a call. OK?'

OK? This was *fantastic*! Not only had I not been thrown out of the office, I had actually arrived at the 'possibility' of some work in the unspecified future. I was *on fire* – such a conflagration, in fact, that I could scarcely scrawl my contact details on to a piece of paper for fear that it would burst into flames and set the entire building ablaze like that bit in *The Towering Inferno* when a small electrical fire in a broom cupboard suddenly becomes a skyscraper of incandescent rapture and Robert Wagner's smoky mistress falls out of a window wrapped only in a flaming towel.

Incidentally, since you've brought up the subject of *The Towering Inferno* (thanks for that), did you know that co-stars Steve McQueen and Paul Newman were so concerned that neither should have top billing over the other that they got their agents to count the *exact* number of lines attributed to the fire chief and architect respectively and then got the writers to juggle the script until the amount of dialogue was perfectly balanced? After which, they got the promotions people to agree to a credit system whereby one star's name would appear left but *lower*, the other right but *higher*, on both the movie titles and poster ads, thereby preventing the possibility that *either* actor could be seen as 'second billed'.

And they tell us that communism has no place in Hollywood.

Back in North London, I went home to sit by the phone like a spurned lover awaiting a reprieve from their errant paramour. Every time the damn thing rang I leaped to grab the receiver, alive with eager anticipation, only to be crushed by yet another call from a double-glazing salesman asking if I could feel the winds of change a-blowin' through my living room.

In the end, after a fortnight's self-flagellating torture, I decided to swallow my pride and go back to Southampton Street.

This time I got there early in the morning, having learned from my urban revolutionary days in Manchester that police raids were always conducted at dawn to catch suspects at their most 'unawares'. Once again, Michael was behind the desk, perky and polite, with a saucy glint even at 9.30 in the morning. (We would later become friends, and I remember doing tequila shots and dancing the cha-cha-cha with him at a nightclub underneath St Martin-in-the-Fields – not something I have done with many people.) He had the extreme good grace to recognise me and remember my name, and by the time Geoff got to reception at around 10 a.m. he was offering to make me cups of coffee and telling me what was wrong with my haircut and dress sense (a lot, apparently).

I knew that showing up at the office unannounced a second time was majorly not cool, but like Richard Gere in *An Officer and a Gentleman* I had nowhere else to go. And Geoff, playing Foley to my Mayo, presumably saw the desperation in my eyes and decided to give me a break. Indeed, he went one better than giving me a break – he gave me a *job*, albeit temporary. A job filling in listings duties for *Time Out* stalwarts Wally Hammond and Derek Adams, both of whom were being impertinent enough to take holidays, leaving their respective desks briefly unattended.

I was in.

I was keen.

I was enthusiastic.

I was hard-working.

I was also – it turned out – absolutely *rubbish* at listings.

Despite a conscientious crash course in the minutiae and importance of *Time Out*'s extraordinarily detailed account of the time and place of *every* film showing in London ('I want you to take these lists home … and *worry* over them,' said Wally, who took any inaccuracy very personally) I managed to screw up very badly indeed. In my first few weeks at *Time Out*, rather than just omitting an occasional screening here or there, or slipping up on a film title, I managed to lose an *entire cinema*. This had never happened before, and will surely never happen again. It was a major error – an unparalleled goof which pissed off both the public and the cinema owner, not to mention the publisher of the mag, all at the same time. This was clearly why Geoff had been so insistent in asking whether I could actually 'do' listings – because he needed somebody who really could *do* them, rather than somebody who just *thought* they could do them but who would actually drop the ball spectacularly. After all, it was Geoff who took the angry calls from the cinema, and the punters (not to mention the publisher), and he clearly did not need this kind of aggravation.

I promised to do better and tried very hard to do so. But the unavoidable fact was that I was tragically out of my depth. In Manchester, 'doing' the film listings for *City Life* was a comparatively straightforward process which involved ringing round a few cinemas and politely reminding the manager to post us his or her screening times in prompt fashion. Cornerhouse was slightly more complex, since their films changed on a daily (rather than weekly) basis, but they published a terrifically definitive programme which you could pick up from the foyer on your way into the office and then just input the information straight into the typesetter. But London in the late eighties was a whole other world. For one thing it was *huge* and had what seemed like a billion cinemas, many of which were independent 'rep' (or art-house) establishments such as the Scala in King's Cross which could screen up to twenty different films a week. I used to go to horror all-nighters at the Scala where it was possible to do a dusk-till-dawn *five-film* marathon – particularly useful if you didn't have anywhere to stay for the night and weren't averse to catching a snooze between screenings in tatty velveteen chairs with a cat crawling on your head and the sickly-sweet napalm smell of dope infesting your lungs, pores, hair and clothes. Doing the triple-bill-packed Scala listings for *Time Out* alone could put you in the hospital, and that was just the tip of the iceberg.

Back in those pre-internet days, the magazine prided itself on being the *only* reliable source of screening information times and it literally stood or fell on the quality of its listings. I remember coming into the office one morning and finding Wally freshening up after a night spent at his desk because there simply hadn't been any *time* to go home. It was like the boot camp out of *Full Metal Jacket*, only without the guns and the dodgy shots of the Isle of Dogs.

Inevitably, the workload at *Time Out* took its toll on the staff who would occasionally find solace in the welcoming arms of a liquid lunch. During my brief spell as a *TO* office boy, I never got used to the phenomenon of watching one particularly talented editor and writer order a bottle of wine *with the bill* and then go back to the office where he would put in a solid afternoon's work functioning more creatively, efficiently, and amusingly than I could ever do. I have *never* been able to drink at lunchtime – the minute alcohol invades my bloodstream my neurological system gets the message that all work is over and we're on the slow but inexorable road to shutdown. That's what I *like* about alcohol – the fact that it makes all thoughts of work go away, thereby relieving stress, tension, and anxiety in a wonderfully reliable way. But the idea of trying to work after consuming even a half of lager shandy is anathema to me. I'm just not built that way.

I am, however, wired up to feel profoundly uncomfortable and horribly guilty about doing any job *badly*, and despite the handsome reward of the weekly pay cheques (when the chips are down the capitalist bastards will always treat you better than the breast-beating liberals) I knew that I was letting *Time*

*Out* down. So after scraping by for a few more weeks I cornered Geoff in private and told him what he already knew – that I just wasn't up to the job. He agreed, but with great largesse congratulated me on having owned up to my own shortcomings and promised to honour his earlier offer of writing work. He would later tell me that this had been a turning point – that he would have *had* to fire me had I not offered my own resignation, but that doing so had somehow saved my reputation and made me seem reliably honest rather than just unreliably rubbish.

I learned an important lesson too – when it comes to work, always find the door before they show it to you.

We agreed to muddle through until someone better could be found to handle listings cover, and I found myself spending more and more time in the *Time Out* office with little to do other than answer the phones and 'help out' in vague and frankly unspecified ways while filing the occasional film review and getting under Michael's feet, which became my new favourite pastime. This suited me just fine, because I got to watch *real* journalists at work while making some great friends like Nigel Floyd, with whom I would end up going to Russia with disastrous results (see Chapter Five).

I also got to review some films, generally low-rent genre stuff which (as before) provided my passport to 'proper journalism'. You can say what you like about trash cinema – in terms of my career it has served me better than all the Oscar-winning art in the world. Any idiot can review an acclaimed mainstream blockbuster like *Gandhi* (which prompted my oft-repeated maxim about 'SIR' Ben Kingsley that 'when he's good he's *very* good but when he's bad he's Gandhi') but it takes a special kind of idiot to get the measure of an underfunded piece of gory knock-off schlock, or indeed the *sequel* to an underfunded piece of gory knock-off schlock.

The problem with printed reviews, of course, is that there's something horribly permanent about them, allowing gross misjudgements to be waved in your face years after the initial error has been committed. I have always tended to treat *everything* that appears in print as some kind of journal of record, and have never quite got my head around the idea that yesterday's news is tomorrow's fish and chip papers. And indeed, in the age of the internet, it *isn't* – as Julia Roberts so eloquently explains to Hugh Grant in Richard Curtis' oddly enduring *Notting Hill*.

And so it is with a sense of trepidation that I now reach for the weighty *Time Out Film Guide* which would become the ultimate resting place for all the blather that I and many others wrote for the mag in the pressure-cooker environment of that steam-driven office. I *know* that most of what I wrote for *City Life* wasn't very good, but it also wasn't very widely read and hasn't been properly archived outside of Andy Spinoza's filing cabinets. So, as long as we all felt good about it at the time, then that's all that really matters. But those early *Time Out* reviews *are* still out there in the world, and are indeed accessible online as part of a frighteningly thorough archive of which none of us could have ever dreamed (and for which, therefore, most of us never got paid ...).

But let's stay with print. If memory serves, the first

review I ever had published in *Time Out* was for a cheapie schlocker entitled *Watchers*. All I can remember about it now is that (as the title suggests) there was a running motif about eyeballs – other than that, it was fairly unremarkable stuff. Now, the natural tendency when you start reviewing films is to resort immediately to hyperbole, declaring middle-of-the-road fodder to be somehow exceptional because from where you're standing, frankly, it *is*. I was clearly guilty of this at *City Life*, and hadn't entirely grown out of the habit by the time I arrived at Southampton Street. I remember, for example, declaring in *Time Out*'s sister magazine *20/20* that the Falklands War drama *Resurrected* was 'the most important, and indeed difficult, film you will see this year' – a brash claim which promptly wound up on the film's poster. It has been to my infinite relief that this comparatively little-seen movie's young director Paul Greengrass has subsequently blossomed into one of the most talented and imitated film-makers of his generation, helming the hit *Bourne* sequels, and picking up an Oscar nomination for the 9/11 drama *United 93*. The fact that Greengrass has had such remarkable success, becoming a film-maker who is bankable *and* credible on both sides of the Atlantic, makes my untrammelled praise for his debut feature seem uncannily prescient – indeed, I have never failed to remind Greengrass whenever I bump into him in Soho that I was there *first* and that therefore he owes his entire movie career to me. Yet the truth is that I just got lucky, and the fact that I was so bowled over by a movie which *happened* to herald a major new talent was more down to good fortune than good judgement.

Remember, I'm the guy who predicted (again in print) that in the race for muscle-bound superstardom, Dolph Lundgren would triumph over both Jean-Claude Van Damme and Arnold Schwarzenegger because of the three of them he was the only one who could do a passable American accent.

Dolph and Jean-Claude were recently to be found re-teaming for the action franchise reboot *Universal Soldier: Regeneration*, having both served time in the hellish 'straight-to-video' market.

Arnold, meanwhile, runs California.

Good call, Kermode.

It's partly for this reason that I tend not to revisit my own reviews – the sense of self-loathing and shame is just too much to bear ('Sweet heavens, did I really say *that*?!'). But flicking through the *Time Out Film Guide* I discover that I pronounced *Watchers* to be 'good cheap nonsense', an assessment by which I'll stand. Elsewhere the remnants of my work in the *Guide* are marginally less harrowing than I had imagined – which says more about the quality of *TO*'s editors than it does about my writing. I did get to have a crack at a couple of mainstream movies, such as *Star Trek V: The Final Frontier* ('warped factor five' – boom boom), but the two reviews I'm most proud of from this period are of solidly marginal fare: *Surf Nazis Must Die*, which I really hated; and *Piranha Women in the Avocado Jungle of Death*, which I gave an enthusiastic thumbs up!

As I intimated previously, there's really nothing remarkable about being able to identify a 'proper' film like *Schindler's List* as an 'important' movie about the Holocaust (although the true value of Spielberg's movies is always inversely proportional to their seriousness – hence *War of the Worlds* is a better film than *Munich* in the same way that *Jaws* beats *Schindler's* any day). But it's quite another thing to be able to pass judgement on the similarly Third Reich-themed *Surf Nazis Must Die*, a film whose title announced that it was utter garbage, but which might actually have turned out to be brilliant by mistake (which it didn't). Equally, while everyone quacked on endlessly about how important *The Accused* was in putting serious gender issues up there on screen, far fewer trumpeted the merits of *Piranha Women* which was widely imagined to be an unpolished turd but which was actually a very witty feminist satire with more to say on the sex war than most films of the eighties.

Things were made particularly complicated in this period by the rise of home video and the subsequent expansion of the knowingly trashy – and thus allegedly postmodern – genre market which threw up titles like *A Nymphoid Barbarian in Dinosaur Hell* ('Where the prehistoric meets the prepubescent!') and *Hollywood Chainsaw Hookers* ('They charge an arm and a leg!'). Brand leaders in this area were Troma films, who had made a killing distributing the retitled cheapie sleaze-fest *Blood Sucking Freaks* (formerly *The Incredible Torture Show*) against which our old friends Women Against Pornography had campaigned in the US.

Capitalising on the negative publicity of their early success, Troma had cashed in on the burgeoning belief that some movies (like Ed Wood's infamous *Plan 9 From Outer Space*) could be 'so bad they're brilliant' and proceeded to distribute a string of films whose titles suggested rancidly rotten delights aplenty. In some cases, they simply bought off-the-shelf grot and repackaged it for the 'cult' market' – like *Rabid Grannies* whose protagonists, as Nigel Floyd pointedly observed, were in fact 'possessed aunties'. They were also Belgian (like JCVD, Plastic Bertrand, and Tintin) and were originally named *Les Mêmes Cannibales*. But more importantly they were rubbish. As was *Surf Nazis Must Die*, which I described in my characteristically temperate *Time Out* review as 'Utter horse shit'. Even accounting for the lowered expectations engendered by Troma's reputation for unwatchable dreck, *Surf Nazis* was a massive viewing disappointment, and I'm proud to have said so. By comparison *The Toxic Avenger*, in which a janitor falls into a vat of slime and becomes a mop-wielding melty-headed anti-hero, was almost bearable. Almost, but not quite. Yet to this day there are airheads who will tell you that *Surf Nazis Must Die* is a must-see 'cult classic', morons who were taken in by Troma's extraordinary talent for hyping junk, and who still think there's something hilariously rebellious about watching genuinely terrible films.

Part of the reason for Troma's success was the fact that co-founder Lloyd Kaufman was actually a terrific talker who was great fun to be around – unlike his movies. When the NFT ran a somewhat misjudged Troma retrospective in the early nineties Kaufman tore the place up, his resemblance to Mel Brooks proving to be more than merely physical. The audience positively rocked with laughter which was only quelled when one of Lloyd's bloody awful movies started playing. I also had the strange pleasure of interviewing performance artiste and *Toxic Avenger* sequel star Phoebe Legere who tried harder than anyone I have ever met to appear zany, madcap and weird, thereby leaving me with the impression that she was fantastically ordinary and a bit dull. Our interview took place on the balcony of a waterfront hotel in Chelsea where Phoebe greeted me in electric pink leggings and a tutu, a large piano accordion strapped across her chest which she played whilst unsuccessfully attempting to affect an air of casual insouciance. To her credit, she didn't appear to actually *like* (or even to have *seen*) the *Toxic Avenger* movies in which she featured, so maybe she was smarter than she seemed. Frankly, if *I* was promoting movies that bad, *I'd* take up playing the piano accordion.

In truth, despite what the fans will tell you, movies which are actually 'so bad they're brilliant' are rarer than hens' teeth, and are almost *never* the result of someone setting out to make a cult movie in the first place. Cross-dressing cult hero Edward D. Wood Jr, now widely hailed as the world's worst film-maker, seems to have genuinely believed that both *Glen or Glenda* and *Plan 9 From Outer Space* were going to be decent shoestring-budget movies and would have been appalled by his posthumous elevation to world-beating crap status. That's what makes Tim Burton's affectionate biopic *Ed Wood* such a monochrome delight – the fact that its subject (energetically played by Johnny Depp in one of his finest screen roles) is a wild-eyed dreamer rather than a cynical old hack.

In the best scene from *Ed Wood*, Depp's titular anti-hero

storms off the set of his latest low-budget disaster because the financiers are interfering with his vision, but his sour mood turns to elation when he spies his hero, Orson Welles, drinking quietly in the darkened corner of a nearby bar. Still attired in full Angora-sweatered drag, Wood strides over to shake Welles' hand and share his troubles, and rather than laughing at him Welles offers a sympathetic ear. His own career, the maestro admits, was dogged by studio interference, with *Citizen Kane* (which critics now regularly label The Greatest Film Ever Made) being the only film on which Orson got final cut. But, Welles tells Wood, it is important not to give up – never to abandon your dream or lose sight of your vision. Wood is so fired up by his idol's wise words that he gets straight up and storms back into the studio to make what would become the winner of the Golden Turkey Award for Worst Film Ever. 'This is the one!' beams Depp's Wood with glee. 'This is the one I'll be remembered for …'

The only example I can think of in recent years of a film that is genuinely 'so bad it's brilliant' is *Mamma Mia!*, the screen adaptation of the surprise hit stage play in which a collection of Abba songs are clumsily arranged around a hideously literal narrative to perversely crowd-pleasing effect. I never saw the stage show, although a close friend whose judgement I trust told me after opening night that it was worse than *Carrie: The Musical*, a horror-film adaptation (via Stephen King's novel) in which showering high-school girls threw tampons at each other while chanting 'Plug it up! Plug it up!' to a toe-tapping beat. *Carrie: The Musical* was so legendarily terrible that it spawned the catchphrase 'Not since *Carrie* ...' although my friend assured me that this would now be superseded by 'Not since *Mamma Mia!...*'

But it was not to be. Despite some stinky reviews *Mamma Mia!* became a smash hit stage play on both sides of the Atlantic, attracting the great and the good with its unique feel-good mix of indescribably bad scriptwriting and indestructibly good pop songs. Meryl Streep has publicly declared that the play helped her to get over the trauma of 9/11, its relentlessly escapist optimism proving the perfect antidote to the horrible realities of modern international terrorism – apparently. Indeed, it was as a result of her writing to the producers to tell them how much she had enjoyed the show that she wound up starring in the godforsaken film adaptation which has gone on to become the most successful British-backed movie *ever*.

Now, only a certifiable maniac could claim that the film of *Mamma Mia!* is actually any good. It isn't – it's knee-tremblingly terrible in every conceivable respect. The plot, if one may call it such, goes like this: a former Chiquitita-turned-ageing-Dancing-Queen faces her Waterloo when her Nina Pretty Ballerina daughter discovers that her Mamma Mia *doesn't* know which Man After Midnight Gave her Gave her Gave her a child. After sending out an SOS to her Honey Honey, the Angel Eyed kid decides to Take a Chance on three potential suitors to prove their possible parentage, with the Winner Taking It All up the aisle at her impending nuptials. Voulez-Vous? Not 'arf, pop-pickers.

If you think the plot sounds ropey, try getting your head

around a cast which pairs up stalwart Scandinavian thespian Stellan Skarsgård (in a role reportedly turned down by Bill Nighy) with rumbustious British treasure Julie Walters who (according to legend) triumphed over an equally well-known comedian who was told at the auditions that the role was hers unless she sang 'like a cow in labour' – which, it seems, she did. Oddly, the bovine procreation rule doesn't appear to have been extended to Pierce Brosnan who is without doubt the worst 'singer' ever heard in a sound motion picture, *ever* – and I'm including in that hallowed list Charles 'no neck' Gray in *The Rocky Horror Picture Show* and Peter Boyle's monster-clumping massacre of 'Puttin' on the Ritz' from *Young Frankenstein*. Is that the *QE2* docking – or Pierce 'Any Key Will Do' Brosnan searching for a middle C? The moment in *Mamma Mia!* when I realised that Pierce was actually going to take a running jump at 'SOS' sent me quite literally (as opposed to metaphorically) into the head-between-the-knees-thank-you-for-flying-air-atonal brace position. 'Sooo weeeheeen yrrrrrrr nrrrrrrrrrrrr meeeeeee,' screeched Pierce at the top of his paint-peeling voice, 'da-ha-haaarrrrlin cayant ya hrrrrrrrrrrr me ESSSSS OOOOOO ESSSSS!' Duck and cover! Run for the hills! Hide under tables and keep your face away from the screen for fear that your ears will be melted off by the buttock-clenching squonk-fest that is Brosnan's singing. Screw nuclear weapons, if North Korea or Iran ever start to get antsy again we could just drop Pierce behind enemy lines to sing a few bars of 'I Have a Dream' and surrender would surely follow apace. Also, he could prove a useful deterrent against global warming because the temperature of the screening room I was in dropped about a million degrees the minute Brosnan took a deep breath and let fly. The iceberg lettuce in my sandwiches stayed crunchy fresh for a week.

While Pierce was taking it upon himself to redefine the parameters of the popularly accepted rules of musical engagement, Muriel, Her Majesty Mrs Strepsil, was going at the works of Benny and Björn as if they were the outpourings of the Bard himself. Her interpretation of 'The Winner Takes it All' owed more to the murder scene from *Macbeth* than to the pure pop traditions of Eurovision. When Muriel said/sang that 'I don't wanna talk …' you understood that she *really did not want to talk*. At all. Ever. *EVER*. Agog, I waited for her Shakespearean take on Abba's worst Scando-English lyric 'A big thing, or a small' and was not disappointed. By the time the song was finished the palms of my hands were bleeding, my uncut nails having dug into them in a fever of pseudo-stigmatic ecstasy.

To be clear, the film is awful. And yet, and yet, and yet …

Somehow, in the middle of all that awfulness, something wonderful happened. As the tidal wave of poop crashed over my head, the world seemed to perform a peculiar axis-altering tilt whereby north became south, black became white, pleasure became pain, and (against all the odds) good became bad – and vice versa. Even as every critical faculty I possessed told me to run screaming from the theatre *right now*, I felt my heart swelling, my eyes welling up, my pulse starting to jump, and my general aura going all pink and cuddly. I presume this is what it is like taking heroin – really bad, but in a way which is strangely appealing at the time. I say 'I presume' because all I know about heroin is what I learned from Lou Reed and *Trainspotting*, namely that the soundtrack is nice but you end up screaming in a pool of vomit while swivel-headed dead babies march across the ceiling, or chasing cack-encrusted suppositories round the U-bend of an Edinburgh public toilet. Neither of which sound great.

But *Mamma Mia!*, for all its hideous flaws, had miraculously started to sound absolutely *brilliant*. It is a fitting testament to the power of Benny and Björn's songwriting that their work appears to be unassailable even when James Bond himself has been licensed to kill their songs. When you do this sort of thing to the Beatles' back catalogue you wind up with William Shatner gaily massacring 'Lucy in the Sky With Diamonds', leaving Lennon and McCartney looking every bit as stupid as Captain Kirk. But the Abba songbook is made of sterner stuff, and no amount of inappropriate celebrity honking can dispel the magic of those pure pop classics. By the time La Strepsil started rhapsodising that her daughter was 'Slipping Through My Fingers' I was in floods of tears – tears of laughter, tears of joy, tears of (let's be honest) *shame*, but tears nonetheless. And as I looked around the darkened auditorium at my fellow cowering critics, I realised that I was not alone, although several of my wet-faced comrades would thrice deny their uncontrollable physical responses as the cockerel's crow heralded the arrival of their crucifying reviews in the morning papers.

Don't get me wrong – *Mamma Mia!* is rubbish. But rubbish the likes of which we shall not see again for some time. And rubbish which somehow left in its wake a trail of resplendent joy and bonhomie which would have satisfied Morecambe and Wise's oft-sung request that we bring them fun, sunshine, and love, and leave Ken Dodd thanking the Lord that he'd been blessed with more than his share of happiness.

*Mamma Mia!* went on to become the fastest selling DVD ever in the UK, although I remain convinced that in order to appreciate it fully you had to see it with an audience. We were on holiday in Cornwall when *Mamma Mia!* came out, so Linda and our daughter went to see it at the fabulous Screen Seven of the Regal Cinema in Redruth (tag line 'Stairway to Seven') and had a ball. Meanwhile I endured *Transformers* with our son who enjoyed the robots hitting each other but couldn't understand what useful role was served by Megan Fox. I tried to explain to him that the film was directed by Michael Bay who is, in his father's twisted opinion, the Antichrist and Enemy of Cinema, but he still wanted to own it on DVD the day it came out. Hey-ho.

Back to Southampton Street, and *Time Out*, and *Piranha Women in the Avocado Jungle of Death*. In case you don't know (and there's little reason why you would) *Piranha Women in the Avocado Jungle of Death* was actually a UK retitling of an American movie called *Cannibal Women in the Avocado Jungle of Death*. The film had undergone its subtle name change in order to circumvent the peculiar prejudices of the British Board of Film Classification (BBFC) who, in the mid-eighties, had acquired the state-legislated power to rate, cut, and ban all videos released in the UK. Unfortunately, during the pre-regulated 'video nasties' scare, a number of titles including the word 'cannibal' had been seized by the police and prosecuted under the Obscene Publications Act – titles such as *Cannibal Holocaust*, *Cannibal Ferox*, *Cannibal Apocalypse*, and the immortal *Prisoner of the Cannibal God* which starred bonafide screen legend Ursula Andress. Under the iron rule of the ever vigilant James Ferman, the BBFC had been given instructions to look very carefully at anything which invoked the spectre of the 'video nasty', and apparently this jumpiness extended to *any* movie – no matter how innocuous – which sounded even vaguely disreputable, particularly if their titles contained a tabloid-baiting buzzword like 'cannibal'. Thus Colourbox, an independent company who had picked up the rights to *Cannibal Women* cannily changed the title to *Piranha Women* in order to ease the video's progress through the censors' offices.

The other word that our censors got a bee in their bonnet about was 'chainsaw', thanks to the notoriety of *The Texas Chain Saw Massacre* and its variously banned sequels. This led to one of the maddest pieces of video retitling (again by Colourbox) for Fred Olen Ray's harmless splatter spoof *Hollywood Chainsaw Hookers* which had the actual word 'chainsaw' taken out of its title and then replaced by a small outline drawing of (you guessed it) a chainsaw! Thus, although the cover art featured a small silhouette of a chainsaw and a gaudy picture of scream-queen Michelle Bauer in underwear and heels brandishing a bloody huge chainsaw, technically the *word* 'chainsaw' never actually appeared anywhere so the video didn't get banned. Stupider still, the film was now officially called *Hollywood* ***** *Hookers* which made it sound like a porn flick, although I'd love to see someone attempting to 'relax' in a gentleman's way to a film in which anything that comes up comes *off* – if you see what I mean.

As for *Piranha Women*, the actual content of the film (sex, nudity, violence, flesh-eating, etc.) was solidly tame. In fact, the movie had very little to delight either the gore-hounds or the hand-shandy brigade, despite leading lady Shannon Tweed's centrefold status. What it *did* have was a really decent screenplay by writer/director 'J. D. Athens' who later turned out to be J. F. Lawton under a pseudonym. Lawton would go on to write a darkly interesting script entitled *3000* about a rich man who hires a prostitute to pretend to be his girlfriend for the titular fistful of dollars. The premise smacked of *Pygmalion* (and therefore of *My Fair Lady*) although Lawton's story ended with the hooker going back to her downbeat street life rather than joining the rich man in his vacuously extravagant champagne lifestyle. After various rewrites which effectively removed all the unpalatable rough edges, *3000* finally made it to the screen as *Pretty Woman* – one of the biggest money-spinning blockbusters of the decade. Lawton would subsequently pick up writing credits on movies starring everyone from Steven Seagal, Keanu Reeves and Morgan Freeman to Martin Landau and Robert De Niro. But that was all in the future – back in the late eighties he was just another goofy pseudonymous B-movie chancer, with nothing to distinguish him from the terrible Troma pack other than the fact that his movie was actually pretty good.

The story of *Piranha Women* goes like this – following a Vietnam-style military debacle, ethno-historian Dr Margot Hunt is sent by the CIA into the avocado jungle in search of eminent renegade feminist Dr Irma Kurtz, a former chat-show stalwart turned man-eating Piranha Woman who has 'gone native'. Accompanying Hunt on her quest is bozo guide Jim, played with gusto (and luxurious mullet) by Bill Maher, and pneumatic airhead student Bunny (Karen Mistal). As they journey into the heart of darkness, Hunt and her colleagues encounter a tribe of emasculated males named the Donahues, and a splinter radical feminist tribe who have declared war on the Piranhas following a dispute over which sauce best accompanies freshly peeled man (they favour clam dip over the Piranha's dressing of choice, guacamole). After various shake-and-bake shenanigans, Dr Kurtz refuses to return to civilisation, recalling 'the horror, the horror' of appearing on the David Letterman show.

For anyone who had witnessed the breast-beating infighting of radical eighties gender politics first-hand, *Piranha Women*'s central condiment conceit was pretty funny, unlike all the *Surf Nazis* and *Rabid Grannies* of this world whose only jokes were their titles. I laughed pretty consistently at *Piranha Women* and went on to say so in print in *Time Out*, after which I thought no more about it.

Until, a couple of weeks later, I met a feisty young woman named Cass who worked for Colourbox video in the role of press-officer-cum-general-Ms-Fixit. I'd been receiving press releases from her for a few months, and because I like to put names to faces we had agreed to meet up for a drink in Wardour Street, just across the road from Colourbox's fantastically unglamorous office. Cass arrived bearing a bag of VHS preview tapes (this was in the days before DVD, remember, when videos were still considered to be handily compact) of forthcoming straight-to-video releases including the abysmal *Oversexed Rugsuckers From Mars* which turned out to be so utterly rotten that even Colourbox didn't much fancy releasing it. We talked about the company's battles with the censors over titles like *Intruder* (a mild store-bound slasher that had been hacked up by the BBFC) and she promised to slip me an uncut preview tape if she could find one. Then, as we were finishing our drinks, she said in an off-hand manner: 'The funny thing is, ever since that *Piranha Women* review came out I've had people asking what strings I had to pull to get a good review in *Time Out*. It's hilarious. I told them I had nothing to do with it – that some bloke called Mark Kermode just apparently really liked the film. I told them I'd never even met you.'

'And what did they say?'

'They said, "Good thing too. You don't want to be hanging around with the kind of bloke whose idea of a really good movie is *Piranha Women in the Avocado Jungle of Death*." Ha ha ha!'

Over the next few years I came to know, respect, and really *like* Cass (or 'Cassie', as she was better known). She was terrifically energetic, always good-natured (not easy when your job involves dealing with journalists, who are generally miserable gits) and most importantly, refreshingly honest. She worked hard at her job, and in all the time I knew her she never once tried to spin me a line about how great a movie was – she simply alerted me to its existence and imminent release (or non-release in the case of *Oversexed Rugsuckers From Mars*) and left it at that. She was great. And then she died, quite suddenly, of an undetected condition, at a shockingly young age. I always think of Cass whenever the subject of *Piranha Women* comes up, which it does with increasing frequency. There's something strangely poignant about the fact that its key players went on to have such stellar careers, and it reassures me to think of Cass laughing heartily in that pub about the inherent ridiculousness of the movie business.

Alongside the prestige of appearing in print, *Time Out* was soon to open another door for me. One day, I was working in the office, filling in for Derek Adams who was taking a couple of weeks' well-deserved leave. Derek, it turned out, was a drummer and for a while he and I had toyed with the idea of forming a garage band, bashing out old rockabilly standards and wondering whether the world was ready for a British answer to the Stray Cats, who were themselves an American answer to the Polecats. As I sat there methodically screwing up the listings (I had improved, but not that much) the phone rang and I answered it ...

At which point, one of two things happened.

In the version of this story which I *remember*, and which

I have repeated ad infinitum to anyone who will listen, the voice on the other end of the phone asked for Derek Adams. I told them he was away for a fortnight but that I'd be happy to help.

'Oh,' said the voice.

'Oh, what?' I asked, politely.

'Oh, it's just that we need someone to do some video reviews for us this Sunday. On LBC Radio.'

There was a moment's pause – probably not even that – before I leaped unbidden into the fray.

'I'll do it!' I announced.

'Really?' said the voice, somewhat uncertain. 'But we need someone with radio experience ...'

'Oh I've got that,' I lied, 'loads of it.'

'Have you? Where from?'

'Oh ... Manchester,' I answered vaguely, figuring that nobody who worked in the media in London would have any idea what happened north of Watford.

'Right,' said the voice. 'Great. Well then, can you be here by eight o'clock on Sunday?'

'No problem,' I answered confidently. '8 p.m. Sunday I'll be there. Incidentally, where is "there". Or "here"?'

'"Here" is our studios in Gough Square, up by Fleet Street. And it's not 8 p.m., it's 8 *a.m.* We're a breakfast show.'

'Great. No worries. I *love* breakfast,' I babbled. 'See you at 8 ... *a.m.*!'

That's the version of the story which would appear in the TV Movie of My Life, providing a wonderfully serendipitous moment in which my future as a radio broadcaster would be sealed by being in the right place, at the right time – even if I was the *wrong* person.

However, the respected broadcaster Sarah Ward, who co-presented LBC's weekend breakfast show with Ed Boyle back in the late eighties, assures me that this story is baloney. According to Sarah, someone from her programme called me after she and Ed read my reviews in *Time Out* and decided to give me a broadcasting break. Whatever the truth – whether they were looking for me or Derek – I *know* that I lied to them about having 'radio experience' because the awful consequences of that lie still haunt me to this day.

For reasons which I have never fully understood, I had a pretty clear but utterly fanciful view of the way live radio worked. Here's what I thought would happen: I would arrive at the studios at the appointed hour of eight o'clock to be met by a helpful assistant who would show me into a large boardroom generously furnished with coffee and croissants. Into this room would file the assembled team of broadcasters who would jointly present the breakfast show which probably kicked off around 9 a.m. Before the broadcast began, we would all be introduced to one another and swap a few casual niceties before settling down to discuss the business of what we would actually talk about 'on-air'. To this end, I would bring along a large sheaf of notes with several suggestions of videos on release which may be of interest to the listener. We would discuss these possible candidates, with me probably flying the flag for more obscure fare like *Piranha Women* while the presenters would doubtless argue for some more mainstream titles. After an exchange of polite banter, we would agree on a happy compromise, and I would retire to gather my thoughts (and my notes) before going 'on-air' at a leisurely pace sometime around ten o'clock.

Here's what actually happened.

I arrived at the LBC studios in Gough Square at the appointed hour of 8 a.m. So far so good. I rang the doorbell. No answer. I rang it again. Again, no answer. I started to think I was in the wrong place. Then, just as I was preparing to leave, a voice on the intercom said: 'What?'

'Oh, hi,' I replied, struggling to sound unflustered. 'It's me, Mark Kermode. From *Time Out*. I'm here to do the video reviews.'

No answer. Just a buzz. I pushed the door. It opened, and I stepped inside.

Nothing.

No one.

Then a noise. A door opening and closing. Someone running down a corridor. Another door banging. Then, suddenly, someone grabbed me by the arm and propelled me down the corridor whilst speaking very fast and somewhat agitatedly …

'… news overran so we couldn't come and get you, thought you'd make your own way to the studio, bit of a panic this morning, breaking news blah blah blah, that door there, yes yes yes, *that* door, blue mike, bye …'

And the next thing I knew I was in the studio. And on-air. Live.

Jeezly buggers!

'And now,' said a voice which was either in my head, or

out there in the 'real world' or both (I really couldn't tell) 'here's Mark … *Commode*, with the video review. So Mark, what's out …?'

You know that dream that everybody has (or at least I *assume* that everybody has) about waking up naked in the middle of your maths O-level exam (no? nobody else? Just me then …)? Well, it was like that, only LIVE ON-AIR and crucially *NOT A DREAM*. And faced with this frankly unforeseen circumstance, I did what I believe any other thoroughly unprepared person would do.

I panicked – vociferously.

With nothing but the sound of my own blood thrumming deafeningly in my ears I started to speak, to babble, to spew forth sounds which occasionally had meaning but equally often were just pure animal noise. You know the yelping sound that a dog makes when you accidentally trap its paw under the foot of your swivel chair while it attempts to warm itself around the electrical snug of your malfunctioning computer (no? just me again, then…)? It was like that, only *human*. Just about.

I started to talk about anything that came into my head, and a lot of stuff that just went straight to my mouth, entirely bypassing the higher cerebral cortexes. I held forth like a zealous worshipper suddenly moved by the spirits to speak in tongues in a Pentecostal church, vomiting fluent drivel which merely needed a divine interpreter to turn it into something comprehensible by carbon-based life forms. Somewhere in the middle of it all I think I mentioned some videos but to be honest I'm really not sure. For all I know I recited *The*

*Canterbury Tales* in original fruity Middle English. It was the closest I have ever come to experiencing demonic possession first-hand, although unlike Linda Blair I couldn't claim afterwards that 'the Devil made me do it'. The babbling went on for what seemed like hours, days, months, but was in fact only three and a half minutes of actual air time. At the end of which a light flashed in the centre of the room, the still unidentified presenter (who turned out to be Sarah) said something like 'Thank you Mark. And now, sport ...' and a hand at my elbow guided me out of the studio, down a corridor, through a metal door, and out on to the street.

The door slammed shut.

It was all over.

It was seven minutes past eight.

I felt like I had been mugged.

I decided to ring my mum, who had been alerted to my radio debut with instructions to tune in. Apparently she had complied.

'Hi Mum.'

'Oh, hello.'

Nothing else. Just 'hello'. No 'That was nice' or 'Well done' or 'Oh you sounded so relaxed' – all off-the-peg maternal compliments that everyone knows are utterly untrue but which somehow make you feel better about things which have gone really badly. Like when you come last in the sports day sack race or fall off the stage while trying to play the French horn in the school concert or fail your French exam for the *second time*. Everyone knows you've done rubbish – most of all yourself – but your mum is allowed (nay *required*) to lavish you with well-meant but utterly undeserved praise before offering to buy you an ice cream and let you stay up late to watch *Star Trek* to make you feel better. But there was none of that. Clearly she'd forgotten about the broadcast. A blessing.

'So, you missed it then?' I said casually, planning to shrug the whole thing off safe in the knowledge that no one had been listening. It was, after all, only a local station.

'Oh no,' replied Mum, slightly indignantly. 'I got up specially and listened to the whole programme from six o'clock onwards. I thought you might be on at any time and I didn't want to miss it.'

'So you did hear it then?'

'Oh yes.'

Still nothing else. Blimey O'Reilly, it must have been bad.

'So you heard it, *and* ...?' I prompted desperately.

'Oh, the signal was very clear,' said Mum, clearly putting on a brave face and struggling to accentuate the positive. 'Yes, *very* clear. I was worried that I wasn't going to be able to find it, because I only really listen to Radio Two usually. But I looked up the frequency in the newspaper and I found it quite easily. So that was good. And, as I said, very clear.'

Great. The signal was good and clear. This was even worse than I thought.

'And what about *me*, Mum?' I finally blabbed, unable to restrain myself, 'How was *I*?'

'Oh, very clear,' she said again, brightly. 'Yes, very clear indeed. I could hear every word. It was as if you were right here in the room. That's how clear it was.'

'But was I *any good?*' I almost screamed. I *knew* that I had been utterly awful but the fact that not even my mother could bring herself to lie about the extent of the on-air catastrophe was really giving me the willies. Central London is a lonely place to be at ten past eight on a Sunday morning, and I was starting to feel as if my incompetence had somehow unleashed a seismic blast of destruction and despair which had cleared the streets (there were neither cars nor pedestrians in sight), leaving a pall of hopelessness hanging over the city. The only time I've ever known London so quiet was years later when *The Culture Show* decided to restage the post-apocalyptic opening to Danny Boyle's *28 Days Later* and I got to walk through a deserted Trafalgar Square at 4.30 a.m. thinking that the capital was actually quite palatable as long as there weren't any people in it. Standing around outside the radio station on that lonely Sunday morning, however, I would have been grateful for any sign of human life. There was none.

'But, other than the clarity of the sound, which of course I am thrilled to hear about, was I actually *any good?*'

There was a brief but howlingly noticeable pause.

'Oh, yes.'

Silence.

'Really?'

'Yes. If a bit … gabbly'

'"Gabbly"?'

'Yes, you know … you gabbled a bit.'

'A *bit?*'

'Well, a lot, actually. Since you ask. But it's probably

just me, I'm not used to listening to people speaking so …'

'Gabbly?'

'Yes, as you say, gabbly. And fast. Fast and gabbly.'

This was terrible.

'But the signal was very clear,' Mum ventured again bravely. It was no use. Clearly the entire fleeting episode had been career-threateningly poor. I had learned an important lesson – I was absolutely *awful* at radio, and I wouldn't be doing it again in a hurry.

Or so I thought. But a couple of weeks later I was back in the *Time Out* office, still answering the phones on Derek Adams' behalf, when an uncomfortably familiar voice said, 'Hello, is that Mark … Commode?'

'Close enough,' I replied, suspiciously. I recognised the speaker as someone from LBC; presumably there had been complaints and now they were ringing to offer an official reprimand. I deserved nothing else. But instead I got this: 'Oh hi, look, it's a short month this month and we need to do our video reviews a week early, which will be next Sunday. Same as before. Could you do it again?'

Clearly there had been a clerical oversight and no one had informed this person of my former foul-up. They couldn't have actually *heard* it because if they had they wouldn't be offering to let me repeat the offence. But that was exactly what they were doing. And even as every atom of my being screamed, 'No no *noooo*, never again, never never never *not ever no*,' my mouth blithely said 'Yes' and that was that.

But this time it would be *different*. This time I knew what to expect. This time I would be *prepared*. Indeed, this time

I would make amends for the previous tragedy and perhaps rescue my dignity in the process. It was a second chance, a last-minute reprieve, a stay of execution, an opportunity to snatch victory from the jaws of defeat ...

That's it – I'm all out of clichés. Just choose the one you find least trite and hackneyed (or insert one of your own) and that's what it was.

So, over the next few days I 'prepared' myself for my forthcoming radio rematch. Having figured out exactly how long the slot would last (just under four minutes on the evidence of last time) and resolving to speak m-u-c-h s-l-o-o-o-o-w-e-r than before I calculated that it wouldn't really be possible to talk about more than two videos – unlike the eight through which I appeared to have cantered on my debut. I duly chose two titles, both of which were reassuringly mainstream (no more *Piranha Women* this time, thank you very much) and I sat down to write a script which I timed, and rehearsed, then trimmed and edited and timed and rehearsed some more. It was amazing just how little you could actually say in four minutes if you were talking at the pace of the speaking clock, but I was determined to right the wrongs of yore and the most grievous wrongs were clearly the incomprehensible speed and unmanageable substance of my first outing. By the time Sunday rolled around, I was as practised, sonorous, and ponderously low-key as a churchgoer reading from the gospels at the lectern on Good Friday, desperate not to stumble over some hotly debated theological point, and determined that the deaf pensioners in the back rows would be able to hear every word.

I arrived at the radio studio early – 7.30 a.m. to be precise – in order to give myself time to gather my thoughts and take several deep breaths. After the usual routine of pushing the bell and getting no answer I was finally allowed in by someone who was clearly baffled to see me. 'You're not on till after eight,' they said with some agitation as they ushered me into an anteroom outside the studio that looked as though it had been used as a mobile military hospital, so total was the chaos and carnage. 'Did someone tell you that you were on earlier?'

'Oh no,' I replied. 'I just wanted to be here in good time, you know, to "get in the zone" or whatever it's called. Soak up the atmosphere.'

They looked at me as though I was mad, then apparently decided that I was taking the piss, turned on their heels and clumped back into the studio. From the clock on the wall I could see that there were at least twenty-five minutes to go before I was needed, and I suddenly had that sense of being in a doctor's waiting room, about to receive some extremely unpleasant test results. 'Ah yes, Mr … Commode is it? We've got your blood samples back and I'm afraid it's bad news. Very bad news. Yes, it seems that you have a severe case of *criticus totalis fraudulenta* with an underlying bout of *radioramblus incompetentis*. Unfortunately it's terminal – you'll never broadcast in this town again. Now, take these two paracetamol and go crawl under a rock and die …'

Whilst it had seemed very sensible to arrive early, I was now starting to realise the benefits of just turning up and going straight on – at least you didn't have time to sit there sweating bullets while the second hand slowed to a crawl and time expanded infinitely before you. By the time 7.45 rolled around I was on the point of puking. What the hell had I been thinking? I'd already proved that I couldn't do this in front of several thousand listeners including my mother. Why on earth was I putting myself through this humiliation again? In what would become a common experience I realised that if the radio station suddenly suffered a massive power cut and I was sent home without having had the chance to broadcast I would be relieved and delighted. I started unconsciously praying for just such an eventuality, imploring the heavens to rain down fire (only a *little* fire, obviously, not enough to *hurt* anyone – just enough to cause an electrical malfunction). Unfortunately, I have always believed vociferously in a non-interventionist God, and if the Almighty was listening he took this moment to prove to me that I was right by doing absolutely nothing; 'Sorry, but apparently I don't intervene. Your words, not mine. Have a nice day.'

Over the next half-hour I aged about fifty years, losing half my body weight in sweat that poured from my palms, armpits, and other embarrassing glandular areas like Albert Brooks experiencing his on-air flop-sweat meltdown in *Broadcast News*. By the time it was finally my turn to go on, I looked like I'd been for a refreshing pre-broadcast swim without first removing my clothes. I didn't so much walk into the studio as ooze, before pouring myself like a puddle into the handily water-resistant chair behind the 'blue microphone', my fluid body held together by nothing more than surface tension.

But amazingly, despite my reversion to liquid form, the hours and days of practice, practice, practice paid off. I took a deep breath, unfolded my scripted sheet of notes, waited for Sarah to say, 'So Mark, what have you got on video for us this week?' and then started to read. Slowly and surely. Clearly and precisely. Factually and informatively.

Or, put more simply, boringly.

To be honest, I had no idea how it was going – the only sound I could hear was that of my heart beating out a percussive accompaniment to the chorus of '76 Trombones and a Euphonium'. But as each successive paragraph went by I knew that I was not cocking it up as before. I was not gabbling, I was not speaking incomprehensibly fast, I was remembering to breathe, and (most importantly) I had a script with a beginning, middle and end, and a well-rounded exit strategy. So when I finally got to the bit which read 'and that would be *my* pick of the week, now back to you, Sarah.' I was feeling pretty damned pleased with myself. As I finished, my physical body seemed to re-coagulate back into semi-solid form and I was able to evolve upward out of my chair, like an amphibian climbing out of the protean slime, and exit in the manner of some higher ape form doing an almost passable impression of early Stone Age man.

I had got away with it. I had not been totally rubbish. I had managed to read my entire script from start to finish without stumbling, and had kept pretty close to time in the process.

I had been … professional!

I was heading for the door which led back on to the street whence I had been thrust so rudely last time when a woman whose face I didn't recognise came out of the control room. She may have been the producer, or the assistant producer, and for the purposes of this story, she will be played by Kelly Macdonald, or someone of equally arresting reputation.

'Hi,' she said gaily, with just a hint of unsettling concern.

'Oh, hi,' I replied (clearly being on the radio had turned me into a fabulous wit and raconteur).

'Just wanted to make sure everything was OK?'

Hmm. That sounded less than congratulatory. Perhaps I *had* been rubbish.

'Oh yes, fine by me,' I said, attempting to sound as if I did this all the time and it hadn't been a big deal or anything – I had, after all, falsely told everyone that I had 'loads of radio experience'.

'Is anything … *wrong*?' she asked, again more concerned than interrogative, which was in itself rather disconcerting.

'Um, no I don't think so,' I flannelled. 'It all seemed to go alright … didn't it?'

'Oh yes,' she replied. 'It was "alright". It was perfectly … "alright".'

'So it *was* … alright?'

'Yes, like I said, "alright" is what it was. It's just that …'

Here we go. Here comes the tidal wave of recrimination and blame. Here's the broadside about the number of complaints they got last time they put me on-air; about how I clearly lied to them when I said I knew my way around a radio station; about how the station's bosses were now threatening to fire people for putting an eejit like me on their radio station and about how I was never ever going to be allowed back into the building. Well, hell, I deserved it. I had gone and blagged myself into a job I was clearly not capable of performing, exactly as I had done with the *Time Out* listings fiasco and the lost cinema and the angry punters on the phone and all the rest of it. The LBC bosses may even have spoken to Geoff Andrew and had their suspicions about me being a lying useless fake confirmed.

'It's just that,' she resumed valiantly, 'we all kind of liked it last time when you sort of pretended that you didn't know what you were doing.'

'Pardon?'

'You know, last time when you did that thing about pretending to be making it all up on the spot, as if you'd just walked into the room and said the first thing that came into your head.'

'*What?*'

'The *goofy* thing. The *funny* thing. The "I've got no idea what I'm doing here but I'll give it a try anyway" thing. Your *act*. I mean, we all *know* it's an act, but we thought it was funny.'

I was stunned (yet again). And shocked. Shocked *and* stunned. Positively Rutled.

'You thought it was ... funny?'

'*Oh yes*, but in the way you intended obviously. We were laughing our heads off in the control room. At one point I think the engineer even started to think that you weren't putting it on. But it was really entertaining, even if you weren't interested in the videos which, let's be honest, most people aren't.'

'Aren't they?'

'No, not really. After all, it *is* first thing on a Sunday morning. Most people are just tuning in to be entertained. Which was sort of the problem today.'

'You didn't like what I did today?'

'Oh no, like I said it was fine, absolutely fine. If a bit ... boring.'

'Boring?'

'Yes, well, you know, a bit downbeat.'

'But I *did* review the videos.'

'Yes, you did review the videos.'

'And my reviews were considered, and balanced, and sensibly delivered.'

'Sensibly delivered. Yes.'

'But you didn't like them?'

'Not as much as the funny ones, no.'

'So you *wanted* me to be funny?'

'Well, yes.'

'And to sound as if I didn't know what I was doing?'

'Yes, sort of.'

'And to speak as if I was making it up as I go along?'

'Well,' she said, drawing herself closer, somewhat conspiratorially, 'we'd just prefer it if you didn't sound like you were reading a script.'

'Which I did today?'

'Yes.'

'Because today I *was* reading a script.'

'Apparently so.'

'Whereas last time I wasn't.'

'No.'

'I was just "making it up".'

'Exactly.'

She smiled brightly, shook me by the hand (firm but fair) guided me toward the exit, and the next thing I knew I was back out on the deserted street with the same feeling of having been unsuspectingly violated.

Several years later I would come to recognise the wisdom of this advice, and to accept that I have probably built my entire radio career around the principle of 'pretending not to know what you're doing and sounding like you're making it up on the spot'. The only thing is I have *never* pretended – I have *never* known what I am doing. It's so much easier when it isn't an act – when you are genuinely incompetent. It also helps when you are right. And I am both of those things. Incompetent, but right.

But standing out on that deserted street in London without even my mother to call for reassurance (I hadn't told her about the repeat appearance after the disaster of the first) I felt nothing other than despair and defeat. I had tried my best to be good at something and I had wound up being even worse than I was the first time round. Hell, as far as I could see I didn't even know the difference between good and bad any more. I was lousy at listings and even worse at radio. I had run away from Manchester only to blot my copybook in London and the walls were closing in. Any minute now someone was going to blow the whistle on my budding career and I was going to be revealed for the talentless fraudster that I truly was.

That I truly *am*.

I needed to escape.

I needed to put clear blue water between myself and my very public failures.

I went home and listened to Dexy's Midnight Runners' third album *Don't Stand Me Down* and heard Kevin Rowland speaking to me and me alone, impeaching me to 'Go west, go west young man …'.

So I did.

# Chapter 4

# CALIFORNIA ÜBER ALLES

Like Withnail & I, who went on holiday by mistake, I arrived in New York more by accident than design.

I was aiming for Los Angeles, following in the footsteps of my close friend Tim Polecat who was sending back daily reports about how much better it was than England because the restaurants actually understood the meaning of the word 'service' and the garage owners didn't make that oddly British tooth-sucking noise every time they looked under your bonnet meaning you were about to be screwed for a grand and your car wouldn't be ready till Wednesday. Tim used to live in Mill Hill, and it was there that he and I had cemented our friendship over a shared appreciation of the complex time structures and artistic merits of the entire *Planet of the Apes* movie cycle which (as we know) played such an important role in my political education. We had also bonded over a mutual belief that the seventies celluloid car-crash *Caligula* was actually some weird form of masterpiece, rather than just an expensive porno flop with big-name stars like Helen Mirren, Peter O'Toole and Sir John Gielgud talking in between the interstitial Penthouse Pet sex scenes. Several years later I would oversee a clumsy but effective Channel 4 recut of *Caligula* which removed all the hard-core porno shots (which had been stuck in willy-nilly by *Penthouse*-owner-cum-movie-producer Bob Guccione) in a belated attempt to prove that Tim and I were on to something. When Guccione's lawyers started making threatening noises, I took it as proof that we had been right all along.

Tim had recently moved to LA with his then wife Jenny, an aspiring Scandinavian-American model-slash-actress who had already experienced fleeting fame as the woman who opens the fridge in the 'Milk's gotta lotta bottle!' TV ads. Tim, meanwhile, had enjoyed a couple of Top Thirty hits with the previously mentioned rockabilly rebels the Polecats (hence the name, obviously) and had more recently designed the front cover for a 12-inch EP which I had made with a couple of friends under the catchy moniker 'The Trumpeting of Mighty Jungle Beasts'. Despite being 'Second Single of the Week' (or something similar) in *Sounds* and 'hotly tipped' in the *NME*, we had failed to break big, and would probably have split up due to musical differences if we had actually existed as a 'real band'. Which we didn't. So we couldn't.

Back to New York. The plan went something like this. Tim and Jenny would set up base in LA, from whence they planned to dominate the world with their new band Destroy

All Monsters, named after the 1968 Japanese monster movie which featured an assortment of rubbery beasties including Godzilla, Mothra, King Ghidorah and more. Tim would play guitar and sing, Jenny would play bass, and I would help out by making lots of *Day the Earth Stood Still* sci-fi bloop-bloop noises in the background with a range of electronic gadgetry that none of us really understood. We already had a couple of synthesisers and I had my eyes on a theremin at which I could gesture in the virtuoso manner of Jimmy Page in *The Song Remains the Same*. I had no doubt that DAM would be massive – after all, they'd already been on a Saturday morning TV show in the UK where they had been interviewed by a rubber puppet called Gilbert the Green Alien. How could they fail? As for me, I would divide my time between occasional pop stardom and more regular movie journalism, the latter of which would be boosted by the fact that I would be living in Hollywood where everything movie-tastic was happening.

The only fly in the ointment was my own nervousness about moving to America, land of drive-by shootings, ambulance-chasing lawyers and twenty-four-hour terrible television. Also I was completely incapable of organising any form of journey further than a trip to the Phoenix East Finchley to catch a late-night double bill of *The Enforcer* and *Dirty Harry*. So when a neighbour offered me a free standby ticket to New York which he had somehow managed to win through a prodigious consumption of instant coffee, I thought, 'New York is in America. And so is Los Angeles! They can't be far from each other.' And off I went.

Problems started early on. At Heathrow, I was assured

that I wouldn't be allowed to enter America at all unless I had either a) a visa (which I didn't – I thought we had a 'special arrangement' since World War Two), or b) a return ticket to prove that I was going to come back. When I pointed out that my free coffee air-miles voucher did indeed cover the trip back, it was explained that 'free coffee tickets' didn't count. You had to have *paid money* to come back, otherwise it would look like you didn't really mean it. This seemed ridiculous to me – I mean, who *wouldn't* want to come back to a country overrun by ten years of Thatcherism and the advent of the 'snood'? But by the time we'd sorted out our disagreements I was £200 down, a serious dent in my travel plans.

The first standby flight shipped out at three in the afternoon, and pulled into New York around 9 p.m. local time. Before hitting the notoriously unfriendly US customs and immigration desk I had studiously removed all outward signs of my former revolutionary communist affiliations, viz. a hammer and sickle insignia on my leather jacket, a badge with an embossed silhouette of Lenin, and a copy of the *Communist Party Manifesto* which I had been carrying around in an inside pocket for years without ever actually reading it. As it turned out, the guy behind the glass couldn't have cared less if I was carrying a Kalashnikov rifle and singing 'Arise ye starvelings from your slumbers'. This was more than a decade before 9/11, and the main defence issue of the day was whether or not you looked Mexican.

It wasn't until I was in the main concourse, attempting to get a cheap flight to LA, that I began to realise just how big America was. Clearly my initial plan of working against the time difference and being in Hollywood before late tea was not going to work out. Worse still, I had shipped up on the eve of something called Thanksgiving which apparently was 'not a good time to travel, sir' – particularly for those in search of bargain-basement deals. After several hours negotiating, it became clear that my only option was to buy a ticket for the day *after* Thanskgiving, which meant spending a few nights in New York.

'Hey, no problem,' I thought. 'I *know* someone in New York. My old school friend Saul Rosenberg, who's doing postgrad studies at Columbia University. I'm sure he'll be *thrilled* to see me, and to put me up. Unannounced. At Thanksgiving.' OK, so I didn't actually have his number in New York. But I *did* have a number for his mum and dad who lived in Willesden and who would doubtless be *thrilled* to hear from me. After all, they were smart cosmopolitan people who had been extremely nice about allowing our awful band to practise VERY LOUDLY in their front room and they had even been gracious enough to come and see us play an equally eardrum-threatening gig at the Moonlight Club in West Hampstead. Surely calling them up would be no trouble.

Unfortunately, having no head for figures, I had made a catastrophic miscalculation on the time difference and somehow concluded that London was five hours *behind* New York. It isn't – it's five hours *ahead*. But I hadn't figured that out yet.

So I called them.

Saul's mum answered, sounding unaccountably sleepy and not her usual vibrant self at all.

'Hi, it's Mark,' I blathered, 'you know, Saul's friend. From school. Remember me? We used to be in a band together, many years ago, and we rehearsed in your front room. Terrible racket. Anyway, how are you?'

There was a pause.

'Whaaaaaaa?'

Another pause. I tried again.

'Yes, anyway, I'm in New York and I need Saul's phone number. Could you give it to me?'

Silence. The sound of the phone being passed to another hand. A lower voice. Saul's dad. Also sounding sleepy.

'Hello?'

'Oh hi, it's Mark, Saul's Friend. Band. Terrible racket ha ha ha! Anyway, do you have Saul's phone number?'

More silence. Then, 'Are you hurt?'

Strange question.

'Er, no. I just need — '

'DO YOU KNOW WHAT TIME IT IS?'

'Um, yes, it's eleven o'clock here, and you're five hours behind so it's six o'clock there. Isn't it?'

More silence. I thought I heard the phrase 'stupid boy' being muttered in the background. Some banging around. Then the low voice again.

'Mark?'

'Yes?'

'Are you well?'

'Oh, yes thanks.'

'And your mother and father? They are well?'

'Yes, great, thank you.'

'Good. Here is Saul's phone number. And Mark, although you are always welcome to call and we are pleased to help put you in touch with Saul, may I point out that it is in fact four o'clock in the morning here in England.'

'Is it? Oh, sorry. But thanks. And say thanks to Mrs Rosenberg. When she wakes up ...'

Lovely people, the Rosenbergs – slow to chide, swift to bless.

I rang Saul's number. Amazingly, he answered.

'Hi Saul. It's Mark. I'm in New York. Which is great. And I need to come and stay at your place. Until Tuesday probably. So, where are you? And how do I get there?'

Silence.

Then (inevitably), 'Whaaaaaa?'

Oh for heaven's sake.

'Look, I haven't got time to discuss this, and I really don't have anywhere else to go, and hey Saul it's *me*, Mark, you know, *Mark*, from the band, terrible racket, blah blah blah, and I *really need to know how to get to wherever it is that you live*.'

Saul considered this for a moment. It turned out that not only was it Thanksgiving, but also that he was up against some horrible academic deadline and he'd essentially planned to spend the next four days with his head down concentrating on work and the last thing he needed right now was Mark from the terrible-racket band turning up on his doorstep. But to his great credit, he did not say any of this out loud – at least, not yet. Instead he said simply: '83rd and Columbus. Take a taxi.'

'Can't do that,' I replied, omitting the usual niceties about 'thanks a lot, you're a real life saver' etc. 'Don't have the money for a taxi. Don't have the money for *anything* actually. Can't I get a train? Or a bus? Or *something*?'

'Oh for heaven's sake. Right, here's what you do. You get to the subway, you look at the map, and you follow the red line to 79th and Broadway and you get off there and walk. You do not talk to *anybody*. You do not look weirdly at *anybody*. And you do not get off anywhere else. Have you got insurance?'

'No, of course not.'

'Of course not. Right, in that case, you do not cross any roads. If you get hit by a car, tell the ambulance man that you're *me* and that you have Blue Cross. But *don't* get hit by a car.'

I thought about telling Saul that this wouldn't work because if I went to hospital there'd be tests and nakedness and whatnot, and someone would realise that key parts of *my* anatomy did not match up with *his* name and we'd all end up in court and that would not be good because I needed to get to Los Angeles as soon as possible. But the money was running out, so I decided to hold that thought till later.

So, where was the subway? There was a sign with a picture of a bus, a car, and a train, so I figured that had to be a good start. I found a bus and got on it. We travelled around for about forty minutes, stopping at various empty car parks, before arriving back at the airport where we started. Apparently I had missed the train station. We tried again. This time I succeeded. I got a ticket, I got on the train. So far, so good. The train was virtually empty and suddenly I felt like Tom Cruise in *Risky Business* in that scene when Rebecca De Mornay tells him that what she really likes to do is to *ride around on the subway after dark* – if you know what I mean. I looked out of the window and saw nothing but desolation, poverty, and trash. It was brilliant!

The train went subterranean, and if Jason Isaacs were still on board with that TV Movie of My Life he'd probably be wondering about now whether he hadn't accidentally signed up for a remake of *The Taking of Pelham One Two Three* (these being the days before Tony Scott took a sledgehammer to Joseph Sargent's original and did it all over again with more shouting, shooting, and swearing but apparently *without* a camera tripod). By the time we pulled into an underground station I half expected to see Gene Hackman ordering a 'fruit cup' before being craftily given the slip by Fernando Rey in *The French Connection*. (On the subject of which, director William Friedkin once told me that Rey had only got the job as 'Frog One' because he had told his casting agent to 'go get that guy out of *Belle de Jour*', and it wasn't until Rey got off the plane in New York that Friedkin realised he *wasn't* the guy he'd seen in *Belle de Jour* – Francisco Rabal. As William Goldman famously observed, in Hollywood nobody knows anything.) By the time we got to 79th Street, I had somehow mutated into John Travolta in *Saturday Night Fever* and you could tell by the way I used my walk that I had neither the time nor the inclination to talk. The swagger lasted all the way up the escalator until I got to street level, where I was greeted by the sight of someone taking a dump in the snow, clenching his buttock with one hand while simultaneously pan-handling with the other. I realised that I was way out of my depth, and ran the two blocks to Columbus Avenue, entirely forgetting Saul's advice about not crossing roads or getting hit by cars.

Saul's apartment was up on the eighth floor, and by the time I got there, it was close to one o'clock. But by then I was buzzing, and I really wanted to do something you couldn't do in England at this hour. At least not back then.

'Hi Saul. Let's go for a drink!'

Saul started to protest – he had work to do, it was really late, he was really *really tired* – but he soon realised that I'd probably be less trouble if sedated by alcohol, so he gave up and agreed. We walked out into the freezing night, across the filthy snow-covered streets, to a diner where I ordered 'A beer. And a whiskey. Together', and was absolutely thrilled when I got both without argument. I enjoyed this experience so much that I did it again, almost immediately, and by 2 a.m. I was completely smashed, and not a little crazy. Saul sighed, took me back to the apartment, showed me the sofa, and went back to work on his studies.

Sometime the next day I wandered groggily into the kitchen in search of caffeine. I found a cup, a kettle, milk in the fridge, and something which, according to the label, was 'Choc Full O' Nuts!' – a proud boast, although I still can't see why on earth this should be a good thing. Undeterred, I used my English superpowers to concoct a hot caffeinated drinking substance from these alien ingredients, and I was feeling pretty damned pleased with myself when Saul appeared, looked at me, and rolled his eyes heavenwards.

'You know this is a kosher kitchen?' he said, wearily.

'Sure,' I lied. 'No problem.' Having grown up in North London I figured I could do kosher. No bacon. Only bagels. And lox.

'Right. Then you'll have noticed that all the china has either a blue or a red mark on it.'

I hadn't.

'So, for example, that cup you're holding has a thin red line round the top.'

I looked carefully. And he was right – there *was* a red line. Clear as day.

'So the red china is for meat, and the blue china is for dairy.'

I thought about this.

'So I have to drink meat out of this cup?' I asked, before adding feebly, 'Like Bovril?'

'No, but you have to *not* drink dairy out of it.'

'Oh, fine. Well that's no problem, because this is coffee.'

'With milk. Which is . . .?'

'Oh. I see. Sorry.'

'No worries,' Saul smiled. 'Enjoy your drink.'

I did so. When I'd finished, Saul quietly took the cup, broke it on the side of the table, and put the pieces in the bin.

I had been in New York less than twelve hours, and so far I had managed to annoy Saul's parents, mess up his work schedule, and driven him to start destroying his kitchen. I really needed to get to Los Angeles, for both our sakes.

Three days later, I arrived at LAX which looked for all the world like an old thirties sci-fi movie. Only in colour. This was not surprising, since for the last few months I'd been gazing at images of LAX which had been cunningly reconfigured to look *just* like an old thirties sci-fi movie (only in colour) in the video for Destroy All Monsters' first single 'Stranger than Fiction'. (Incidentally, I just checked and that video is now up on YouTube and is, frankly, brilliant. Go take a look, and you'll see why I was so excited.) I was met by Tim and Jenny who drove me to their apartment in Hollywood with tales of just how brilliantly everything was working out here in Sunny California – a place where, they assured me, 'having an English accent is a qualification'. Indeed, Tim had already picked up some design work doing retro graphics for some fairly big movies (he's since become an established film designer, as well as an ongoing Polecat) and Jenny was going to acting classes where some Hollywood thesping guru was teaching people how to be a banana. Or to *behave* like a banana. Or something. Better still, there was a cash-in-hand crewing assignment on the cards doing a video for some dodgy heavy-metal band which would sort out my financial problems forthwith.

Despite (or perhaps because of) his rock 'n' roll past, Tim didn't drink, so I figured that, to celebrate my arrival, we should do the only *other* thing that you couldn't do legally in the UK back then.

'Let's go to a video store and rent *Texas Chainsaw Massacre 2*!'

Like all middle-aged horror fans who cut their fangs in the dark days of the seventies, I had experienced that brief rush of transgressive exhilaration which heralded the dawn of unregulated video in the early eighties, making available a plethora of splendidly grotesque horror fare which had previously been cut or banned outright in cinemas. The heyday was short-lived because a tabloid-fuelled national panic about 'video nasties' soon led to the draconian Video Recordings Act under which we have suffered ever since. But for a few months you could pop to your local cornerstore and be bewildered by the cornucopia of uncertificated filth, degradation and sleaze on offer, an extensive list of which the Director of Public Prosecutions had usefully put together to ensure that you weren't missing anything. Honestly, if it hadn't been for the vigilance of the DPP I'd never even have *heard* of the castrating oddity *The Witch Who Came From the Sea*, and I remain eternally grateful for that list (which became affectionately known as the 'Big Sixty') even if it was actually drawn up as a guide to tell the police which titles to impound. But once the clampdown kicked in, hard-core horror disappeared for another fifteen years, leaving UK fans dreaming nostalgically of titles which some poor unfortunates had actually been sent to prison for copying and distributing.

No kidding.

Not in America, however. No sooner had I mentioned *Texas 2* than Tim pulled into the dungeon-like Mondo Video emporium on Vermont and Sunset where every single tape which had been summarily banned in the UK appeared to be available for perusal and consumption by small children and nuns. *Snuff*, *SS Experiment Camp*, *Cannibal Holocaust*, *Faces of*

*Death* – they were all here, and no one seemed to be in the least bit bothered by their society-threatening presence. With trembling hands I rooted out a copy of *Texas 2* (which, like its predecessor, had been effectively banned by the British censors on the grounds that cuts wouldn't make it any less reprehensible) and took it up to the counter.

'Two bucks,' said the guy behind the till who was wearing a fetching *Corpse Grinders* T-shirt. 'Or you can buy it for five.'

Immediately, I was in turmoil. For less than the equivalent of three pounds in 'real money' I could legally purchase this banned movie, with a proper original sleeve and everything. But then I'd have to take it home, through customs, where I was bound to be spotted and cavity-searched to within an inch of my life, thus forfeiting both the video *and* my dignity. The element of danger was too great.

'Er, I'll just rent it,' I said, pathetically.

'Okey-dokey. Need to see a membership card or ID.'

Damn. I knew it was too good to be true. Of *course* you couldn't just walk into a video store and rent *Texas Chainsaw Massacre 2*. What on earth was I thinking? Damn, damn, damn.

'There you go,' said Tim, handing over his driver's licence, and less than thirty seconds later the deed was done, and I was out on the street clutching *TCM 2* and well on my way to being depraved and corrupted. And it wasn't even teatime.

When we got back to the apartment, I slammed the video into the VCR in a manner creepily reminiscent of James Woods having sex with his fleshy television set in *Videodrome*.

The movie started. I watched it all.

It was terrible.

There was a lively highlight in the opening act in which Leatherface ploughed his chainsaw through the roof of a moving car and cut someone's head and face in half to enjoyably squishy effect. But other than that it was total toilet. Not even Dennis Hopper could dispel the air of dreariness. It just went on, and on, and on ... By the end of the film, I was feeling more depressed than depraved. Still, that's another banned movie ticked off the list, so it hadn't been a complete waste.

The next day, we set off at the crack of dawn and headed for the desert where the dumbo heavy-metal band (whose name I honestly cannot remember) were shooting their hairy video. I should have been excited because, no matter how lousy the music sounded, this was my first experience of an 'authentic LA desert shoot'. We were in the middle of nowhere, but everywhere you looked there were lights, trucks, camera tracks, and swooping cranes, all guarded by burly Hell's Angels types who probably handled security for the Stones back in the days of Altamont. ('Meredith Hunter? Stabbed? Get away!') It was only a video shoot but, in the manner of all things within the nuclear-fallout radius of Hollywood, it had taken on the appearance of a full-blown feature-film set. So why was I so unimpressed?

The answer was the band, who were catastrophic. Full head-trees adorned each preening nincompoop, with poodle perms and cat flaps to a man. Their trousers were horrible, their silly spiky boots even more so, and they sounded every bit as awful as they looked – after three ear-splitting playbacks of the band's ghastly single I was sorely hoping for a surprise visit from the Manson family, the inbred stragglers of which presumably still lurked hereabouts. But this was my first Hollywood film assignment, and I really needed to earn that money, so in an attempt to look busy I went and stood by one of the gigantic wind machines positioned ostentatiously to the side of the stage.

'Be careful with that,' warned Tim, tapping the contraption which resembled a giant aeroplane propeller trapped in a cage and mounted on wheels. 'If you crank it too hard, it'll try to take off. It's basically a plane without wings.' Bearing this in mind, I spent the next six hours gingerly blowing the smallest of sensitive breezes toward the stage, artfully catching the noxious smog spewed out by industriously pumped Mole Foggers, and whisping it around the band's golden locks which flapped and billowed in the breeze. With every take of the song, I detested the band more, and started to fantasise about trapping their hair in the propeller and deftly removing their collective tresses and scalps with one bloody rotation. Perhaps last night's encounter with Leatherface *had* corrupted me after all. What a relief.

Finally, after yet more air-blown preening and primping, the band decided to take a break and retire to their trailer for what I presumed was a relaxing session of communal masturbation. As the drummer manoeuvred his heavily spandexed bum from behind the kit, I found that I could resist temptation no longer, and cranked the handle on the wind machine up to maximum thrust. I presumed that this would cause the machine to race away from the stage at wobbly velocity and I braced myself for the inevitable G-force. Strangely, nothing happened. The propeller sped up, the engine roared a little but the wind machine remained solidly in the same spot. No attempt to take off. No oversized go-carting fun. Nothing. Just more wind and noise. I looked down, and realised to my disappointment that some safety-minded technician had (very properly) anchored the wind machine firmly into the ground, a chain descending deep into the desert sand, holding it in place like a boat in the harbour. We weren't going anywhere.

I looked up into the afternoon sun, and through the swirling sands I noticed a minor commotion on stage. People waving their arms around. Shouting. Lots of hair blowing. And the drum kit (with spandexed drummer still attached) moving slowly, inexorably, backward toward the edge of the stage. It was a surreal spectacle, graceful and beautiful, if a little bit creepy, and I was transfixed. Maybe the heat had got to me, but I can see it now as if witnessing some eerie poltergeist phenomenon – the drum kit being moved by unseen spirit hands. People were shouting but you couldn't hear what they were saying over the calming drone of the wind machine. And anyway, the sight of the perambulating drums was too enrapturing to pay much attention to anything else. There they went, inch by inch, oozing like a giant snail toward an approaching precipice. And then, a moment later, they were gone, gently dropping off the stage, a percussive boat sailing over the edge of the world, its hairy captain at the helm. I shut the wind machine down and wandered off toward a picturesque dune, momentarily serene and at one with the world …

OK, *cut*!

Right, that's what *would* have happened in the TV movie – the drummer being blown off the stage. After all it's a funny image, cinematic and somewhat odd, an ideal clip for the trailer, blah blah blah. But the more I think about it the more I begin to suspect that this episode (which I remember *vividly*) is actually made up – or rather it is 'inspired by real events'. Think about it: how likely is it that any scene happening in 'real life' would have such a neat set-up, arc, and comic denouement? It's like that urban legend about a 'celebrity' forgetting to unclip a radio microphone and being overheard moaning earthy obscenities whilst on the toilet; or the story about the even more famous movie star being admitted to hospital with a rodent stuck up his tradesman's entrance; or the one about the equally celebrated pop star whose stomach was pumped and … well, come on now, you know the rest, don't you? I don't *need* to tell you the names involved because you've all heard those stories before. And even though you *want* them to be true, deep down you know they're *not* because, dramatically speaking, they are simply *too good to be true*.

Rule Number One: if it reads like a movie script, it's almost certainly a myth.

And in the case of that drummer, I'm pretty sure that if anyone blew him off stage it wasn't me, but Jason Isaacs in the wildly fictionalised Movie of My Life.

You see, I really *did* point the big wind machine at the drummer with the horrible hair and spandexed buttocks and his drums really *did* shake a little bit. I think a cymbal may even have fallen over. I *know* this to be true not only because I can *remember* doing it (which, as we have seen, proves *nothing*) but because I can remember having a conversation about it with Tim who was actually there at the time and thus offered independent third-party verification. But when we get to the bit about the drums sailing off the stage it all starts to sound rather too visually orchestrated to be true. Moreover, in my 'head movie' this final movement has changing camera angles and alternating POV shots. I can *see* the cymbal falling over from the viewpoint of someone standing by a wind machine about twenty yards away to the left of the stage, but then my memory cuts to a medium close-up of the bass drum starting to shift on its axis, and thence to a low-angle rear view of the drummer's hair blowing majestically behind him as his backside creeps slowly *toward* the camera. In short, I'm seeing this sequence as if from the vantage point of an editing suite, or indeed from the bank of 'video-assist' monitors behind which movie directors now hide in order to keep an eye on a whole range of cameras rather than striding around the set with a megaphone like in the good old days …

And that means that it's almost certainly pure baloney. It doesn't help that the scene smacks of an out-take from *This is Spinal Tap* (in which drummers regularly spontaneously combust on stage and get killed off in bizarre gardening accidents) or more damningly a passing moment from *Slade in Flame* in which a drunken Jack Daniels falls off stage taking most of Don Powell's drum kit with him. In fact, if I put my mind to it I think I can even match up the exact shot from *Flame* which inspired that 'low-angle rear view' I was mentioning a moment ago. No, the more I consider the evidence the more I'm *certain* that the writer of this screenplay is indulging in what is referred to in the trade as 'dramatic licence'.

Still, it's a good scene – one of my favourites in fact. And since I've apparently already shot and edited it (and Jason is really good in it) I'm leaving it in. And if asked whether or not it is 'true' I will reply serenely that it is a 'composite' dramatic construction drawing on several 'actual events' (I really did once see a real drummer really fall off stage at a real concert) in an essentially 'truthful' – if not entirely 'factual'– manner. Like that bit in the 'true story' of *Frost/Nixon* where the ex-president rings the presenter up in the middle of the night, pissed as a fart, and starts babbling about them being essentially the same kind of guys – the bit that is everyone's favourite scene in the whole movie but which is also pure bunkum from start to finish. That drunken phone call *didn't* happen, but as screenwriter Peter Morgan has so often argued, it *could have* happened. And that movie got nominated for *loads* of Oscars, so if it's good enough for them, it's good enough for me.

'Mr Isaacs to the wind machine please!'

It came as little surprise to discover that, despite my English accent (and despite the fact that I *hadn't* actually blown the bloody drummer off stage) I wouldn't be required for any more casual crewing work in the near future. Still, with $100 in my pocket I felt like Little Richard preparing to rip it up and ball tonight, and duly emboldened I decided to strike out on my new career as an international film journalist. I had always said that if ever I got to LA it would be *easy* to bag some choice interviews which I could sell back home in the UK. After all, why wait for film-makers to do the press junkets in Blighty when they were all *right here* in Hollywood just waiting to speak their mind to a spunky British scribe? It sounded straightforward. And oddly enough, it was.

I began with a call to Wes Craven's office, for which I had acquired an address and phone number from the Directors Guild of America. During my brief stay in New York, I had endeavoured to stay out of Saul's hair by visiting the local cinemas to see movies which wouldn't be released in the UK for months (or maybe years) to come. Top of my list was *Shocker*, a film about a serial killer whose execution by electric chair turns him into a high-voltage phantom, able to rip heads through phone lines and power cables. Daft, but fun. Craven's best-known work was the chiller *A Nightmare on Elm Street*, which gave the world the spectre of Freddy Krueger, and redefined the 'plastic reality' of modern horror cinema. But there was something more controversial lurking in Craven's back catalogue which still remained beyond the pale of British law.

A return trip to Mondo Video had secured a copy of *Last House on the Left*, an uncomfortable mix of earnest art-house invention (the plot is lifted from Ingmar Bergman's *The Virgin Spring*) and leery grindhouse gore (rape, torture, disembowelling) with bizarrely ill-judged interludes of chicken-flapping comedy. Like *Texas Chain Saw*, *Last House* had long been banned in Britain, and it was easy to see why; our censors were never going to take kindly to a film which looked so disreputably shabby, and featured scenes of chainsaw-wielding carnage and death by blowjob. Even hardened stateside sensibilities were offended, with audiences in New York reportedly storming the projection booth, hell-bent on ripping the print from the projector and slicing it to smithereens. All this was, of course, great publicity for the film-makers, who marketed *Last House* with the immortal tag line: 'To Avoid Fainting, Keep Repeating It's ONLY A MOVIE …'

Watching *Last House on the Left* at Tim and Jenny's flat was a somewhat grubby experience which they politely left me to enjoy on my own. The next morning, I rolled up to Craven's sunny office on Wilshire Boulevard where (to my surprise) he had agreed to meet me and talk about 'whatever you like, kiddo'. He greeted me warmly, I pulled out my tape recorder, and for an hour we shot the breeze about cinema and censorship. He was warm, witty and intelligent, and I was utterly seduced. He talked about *Last House* as if it were made yesterday, describing it as an angry response to TV images of the Vietnam War, discussing the visceral elements in terms of confrontation and catharsis, and remembering the intestine-ripping scene that 'you only see very briefly' because it's actually a bicycle inner tube. Of the film's vociferous detractors, he championed the protestors' right to tear up his movie if they felt moved to do so, whilst railing against the official ratings boards for being biased against low-budget movies. His position, in short, was that while he abhorred state censorship, he applauded spontaneous community action.

He was my new best friend.

Unbeknownst to Craven, this 'friendship' would backfire spectacularly in future years when my enthusiasm for his work ironically caused British censors to lay into his film with renewed enthusiasm. Having been banned for nearly thirty years, *Last House* found its way back to the newly liberalised British censors in 2001, when they finally agreed to pass it on video with only sixteen seconds of cuts. Spurred on by my encouraging words, the distributors decided to go to the Video Appeals Committee, where a group of media-literate concerned bods (including *Blue Peter* stalwart Biddy Baxter!) heard arguments for releasing the film uncut on the grounds of its great historical importance. Central to their case was an erudite essay written by an acclaimed 'specialist witness' (i.e. me) which contextualised the film within the evolution of the modern horror genre, and verified its status as a key work of American independent cinema. It was a bravura polemic – weighty, profound, and forthright.

And they were having none of it.

After considering the evidence, the good folk of the Video Appeals Committee reported that in their opinion the sixteen seconds of cuts which we were contesting were in fact far too lenient for such a revolting and frankly indefensible film. As a result, the BBFC not only upheld those cuts – they *doubled* them! Thanks to my earnest outpourings, I had effectively prevented *Last House* from being released in an all but uncut form.

With friends like me, who needs enemies?

(Since then, the BBFC have looked at the movie *again* – this time without the aid of my learned input – and decided that it *is* now fit to be released uncut after all. Some would say that it was the passing of time which caused them to reverse their earlier decision. Others would argue that I was the problem all along.)

Back in LA, I turned my attention to Sam Raimi. Today, Raimi is one of the most financially successful film-makers of all time, thanks to his blockbusting Spider-Man movies, all three of which enjoyed record-breaking openings worldwide. In the eighties, however, Raimi was still best known as the creator of *The Evil Dead*, a low-budget splatter comedy which had been deemed legally obscene by several British courts, and had become the bête noire of anti-'video nasty' campaigners like Mary Whitehouse. The British censor's report on *The Evil Dead* is one of funniest pieces of 'serious' literature ever written, as sober adults struggled to defuse the delightfully disgusting power of a deliberately stupid movie with a series of increasingly impotent alterations.

'Reduce sight of Shelley chewing off her own hand' the report reads po-facedly, before going on to insist that the distributors 'remove close shots of Scotty chopping Shelley's hands and legs off' and 'reduce to minimum fluid spewing from Linda's mouth after falling on dagger [and] trunk gushing blood after head cut off'. Call me childish, but doesn't reading that make you want to run off and watch *The Evil Dead* uncut *right now*?

When Radio Four asked me to appear on a programme called *With Great Pleasure* (imagine *Desert Island Discs* but with books) in 2008, I agreed on the understanding that I could include the BBFC's report on *The Evil Dead* as one of my favourite works of literature of all time. To their great credit, the BBFC granted me permission to make them look ridiculous in public by getting actress Amelia Bullmore to read out the cuts list to a packed theatre audience in the style of Joyce Grenfell. 'Remove *entirely* the second shot of headless torso spurting blood on man's face as he lies on top of it,' Amelia recited in schoolmarm-ish tones, to the delight of the audience, all of whom seemed to find this as funny as I did. Sadly, the radio audience never got to share the joke; when the powers that be at Radio Four heard the tape of the recording, they decided that even the *description* of what had been cut from *The Evil Dead* was too revolting for daytime broadcast and it all got cut – again! Meanwhile the BBFC had gone ahead and given *The Evil Dead* a clean bill of health *uncut*, and I have the censor's certificate at home, framed and hanging on the wall, to prove it.

When I first met Raimi, he was hard at work putting the finishing touches on *Darkman*, the movie that would effectively herald his move from the fringes of 'esoteric' film-making to the very heart of the mainstream market. Like Wes Craven, Raimi was surprisingly eager to talk to some previously unheard-of young hack, and I was beginning to think that Tim was right about the English accent being some form of all-access visa. Certainly I had no way of proving to Raimi that I was worth an hour of his time – for all he knew, I could just have been some time-wasting horror fan who wanted nothing more than to meet his genre idols. Come to think of it, that's pretty much what I was. Except that when I got back to the UK I did indeed write the interview up for *Time Out* where it commanded a couple of pages of space, not to mention bagging a front-cover feature (my first) in the specialist horror magazine *Fear* which – like so many other organisations I have worked for – would eventually go down in flames.

The 'curse of Kermode'.

The fact that Craven and Raimi, both of whom had helmed notoriously 'nasty' and 'obscene' films, turned out to be such nice intelligent people pretty much set the tone for the rest of my journalistic career. In the twenty years since I did those first stumbling interviews, I have met hundreds, if not thousands, of film-makers, and based on my (admittedly selective) experience I have reached the following conclusion: the nastier the movie, the nicer the people who made it (and possibly vice versa). Unlike the spoiled-brat superstars of mainstream Hollywood cinema, horror films tend to feature hard-working actors like Gunnar Hansen, who played the terrifying Leatherface in the long-banned *Texas Chain Saw Massacre*, but who came across as a lovely soft-spoken bloke when I interviewed him for the Channel 4 documentary *Scream and Scream Again*. Slasher cinema's grisly special effects are dreamed up by painstakingly talented make-up artists like Tom Savini, a thoughtful soul who (it was rumoured) once made a latex severed head *so* authentic that the police thought it was real and radioed in a murderous decapitation. And the fans who *watch* these movies are invariably the most innocuous and introverted bunch of misfits you'll ever meet in a cinema, no harm to anyone but themselves. Even that gore-hound's bible *Fangoria* magazine (aka 'Exploding Heads Monthly') is edited by all-round New York good guy Tony Timpone who shows up at horror conventions with his equally lovely wife Marguerite, herself a huge fan of Herman's Hermits and all things quaintly Victoriana. These people are splendidly warm and cuddly company and I would commend them to you unconditionally. Jeffrey Katzenberg on the other hand, the movie mogul behind all those 'family orientated' animated hits like *Shrek*, is … well, *not* cuddly. Somewhat *spiky*, in fact. I once did an onstage event with Katzenberg in Bristol at which he was meant to be discussing his deep love of animation, but he sneered and called me an idiot when I told him that I thought *Mary Poppins* was a masterpiece.

Sorry, but anyone who doesn't get *Mary Poppins* has no soul.

Anyway, back to my West Coast adventures. By day four I was starting to think that moving to LA might not be such a bad idea after all. Not to be a pop star – although obviously if DAM took off, then so be it – but as an International

Film Journalist. I really liked the sound of this phrase, particularly the 'International' bit. And the 'Journalist' bit too, come to that. It sounded so much better than 'film critic'. For a brief, deluded moment, I convinced myself that I was actually the kind of person who *could* pull off this glamorous transatlantic lifestyle, seeing films in the US, filing copy in the UK, jetting back home every few months just to gloat about how fabulous my sun-drenched life had become.

Of course, this was all just nonsense. I am not that person, and never will be. I grew up in Barnet and my conceptual map of the world goes: Southampton, Soho, St Albans, Manchester, the Isle of Man, Cornwall; everywhere else. Oh, and Liverpool, for personal reasons. And Shetland. And ... well, lots of other places actually, but none of them in America. Except for Georgetown.

Ah, Georgetown. For reasons which I have already explained, *The Exorcist* ('The greatest movie ever made', Mark Kermode, Radio One) has cast a long shadow over my life. So as I gazed out over the smog-filled streets of Los Angeles, with interviews with Wes Craven and Sam Raimi safely captured on my trusty Dictaphone, I knew instinctively what the next step in my International Film Journalist career must be. I picked up the phone, inhaled deeply, and took a running jump into the abyss.

'Hello, my name is Mark Kermode. I'm a journalist from London, working for *Time Out* and other top publications. And I'd like to interview Linda Blair, please.'

'OK,' said the ever so slightly waspish voice at the end of the phone. 'And what did you say your name was?'

'Kermode. Mark Kermode. I'm a journalist from the UK. And I'm a really big fan of Linda Blair. I've seen everything she's ever made. Not just *The Exorcist*, ha ha ha. No, no, I've seen 'em all!' And I started to list them. '*Roller Boogie*, *Hell Night*, *Wild Horse Hank*, *Sarah T: Portrait of a Teenage Alcoholic*, *Witchery*, *Born Innocent* (cut *and* uncut, of course), *Up Your Alley*, *Airport 75*, *The Heretic* (both versions), *Chained Heat*, *Red Heat*, *Savage Streets*, *Savage Island* ...'

I stopped suddenly, realising that I was starting to sound like a mental case. Or a stalker. Or a stalking mental case. Whatever. Either way, this was not good – particularly since Blair had reportedly been handling death threats from marauding loony-toons ever since *The Exorcist* made her a demonic child star at the age of fourteen. Hard though it is to believe, some cinema audiences apparently have a problem distinguishing fiction from reality, and thus Blair's brilliantly convincing portrayal of a possessed child led some morons to believe that she was actually the Devil. Duh!?

According to legend, at the height of all this insanity the police even sent a special agent round to live with Blair to protect her from the unwanted attentions of whackjobs. To this day, there are still people who believe (and indeed *report*) that Blair went mad as a result of appearing in *The Exorcist* – that she ended up in an asylum and her mother was struck by lightning. So the last thing she needed right now was yet another fruitcake on her case – albeit a fruitcake with an English accent.

In the silence that followed, I realised that I had almost certainly blown it. Might as well just hang up.

Yet Blair's agent (who used to work in fashion – who would've guessed?) was seemingly unaware of this paranoia-inducing area of his client's past.

'Well, that's just *great*!' he burbled happily. 'When would you like to meet?'

I was thrown. Completely sideswiped. I never expected him to say *yes*. OK, so Craven and Raimi both agreed quickly enough, but this was different. Blair was … a star!

'Er, hello?'

'Yes, hello. Sorry. What?'

'I said, when would you like to meet? Can't do tomorrow – busy, busy, busy. How about Thursday?'

'Thursday?' I attempted to affect an air of casual disregard, like that one Tony Curtis uses after Marilyn Monroe snogs him on a yacht in *Some Like It Hot*. I failed – I sounded more like Dick Van Dyke.

'Yes, I believe I *might* be able to "do" Thursday.'

'Well, that's just *great*!' he said for the second time. 'Whereabouts?'

I floundered. Raimi and Craven both just told me to come to their offices. Easy. But now suddenly I had to suggest a 'whereabouts'. Where does one usually have a 'whereabouts'? Hereabouts?

'Um, how about Tim and Jenny's place?' I blurted.

'"Tim and Jenny's Place"? Haven't heard of it. What food do they serve? Linda's vegan, you know.'

'Oh that's OK,' I laughed. 'It's not a restaurant. It's just my friend's flat. Sorry, "apartment". It's great – it's just off Sunset and — '

'*Whhhhaaaaat?*' shrieked the man on the end of the phone who had suddenly hit the correctly protective tone towards his client which I thought would have been appropriate about two minutes ago. 'I am *not* going to send Linda Blair to someone's *apartment*. Are you *mad*?'

Apparently so. Of course I was mad. What the hell was I thinking? I'd blown it again.

Damn.

Bugger.

Bollocks.

But no …

'*Sooo* … how about the Riverside Café, Riverside and Cahuenga? You know it?'

'Oh yes!' I lied. 'Good choice!'

'Well, that's just *great*! She'll see you there at 5 p.m. Thursday!'

And with that he was gone.

I arrived at the Riverside Café at 4 p.m., a full hour before the appointed time, terrified that I wouldn't be able to find the place, and convinced that this was all going to end badly. In an effort to appear less strung out than I clearly was, I drove around the block a few times, hoping to make myself fashionably late, allowing me to rush in as if hot-foot from some equally prestigious assignment, babbling apologies for my tardiness.

Finally I parked (horribly) and stepped into the

restaurant. I looked at the clock. It was 4.03 p.m. Bother. I considered going out and coming in again, but that smacked of Michael Palin in Monty Python's Spanish Inquisition sketch and that's *not* what I was aiming for at all. So instead I just stood there like a lemon.

The restaurant looked like a set. *Everything* in that town looked like a set. Those weren't real customers over there – they were *extras*. And they weren't *eating*. They were just fiddling around with fake lettuce. In fact, if you listened close enough, you could hear that they weren't even really *talking* – they were just going 'rhubarb rhubarb rhubarb' (you only get paid full SAG rates if you say 'real words') in what the script presumably described as 'background mumbling'.

'Table for one?' smiled the actress-slash-waitress, who I hadn't seen sweeping up silently behind me, cleverly cutting off my escape route.

'Er, no. *Two!*' I replied, forcefully.

'Two?' she repeated with smirking derision. She knew I was lying. She knew there was no way that a sad sack like me could possibly be dining with anyone *else*. She'd got my number.

'Yes,' I said again, attempting to stand up straight and tall. 'Yes, I will need a table for *two* persons because I have an appointment here with …' (let's see how she likes *this*) 'with … *Linda Blair*!'

She looked at me blankly, still smiling.

'The famous movie star!' I added, perhaps perfunctorily.

She kept smiling serenely.

'The famous star of not only *The Exorcist* (of course),

but also of many other hits (some of them straight-to-video) including *Roller Boogie*, *Hell Night*, *Wild Horse Hank*, *Sarah T: Portrait of a Teenage Alcoholic*, *Witchery*, *Born Innocent*, *Up Your Alley*, *Airport 75*, *Exorcist II: The Heretic*, *Chained Heat*, *Red Heat*, *Savage Streets*, *Savage Island* …'

She dropped the smile.

'Yeah, I know who Linda Blair is. She's not here yet. Take a seat.'

And with that she turned and walked away.

I really needed to stop doing that.

I found my own way to a table which was clearly set for at least five people. I figured this was about right. A table for two would be … well, creepy. I wanted to establish right away that I was *not* a stalker. I was a proper English film journalist with an enthusiastic regard for Blair's whole cinematic *oeuvre*. I was polite and well mannered, and I cared only about the *work*. Which was entirely true. It's just that I cared about the work *a lot*.

My waitress returned, observed the gigantic size of the table I had chosen, and said something indecipherable under her breath. Then she pulled a pencil out from behind her ear.

'Can I getcha anything while you're waiting? For the other *four* people.'

I decided not to rise to this.

'Yes,' I said firmly. 'I will have a bottle of beer please. A cold one, if you have it.'

The pencil went back behind the ear.

'What type of beer would you like, sir? They're *all* cold.'

'What have you got?'

Bad question.

'Amstel, Heineken, Bud, Bud Light, Coors, Coors Lite, Miller, Miller Lite, Pabst Blue Ribbon — '

'*That one!*'

'Which one?'

'The ribbon one.'

'Pabst?'

'Yes. Pabb.'

'Pabb ...ST.'

'That's what I said.'

She really didn't like me. Also, she was *on* to me. She knew I'd never drunk Pabst Blue Ribbon in my life. She *knew* that I only chose it because of that scene in *Blue Velvet* where Dennis Hopper out-cools Kyle MacLachlan by yelling 'Heineken? Fuck that shit! *Pabst Blue Ribbon!*'

I needed to reassert my authority. I needed to shape up. I needed to start acting like I knew what the hell I was doing. What would Jason Isaacs have done? In a move which I find inexplicable to this day, I decided to take everything I owned out of my bag and place it on display on the table in front of me. By the time my waitress came back, I had effectively occupied the entire tabletop with cassettes, batteries, notebooks, maps and bits of string, like someone attempting to play a swift round of makeshift *Risk* without pieces or a playing board.

There was hardly anywhere to put the beer, so she perched it on the far end of the table and then gave me a supercilious smirk. I smirked back, although her smirk was a lot more practised than mine. After she left, I got up from my chair, walked round the vast table to collect my beer, then walked it back to my seat, to the silent hilarity of the restaurant's few other patrons. Clearly, they were used to this sort of thing.

The Pabst Blue Ribbon was really very good and was swiftly really very *gone*. So I ordered another one. When my waitress returned to the table, I did not even deign to look up. I had got the measure of this game. I was not even going to acknowledge her. Ha!

'Mark?'

I looked up.

Blimey Charlie, it's Linda Blair.

I was thunderstruck. Shocked. Speechless. The last time I saw her, she was levitating effortlessly over a thumping, shaking bed, being doused in holy water by petrified Catholic priests while a packed late-night cinema audience quivered and quaked in awe. And now she was right *here*. Right *now*. Right *real*.

'I'm sorry,' she said politely. 'Are you Mark?'

'Yes, I am Mark, exciting yet trustworthy international film journalist, working for a host of important publications including London's prestigious *Time Out* magazine. How nice to meet you, Linda Blair, versatile and talented actress. I have seen all of your movies and look forward to discussing them with you. Please sit down.'

This is what the voice *inside* my head said. Unfortunately, the voice *outside* my head – the one that everyone in the 'real world' can hear – failed to respond, largely because my face had stopped functioning. I looked like a dead person.

'Sorry,' Blair said again. 'My mistake.' And she started to walk away.

With gargantuan effort, my brain *commanded* my mouth to snap to attention, get a grip, and resume normal communications with the outside world. As Blair headed off into the restaurant, I summoned up what it was left of my *savoir faire*, and launched into the verbal void.

'Isssssaahhmmurkkk!' I announced in something approaching a yell. She turned round again.

'Sorry?'

'Yes, I am Mark,' I grunted torturously, presumably with the expression of someone solving a complicated quantum physics equation while simultaneously passing a particularly large kidney stone.

'Oh. Hey. I'm Linda Blair.'

And indeed she was. I gestured wildly at the table in front of me, where I seemed to be having a front-lawn sale of everything I owned in the world. She surveyed the carnage, smiled (ironically?) and took a seat at the far end of the table. Clearly it was a good choice going for the five-seater. She didn't want to get any closer than that, and frankly I couldn't blame her. If I were in her shoes, and I had been sent to meet *me*, I would have gone straight home and fired my agent, before ringing the police department and asking if that nice officer was still available for house duty.

But, whether out of pity or professionalism, she settled herself down, ordered a salad from the waitress ('Oh hi Linda, how ya doin? The usual?' – all sunshine and light now, the double-crossing bastard), took a deep breath and said,

'So, whaddya wanna know?'

And for the next ninety minutes I interviewed Linda Blair. And she was great. Funny, intelligent, self-effacing, full of quotable stories, always ready to laugh at herself, profoundly aware of her own limitations, and just genuinely really nice. Despite my wobbly start, she put me at my ease, and together we meandered conversationally through the highs and lows of her career. With no hint of self-pity she told me about the weird life she had led in the wake of *The Exorcist*, recalling how people would recognise her in supermarkets and run screaming into the street. 'I was a normal kid,' she said, 'and I wanted to be pretty. But all people ever said to me was, "Wow, can you really spin your head around and throw up?"' She talked openly about some of the less than splendid straight-to-video sleaze she had made in the eighties ('we were filming *Red Heat* in a sewer and the camera tripod had one foot in the river of poop') and even apologised for *Savage Island* – an Italian women-in-chains cheapie for which she had recorded wraparound intro-outro scenes which allowed the makers to market it (spuriously) as 'starring Linda Blair'. Now she was branching out into comedy, and had great hopes for the forthcoming *Exorcist* spoof *Repossessed* in which she co-starred with her funnyman idol Leslie Nielsen, but which, heartbreakingly, would turn out to be utter pants. Hey-ho.

As the interview drew to a close, I asked her what *The Exorcist* meant to her after all these years, and she shrugged and said, 'Well, you know, there isn't a day goes by that someone doesn't ask me about that film. So to me, it's like my left arm – it's just *there*.'

As we parted, she said that she'd really enjoyed the interview and hoped I wouldn't write another one of those stories about her going mad and being sent to an asylum and her mother being struck by lightning. Then she gave me a signed photograph of herself, in a swimming pool, in an affectionate embrace with a dolphin. She looked really happy in the picture – presumably dolphins don't care about the bloody *Exorcist*.

'Oh, and my agent said something about you staying with some people called Tim and Jenny?' she added.

'Er, yes,' I replied sheepishly. 'Sorry about that, it's just that — '

'So I got these for them too!' she said brightly, handing over two more photos of her and the friendly sea mammal for my hosts. 'Send me a copy of the article!'

Which I did.

Back in London, I filed the interview for *Time Out*'s newly launched monthly magazine *20/20*, where it made a good-looking double-page splash. She came out of the interview very well, and everyone in the office commented on how surprised they were by what a smart, self-effacing woman she seemed to be, particularly since they'd all heard that she went mad and wound up in an asylum after her mother got struck by lightning.

I would meet Blair again in 1998 when filming *The Fear of God*, the first documentary I ever made for BBC TV. She remembered me (or at least she *said* she did) and seemed pleasantly surprised that the weird-looking befuddled hack she'd talked to all those years ago in the Riverside Café had somehow managed to carve himself out a career *on camera* with a reputable broadcaster.

'So, I guess things worked out alright for you?' she quipped gaily.

'Yes,' I replied, 'thanks partly to you. You did me a favour all those years ago. You took the time to give me a really nice interview. And I did well out of it. It got some attention. It got me more work back in England. I ended up writing a book about *The Exorcist*. One thing led to another. And so now...'

'And so now here you are!' laughed Blair.

'Yes,' I replied, 'here I am.'

And, indeed, there I was.

# Chapter 5

## BAD MUTHA RUSSIA

Russia. It seemed like such a good idea at the time.

Eisenstein. Tarkovsky. Klimov.

And Woody Allen's *Love and Death* … sort of.

It was 1992 and I was back in London, still filing for *Time Out*, but now also faxing copy to that aforementioned horror-obsessives' handbook *Fangoria* magazine in New York. The former paid the bills and gave me enough of a profile to be able to wrangle my way into movie preview screenings, but it was the latter which fuelled my sense of fanboy pride. As a fledgling genre fan I had kept a pile of dog-eared *Fangos* under the bed where more well-adjusted youths would presumably stash drugs and pornography. There was indeed something furtively dirty about the double-page pictorial spreads of severed limbs and monstrous bodily mutations which packed each new issue of Fango. Whereas old-style horror mags like *Castle of Frankenstein* and *Famous Monsters of Filmland* had feigned disgust or disdain at the genre's more lurid excesses, *Fango* embraced splatter with a refreshingly punky relish which echoed the battle-cry from David Cronenberg's *Videodrome*: 'Long Live the New Flesh!'

The first article I filed for *Fango* was an interview with British star Charles Dance who had just played the male lead in *Alien³* which had been severely compromised (i.e. ruined) by lumpen-headed studio interference. That article had earned me a *Fango* front cover but I had my sights set on something altogether more meaty: a substantial set report, perhaps, with a distinctly British flavour – something my better-established American counterparts couldn't get their hands on. Such an assignment duly materialised in the form of *Split Second*, a sub-*Alien* low-budget rubber monster movie set in a waterlogged near-future London, starring Rutger Hauer (a legend thanks to *Blade Runner*), Kim Cattrall (latterly of the ghastly *Sex and the City*) and Michael J. Pollard, best known as 'the weird one' out of *Bonnie and Clyde*. The film was directed by Tony Maylam who had acquired cult status amongst British horror fans for helming the briefly banned but otherwise unremarkable 'video nasty' *The Burning*.

Hauer was fun, having been around the exploitation block enough times to know the value of being polite and pleasant in interviews. Years later I would enjoy Hauer's company more fully whilst making the documentary *On the Edge of Blade Runner* for Channel 4. Hauer, who stole that film out from under Harrison Ford's nose, was terrifically candid, claiming that Ford had never got over the fact that 'he thought he was playing the hero, but his character was just a guy who fucks a dishwasher and then falls in love with it'. Ford declined to comment.

Kim Cattrall had just completed work on *Star Trek VI* and like Hauer knew the importance of keeping the geeky fans onside. The wild card, however, was Pollard, who gave me my first taste of a genuinely unusable interview. Having presumably been strong-armed by the producers to earn his keep by talking to the oiks of the genre press, Pollard agreed to spend fifteen minutes with my colleague Alan Jones (who filed for the more upmarket *Cinefantastique*) and me in his fantastically unimposing trailer. Thrilled to be in the company of a genuine star, we asked him about his role in *Split Second* as 'The Rat Catcher', only to be told: 'I'm on the Madonna album!'

'Pardon?'

'I'm on the Madonna album!'

'You're ... sorry, what?'

'I'm on the Madonna album,' Pollard said a third time, before adjusting his voice to a high-pitched enigmatic squeak and barking: '*Calling Dick Tracy!*'

I turned to Alan for support. He'd been in this game longer than I had. Surely he'd know what the hell was going on.

'You mean ... you're on the soundtrack album to *Dick Tracy*?' said Alan, clearly struggling.

'That's right!' squealed Pollard gleefully. '*Calling Dick Tracy!*'

And he was. Apparently a sample of his voice could indeed

be heard 'on the Madonna album', providing one of the LP's undoubted highlights. Beyond that we got *nothing* out of him – certainly nothing about *Split Second*. He was the Keyser Soze of unquotable interviewees.

In the wake of the Pollard experience I learned that there really is no point attempting to interview actors about movies in which they aren't really interested (publicists take note) and which they were presumably only doing for the money. Nothing wrong with that – we've all got to work, and with most actors *out of work* for *most of the time* no one can be criticised for earning an honest crust. Personally I've never had any problem with people doing trash to pay the bills, and if they don't want to talk about their trash, then hey, fair enough (although some of them are apparently 'contractually obliged' to do so). Conversely, Julian Sands once snapped at me on the set of the ultra-low-budget British bloodsucker *Tale of a Vampire* (which was 'arty' rather than 'trashy') when I joked that no one could accuse him of doing this film 'for the money'. Knowing that I was from *Fangoria* – a publication of which he may well have disapproved – Sands scowled and replied tartly, 'I don't do *anything* "for the money". Do *you*?' I felt like saying, 'Well actually yes, I hang around on movie sets like this in the middle of nowhere for hours on end just waiting and waiting in the hope that I can spend ten measly minutes talking to some actor who gets hoity with me because they think that they're "above" anything as sordid as earning a living and don't seem to realise that I'm just doing a job which will actually help their movie find an audience and possibly even make money.' But I didn't.

Because I needed to be nice to him so that he would continue to speak to me and so that I could go home at the end of the day and file an interview with him for *Fangoria*.

For the money.

It occurs to me now that Sands' fleeting offhand comment (which was probably utterly uncharacteristic and which he doubtless cannot even remember) may well have played a big part in my ongoing inability to appreciate his marvellous acting talents ever since, and to provoke me to mock him in public on numerous occasions in my role as an apparently unbiased film critic. In which case I owe him an apology.

And vice versa.

Anyway, back to Russia – via Italy. Sometime after filing the *Split Second* set report I got a phone call from Mariano Baino, an aspiring film-maker whom I had met before and been impressed by, for two reasons. The first was that he had made an admirably atmospheric short film entitled *Caruncula*, which was twisted and evocative in all the right ways (acclaimed horror novelist Ramsey Campbell called it 'a small masterpiece of sustained perversity') suggesting a burgeoning directorial talent. The second and equally important reason was that Mariano was actually *Italian*, which was to horror what being Dutch or Swedish was to porn. In effect being Italian was a qualification, a badge of honour to be worn with pride. While Britain had given us Hammer and America had given us *The Exorcist*, Italy had spawned the '*gialli*', a stylish and lurid brand of screen thrillers which took their name from the 'yellow' cover designs of the pulp paperbacks which inspired them.

From the maestro Mario Bava (who predated everything from *Friday the 13th* to *Alien* with stylish B-movies like *Bay of Blood* and *Planet of the Vampires*) to genre darling Dario Argento (whose films were bloody and beautiful in equal measure), Italy could rightly lay claim to having put the Art into exploitation cinema. Even Ruggero Deodato's *Cannibal Holocaust* (which featured unforgiveable scenes of animal cruelty) effectively prefigured *The Blair Witch Project* with its central morbid 'found film' motif. Add to this a string of die-hard weirdies like Aldo Lado's *Short Night of the Glass Dolls* and Massimo Dallamano's *What Have You Done to Solange?* (both of which I would later proudly introduce *uncut* on Film4's Extreme Cinema strand), and having an Italian driver's licence became the equivalent of owning an all-access pass to the hearts and minds of the horror cognoscenti. Hell, we'd even forgive them for the misogynist dirge of Lucio Fulci's loathsome *New York Ripper*, a film so staggeringly adolescent that even spotty male horror fans seemed embarrassed to praise it, resorting to carping on about Francesco De Masi's 'interesting' score, as if this somehow mitigated the movie's irredeemable awfulness.

Mariano invited me and my colleague Nigel Floyd to meet him in Pizza Express by the side of the British Museum where he told us all about his upcoming first feature – a ghostly tale of terror entitled *Dark Waters*. It had been co-scripted by an English writer named Andrew Bark who had worked with Mariano on *Caruncula*. Apparently Bark's original ten-page synopsis had been envisaged as an H. P. Lovecraft homage set in northern England with an American lead. But by the time

Mariano pitched the movie to Nige and me the main action had moved to the Odessa Catacombs out in Ukraine, and the story centred on an English-raised girl returning to a remote island convent where her mother had died in childbirth, and which now harboured a dark demonic secret.

Like so many charismatic film-makers, Mariano talked a *really* great movie. He brought the story of *Dark Waters* to life right there in Pizza Express, using storyboards and drawings to conjure vivid pictures of terror and amazement like P. T. Barnum's cinematic heir. By the time he'd finished pitching the movie I was ready to remortgage my flat and finance the film myself. But there was no need. Miraculously, Mariano had secured the necessary backing thanks to an unfathomably labyrinthine series of connections involving punk rock and the conversion of roubles into dollars. As a teenager, Bark had been a big fan of black-garbed college kids turned pub-rock punk survivors the Stranglers, a devotion which had continued into later life. Somehow, through his membership of the international Stranglers fan club (who knew?) Bark had struck up a correspondence with a young Russian man, Paul Azov, who shared his passion for the band and who had fallen in with Siberian-born businessman Victor Zuev. Victor had set his sights on financing 'the first Western film to be shot in Ukraine following the collapse of the Soviet Union' for reasons both artistic and fiscal. A low-budget film produced in Ukraine which could then turn a profit in the West would generate hard currency which was painfully difficult to come by in the former Soviet Union. Victor had apparently seen *Caruncula* at a festival in Russia and the unlikely trio were now engaged in a major movie undertaking which would never have happened if 'Peaches' hadn't become a surprise Top Twenty hit back in the seventies. There were even wild rumours of Stranglers lead singer Hugh Cornwell performing a cameo role in the film, although this turned out (unsurprisingly) to be fanciful tosh. But the fact that the film was happening *at all* was still pretty impressive, and since these serendipitous beginnings, things had apparently moved on apace. Mariano had already held auditions in London for an English-speaking lead and had cast upcoming theatre actress Louise Salter, striking and elegant photos of whom were swiftly produced from a large brown Manila envelope. (Salter would later go on to have a small role as one of ten 'Paris Vampires' in the big-budget Brad Pitt/Tom Cruise bloodsucker *Interview with the Vampire*.) The rest of the cast had been selected from local talent in Russia and Ukraine, some of whom couldn't speak English but who (we were assured) would learn the dialogue 'phonetically'. It was to be a truly international undertaking; a Russian/Ukrainian horror movie, directed by an Italian, co-written by a Brit, starring an English woman, with a Baltic supporting cast (including a 'Miss Russia' runner-up!) and all made with an eye on eventual American distribution. What could go wrong?

Being an entrepreneurial soul, Mariano had figured out that if he could somehow get Nigel and me out to Russia, then he could get valuable coverage for *Dark Waters* in a string of influential publications in the UK and US. Between us, Nige and I wrote for *Time Out*, *20/20*, *Fear*, *Fangoria* and *Video Watchdog*, not to mention the radio reports we both now filed for the BBC. For our part, we'd get exclusive access to a horror-movie set whose location and backstory alone seemed guaranteed to provoke international interest. Even if the movie sucked the set reports would be unusual and therefore newsworthy. And Mariano had promised that at least *some* of the pictures would involve blood, so that would keep the *Fango*-reading gore-hounds happy. Plus, we'd get to have fun in Russia and Ukraine – a particularly big deal for me. For years I'd been parading around wearing the meaningless CCCP insignia (Yuri Gagarin badges, hammer and sickle earrings) which had become boringly fashionable amongst armchair student Trots in the eighties – I'd even started hoarding copies of *Pravda* (which was now being reprinted in English) on the basis that it couldn't be any more 'biased' than the Murdoch press which held Britain in its evil thrall. Yet what I actually *knew* about the former Soviet Union wouldn't fill the back of a small postage stamp, and here was a chance to gain some invaluable first-hand experience. More importantly, here was an opportunity to start any future political argument with the phrase 'Well, having actually *worked* in Russia …' or to pull out the cineaste trump card 'In my *personal* experience of Soviet film-making in the post-Wall era …' which I was not about to pass up.

Oh, and the entry stamp would look really cool on my passport.

I was sold.

So, some time later, Nige and I found ourselves at Heathrow airport, boldly setting out on a journey which would take us to Moscow, Odessa, and then on to Feodosiya on the Black Sea, with impressive Cyrillic screeds duly emblazoned in red ink upon our passports. The first leg of the trip went fabulously well, and we breezed through customs at Moscow airport despite my worries that the border authorities would take one look at us and put us straight on the next plane home. For several weeks I'd been studiously practising a speech which I would deliver in just such an eventuality, reassuring them that I was a bona fide British film journalist who had come here to report upon the glorious state of the glasnost-fuelled Russian film industry while simultaneously humming the chorus of the Internationale and striking an appropriately comradely pose – chin raised, back straight, with perhaps a sheaf of wheat draped over a muscular spanner-wielding forearm. But whoever was hiding behind the scary peaked cap at the customs desk never even looked at me, merely taking my passport and sliding it under an ominous blue light into which he stared for a couple of minutes while tapping away at a hidden keyboard, and then returning it without a word. Apparently I was in.

Hooray!

Nigel similarly went through on the nod, and we proceeded to the arrivals lounge where we were met by a man from the *Dark Waters* entourage whose name I cannot remember, but who I shall refer to as Ivan for reasons of stereotypical simplicity.

My opening gambit was tediously predictable.

'Hello, I'm Mark, and I need to make a phone call.'

Ivan smiled kindly. 'Who do you need to call?'

'My wife. Linda. I always call her when I get off a plane

just to tell her I've arrived safely, and the plane hasn't crashed and killed everyone on board. You know. Silly really, but it's sort of a ritual thing and I sort of *have* to do it. Or I can't relax. So, as I said, I need to use a phone.'

Ivan smiled again. 'Linda, is she in Moscow?'

'Oh, no no, she's at home in England. Where we live. Linda and me. And I. And I need to call her.'

'Yes I see,' said Ivan. 'It is not easy to do from the airport. Have you booked?'

'Pardon?'

'Have you booked?'

'No, you don't understand, I don't want to travel anywhere, I just want to make a phone call.'

'To England?'

'Yes. England.'

'Have you booked?'

'No, I don't want to *go* there, I just want to *phone* there.'

'Yes. Have you booked?'

This clearly wasn't working. I wanted to talk about phone calls and Ivan wanted to talk about transport. Either that or he wanted me to book a plane and go straight home. In which case he probably wasn't the only one.

I decided to try another tack.

'OK, I *don't* want to go to England because I just came from there.'

'Right. And now we go to my house in Moscow where we will get food and whatever else you might need.'

'Do you have a phone?'

'Of course I have a phone!'

'Great. So I can call Linda from there.'

'Have you booked?'

This was going to be a long trip.

As it turned out it was Ivan (rather than me) who understood the complexities of my predicament. When we arrived at his apartment on the outskirts of Moscow I was duly shown to the phone where I attempted pathetically to make an international phone call. When I asked what the international dialling code was, Ivan laughed sardonically and then tapped a number into the phone which connected me to a sternly unwelcoming operator.

'*Da!*'

'Oh, hello. Sorry. Um. *Dosvedanya*! No, wrong word – bother. Er, do you speak English?'

'*Da*.'

'Oh, great. I need to make an international call. To England.'

'England?'

'Yes.'

'Phone England?'

'Yes.'

'You have booked?'

'What? What is all this about? Everyone keeps asking me if I've *booked*. What does it mean?'

'It means "you have booked?" Your international phone call. To England. You have booked?'

'Have I *booked* to make a phone call?'

'Yes.'

'No.'

'So, no call. You want to book?'

'The phone call?'

'Yes.'

'To England?'

'Yes.'

'Er, yes I suppose so. How long will it take?'

'Two days.'

'*Whaaaat?*'

'Yes, I know. Is fast. Not so busy right now.'

'Hang on, you're saying it will take *two days to book a phone call*?'

'Yes.'

'But I need to call *now*!'

'Then you must book.'

'Now?'

'Yes, now. And you call in two days.'

My head was reeling. This *couldn't* be true. Surely it wasn't possible that a civilised nation which had defeated the Nazis and been the first to put a man in space didn't have simple international subscriber trunk dialling? But Ivan had been right all along. I really did need to have booked – which I hadn't.

So much for the glorious revolution.

I now faced a dilemma – the first of many. I had told Linda that I would phone her the instant I arrived in Moscow. I had failed in this endeavour. Worse, there was no chance of the situation improving in the near future. I couldn't book a phone call from Ivan's flat because we were due to ship out of Moscow pretty soon en route to Odessa, after which we would continue on through Ukraine and to the shores of Feodosiya. By the time we got there we would have been travelling for at least three days, on to which I would then have to add the *extra* two days it would take to book a phone call. Assuming, that is, that they *had* a phone in Feodosiya, which seemed uncertain. By the time I finally got word to Linda that I was not dead I would be on my way home, and she would surely have succumbed to grieving. In the movie in my head I could see her (played, as I mentioned earlier, by Julianne Moore) waiting by the phone, a photograph of Jason Isaacs propped on the desk with a solitary rose leaning poignantly against it, her face growing darker and more burdened with worry and anguish by the moment …

Of course, in the 'real world' (of which everyone seems so enamoured) none of this was happening at all. Linda (rather than Julianne) *knew* that nothing had happened because there'd been nothing on the news about plane crashes and the like and she just assumed that it was hard to call from Russia. You probably had to book it in advance. But I was now in a state of advancing panic, and *nothing* would calm my agitation. Nothing except …

'Alcohol. I need alcohol.'

'Yes,' said Ivan pleasantly. 'We have vodka. You want some?'

'No, no, no, I can't do vodka,' I said feebly. 'Particularly not Russian vodka. I'm not that rugged. Do you have beer?'

'No, but we can get beer. And see Moscow. We have a few hours. We can see the sights. Your train doesn't leave until 3 a.m.'

'You mean 3 "p.m."'

'No, I mean 3 "a.m." Three o'clock in the morning. Tomorrow morning. About twelve hours from now.' He produced the train tickets and, as always, he was right. Our train was indeed due to pull out of Moscow at 3 a.m. Bloody hell. It was still early afternoon, and the lightly freezing rain outside was starting to abate slightly, unlike my headache. So we headed off into town in search of beer and the 'sights'.

Out on the streets, Ivan held out his hand to the first passing car which promptly screeched to a halt in the middle of the road. The driver wound down the window and exchanged a few pleasantries with our guide, before opening his back door to let us in.

'Is it a taxi?' I asked. 'He doesn't have a sign or anything.'

'No,' replied Ivan, nonplussed.

'He's a friend of yours?'

'No. But he will take us to Red Square.'

'I see. Why?'

'I thought you wanted to see the sights.'

'Oh yes I do, but why is *he* taking us? If he's not a taxi. Or a friend.'

'We will pay him.'

'So he *is* a taxi?'

'No. But we will pay him and he will take us.'

As it turned out, this was how the (non) taxi system

worked in Moscow. If you wanted to get somewhere, and you had some money, you simply flagged down a car. *Any* car. And, for a reasonable remuneration, they might agree to take you to your preferred destination. Sometimes, there would already be other people in the car, perhaps a family with children or elderly relatives. But a mixture of benevolent spirit and earnest entrepreneurism meant that if you had the roubles you could squeeze in with their nearest and dearest and go almost anywhere. Considering the frankly terrible experiences I've had with taxis and minicabs in the UK ('You wanna go *where* mate? At *this* time of day/night/year? You're *joking* incha?') it was surprisingly pleasant, if a little unusual.

So roubles changed hands, spaces were found, and off we bumped in an overcrowded Lada (*every* car was a Lada – clichéd but true). We trundled through uniformly drab streets, past endless municipal housing much of which reminded me of my old Hulme flat in Manchester, and on toward the very heart of what used to be the Soviet Union.

After a while we reached Red Square. It was smaller than I had expected. I could see the Kremlin, which looked a bit like Sleeping Beauty's castle from Disneyland, only without Tinkerbell. But *with* a McDonald's. That's glasnost for you. The rain worsened a little, and the wind picked up a touch. I spied the entrance to a subway station. I'd always wanted to see the Moscow Metro which, according to legend, was decorated with striking Soviet murals and offered a beacon of hope to those who still believed in the potential benefits of state-run socialism.

Eager to shelter from the weather we all piled down the subway steps and found ourselves in a cavernous underground palace, clean as a whistle, spankingly upkept, with the promised artwork gleaming from every wall. It was magnificent. A train howled proudly out of the tunnel and into the station where Muscovites proceeded to board and disembark in polite and orderly fashion. I thought of the horrors of London's Northern Line; of being crammed up against jostling bullying louts between Archway and Tottenham Court Road, of endless delays and signal failures, of ripped posters advertising lousy movies and noxious anti-dandruff products, and of illiterate graffiti forcefully inviting me to 'suk thiz'. I thought of being propositioned by a paedophile at Lancaster Gate on the way home from a shopping trip at the age of eleven, and of Paul Weller getting stuck 'Down in the Tube Station at Midnight' and getting beaten up by Nazis who 'smelled of pubs and Wormwood Scrubs and too many right-wing meetings'. And suddenly the absurd romance of my dreams of Mother Russia came flooding back to me and I was filled with an overwhelming love of Lenin and a powerful desire to defect to the East and spend the rest of my days watching *Battleship Potemkin*. We were, after all, headed for Odessa …

After a while we trudged back up the steps and on to the Moscow streets, cold and wet and tired, and headed back toward the suburbs of Moscow. Here we met Yolena, who would be our translator, guide, and (as would become apparent) guardian angel during the descent into hell upon which we were unknowingly about to embark. Yolena was a student in her early twenties; bright, intelligent, fluent in many languages, solid of character and sunny of disposition.

She had agreed to give up a week of her life in order to chaperone a pair of shabby moaning Brits around her country for almost no pay (but rather for 'the experience') and frankly we did not deserve her. But as yet we hadn't realised just how far out of our depths we had drifted nor just how different things were going to be now that we weren't in Kansas any more.

Yolena took us to her sister's flat, stopping to pick up some misshapen bottles of what claimed to be 'beer' from a 'licensed' vendor on an anonymous street corner. Here we were fed and pampered by our hosts whose hospitality seemed boundless. You can say what you like about the Russian state, about its crap economy and rampant corruption (more of which later) and about the stunning inequality between the rich and poor in an allegedly socialist society, but somehow none of that political venality seemed to have brushed off on the Russian people themselves. They were absolutely lovely.

Then again, we hadn't yet met 'Mr Nyet'.

Looking back on this episode now, one question rings in my head: What on earth were we doing in Moscow in the first place? I don't mean that in the cosmic, spiritual sense, but in a very real and material way. Why were we there? Why? Even before we left Heathrow, Nige and I had *known* that neither Mariano nor any significant members of his crew were going to be in Moscow when we arrived. I'm not even sure now whether they were *ever* in Moscow – although the film would indeed wind up being edited there several months later. We had already ascertained that the 'studio' part of the *Dark Waters* shoot was going to take place in Odessa, which we had fondly imagined to be somewhere 'near' Moscow (in the same way that I had imagined Los Angeles to be 'near' New York). In this age of Google Maps it would take most people about ten seconds to discover that Odessa is actually in Ukraine, and nearer to London than Moscow, by some distance. It is also nearer to Kiev, which has an airport, and (crucially) is also in Ukraine. But in my geographically challenged head I think I had simply imagined that in order to get into 'Russia' (by which I really meant the former Soviet Union – *including* Ukraine) you *had* to go through Moscow, like the magical wardrobe which provided the only access to Narnia. And somehow, even though I *knew* this was not the case, I had conjured a scenario in my head in which our old pal Mariano, with whom we had got on so well in Pizza Express all those months ago, would have 'popped up' from the Odessa shoot to meet us upon our arrival in Moscow and welcome us with open arms before taking us out for a slap-up meal where he could tell us how brilliantly the film was going and how he was going to remember to thank me and Nige *personally* from the Oscar stage when the inevitable plaudits started rolling in. Knowing me (rather than knowing you) this sounds like exactly the kind of foolishly self-aggrandising scenario which I would have cooked up in my head and then convinced myself was true. Or 'based on a true story'.

The only thing that was really 'true' however was that we were now further away from Mariano and *Dark Waters* than we had been when we got on the plane in London – both geographically *and* philosophically. As yet, however, the magnitude of our miscalculation was not quite clear.

Give it time.

At 2 a.m., we shambled back off to the overground train station, tired, bedraggled, and generally not at our best. The station was largely empty and cold but a few seats in the middle of the vast open terminus offered somewhere to plonk our aching bones while we waited an hour for the train to arrive. As with the subway, the overground station was fantastically clean, a feature which sadly had its drawbacks. As we slumped huddled on to those lonely seats a man with a mop appeared, slopping his sanitary way inexorably toward us from a great distance. Like an escapee from a Samuel Beckett play he traversed great swathes of wide-open concourse, making a bee-line through the vast emptiness to the tiny cluster of chairs upon which we perched. He could have spent the next ten years mopping the empty floor around us on which *no one* was seated, but for some reason he wanted to mop the exact spot where we had taken root. So, with a few terse words, he got us all to get up and then proceeded to pack our chairs away in a pile and to mop the floor where they had once stood with the vigour of a murderer cleaning fingerprints from the scene of a crime. We stood, bleary-eyed, staring at him, wondering whether he was going to let us sit down again. But he wasn't. We were going to have to stand. For an hour.

So we stood.

For an hour.

'Incidentally,' I asked in a stuporous drawl as the appointed time drew nearer. 'How long *is* the journey to Odessa? Once we actually get on the train ...'

'Twenty-seven hours,' replied Yolena matter-of-factly.

'*Twenty-seven hours!?*' Nige and I blurted in stunned unison.

'Yes,' Yolena confirmed, in calming tones. 'Twenty-seven hours. We will arrive early in the morning.'

'Early in the morning ... *tomorrow*?'

'Yes. Early in the morning ... *tomorrow*. And now it is time to go to the train.'

As the clock struck three, our train appeared on the platform and we shuffled queasily toward its open doors. The culture shock was staggering. While you could have happily eaten your lunch off that ultra-clean station floor, you probably wouldn't have wanted to take a dump on the dining tables of the train. The toilet (for which we'd been waiting with increasing agitation since the station toilet was closed 'for cleaning', naturally) was monstrous beyond belief. It was, in effect, a rusted tin trumpet voiding openly on to the track below, its sides encrusted with a cocktail of faeces and vomit. The ammonia-heavy acrid stench that festered in that tiny portable torture chamber could have been bottled and dropped on to battlefields with results which would surely have contravened internationally respected rules of warfare. Even if your bladder and bowels were so full that they were about to burst out of your body in the manner of John Hurt's spectacular chestular eruptions in *Alien*, believe me you'd *still* find it preferable to tie a knot in it or evacuate out of the window rather than avail yourself of the on-board conveniences.

They were, to be clear, not nice toilets.

The cabins weren't much better.

They consisted of four fold-down bunk beds, each with a stinky mattress covered with a 'cleaned' sheet. You knew the sheet had been 'cleaned' not because it was actually 'clean' but rather because it was actually wet. At least, I hoped that was why it was wet. Frankly, by that point I was starting not to care. There was already one passenger occupying a lower bunk and noisily eating some non-specific meaty substance so I clambered up on to a top billet and lay down in the dampness, my head filled with dreams of Hampstead Heath and a swift half at the Spaniards Inn. I started to drift into unconsciousness …

… only to be woken almost immediately by the sound of Nigel involved in an increasingly heated argument. I clambered back down from the bunk and out into the corridor where Nige was squaring up against a uniformed guard while Yolena stood between them, clutching three rail tickets and bravely attempting to preserve whatever was left of the peace.

The problem, it transpired, was that Nige and I were British, yet our train tickets had been purchased for us by a Russian. Apparently, foreigners were supposed to pay more money for the privilege of travelling on this particular portable toilet, and the guard was now insisting that we hand over more money which he would presumably pocket. Yolena was level-headedly translating all of this for Nige whose replies were being similarly relayed in the correct language back to the conductor. Through this miracle of multilingual communication skills, Nige was able to understand that the Russian guard wanted to fine him for the crime of being British and the guard was equally able to understand Nige's forcefully expressed reaction to this apparent cultural apartheid. At the point that I arrived on the scene, Nige was asking Yolena to translate the following phrase: 'If I pay you any more money, will it make the train go any faster?'

Yolena wasn't entirely happy about this but Nige wasn't taking no for an answer. Clearly he was as rattled as I was, which made me feel a bit better; it's always good to know that somebody else is miserable too – that's why I like Morrissey so much. So Yolena politely passed on the message to the guard who stared goggle-eyed at Nige's insolence, his face going various shades of red, white and blue. He seemed to be weighing up the merits of throwing us all off the train, and I was pretty much ready to decamp back to the station and have it out with the cleaner about giving us back our chairs, when suddenly he let out an exasperated gasp, turned, and headed off down the train.

'I take it that means no,' said Nige as I ducked back into the cabin, taking refuge once again in the rollicking swallow of the marshy top bunk while the man down below continued to munch contentedly. I really wanted to go home, to be wrapped in the arms of my wife who was surely, even now, making funeral arrangements, certain of my premature demise due to my abject failure to phone her immediately upon my arrival at Moscow airport all those hours (or was it days?) ago. I drifted in and out of consciousness, too tired to stay awake, too cold and wet to sleep.

And that was pretty much the way I stayed for the next twenty-seven hours. Every now and then I would get up and wander down the corridor a while, staring out of the window at the abyss of featureless flat fields and scrubby settlements which seemed to stretch the entire length of the journey. Baz Luhrmann, the director of *Strictly Ballroom* and *Moulin Rouge*, once proudly boasted to me that his home country Australia had 'more "nothing" than anywhere else in the world'. Clearly he'd never been to Russia. Or Ukraine, into which we had slipped without really noticing. For hour after hour, an epic vista of nothingness stretched out all around us. And not just nothingness – but *ugly* nothingness. So much for the majestic wheat fields about which we'd all sung so passionately back in the warm pubs of Manchester. The reality was infinitely more miserable than the trouble and pain inspired by a rented room in Whalley Range. God help the Smiths if they'd have been brought up *here*.

Night rolled into day and back into night with little discernible change. The train lurched slowly across ill-maintained tracks, and every now and then the evil stink-beast would escape from its toilet imprisonment and rampage down the corridors and into the cabins like a mustard-gas attack. My insides heaved and groaned and occasionally my outsides followed suit. I was no fun to be around at all.

Somewhere in the middle of it all I started to develop

a pain in the small of my back which spread slowly up my spine to the base of my neck and then up round the back of my head, finally settling between my eyes and ears like a perambulating tumour. I had noticed that when I stood up I was standing neither straight nor proud, and I was starting to doubt that my hunched demeanour was entirely a result of my parlous psychological state. In short, I thought I might not be putting it on, but might actually have done something *not good* in the region of my coccyx. Sadly, I'd downed my entire supply of both aspirin and paracetamol and was now discovering what it must have been like to be alive before the invention of analgesics. It was not pleasant.

I half slept some more and attempted to prepare myself for the coming adventures in Odessa. Surely that would be thrilling? We could walk up the infamous Odessa steps, dodging the ghosts of the tsars' jackbooted warriors and saving babies in prams as they spiralled ever downward toward a vast fleeing crowd. The fact that the stair-bound civilian massacre portrayed in Eisenstein's *Battleship Potemkin* never really happened (but was 'inspired by real events') mattered not one jot. In our world films *were* fact. So, we'd pay homage to Uncle Sergei and then proceed to the historic film studios where a well-stocked canteen and welcoming toilet facilities would surely await. Duly refreshed (physically, mentally and politically) we would proceed to conduct a string of insightful interviews relating to *Dark Waters*, getting down to the business of proper in-depth 'on-set' reportage which was, after all, our reason for being here. Surely things were about to get better?

Sadly, not.

The train pulled into Odessa station, as our guide had promised, first thing in the morning, and somehow (I forget exactly how) we managed to shuffle our way across town to the Odessa studios. They were, as advertised, both impressive and historic, and it would have been terrific to interview Mariano about working here on his first feature film. Predictably, however, Mariano and his crew were nowhere to be seen, having already gone on ahead to the location at Feodosiya, leaving behind only the remnants of *Dark Waters* techies and the decaying leftovers of papier-mâché sets and special effects.

Peculiarly, despite having been advertised as an 'Odessa Studio' production, the *Dark Waters* team didn't actually appear to have been *in* the studios. According to Mariano's current website (which pays testament to the bizarre conditions endured by *Dark Waters* 'survivors') someone 'sold their allotted studio space in Odessa to a rival production for profit, leaving Baino and his crew with no alternative but to move to another studio near Chernobyl'. This new studio was in Kiev Oblast, about seventeen kilometres away from the defunct nuclear reactor which had famously melted down in 1986, scattering poisonous radiation amongst the surrounding lands. It was within this toxic fallout zone that the *Dark Waters* team had been labouring, their make-up woman carrying a Geiger counter to check for fallout between shots.

Meanwhile, back in Odessa, the only evidence of *Dark Waters*' presence was a set built within a derelict swimming pool just *outside* the main studios, where a climactic flood scene had recently been shot. Here were the rapidly rotting remains of the crypt-like sets which would be intercut with location footage of the celebrated Odessa Catacombs, thousands of kilometres of underground labyrinths in which Ukrainian partisans had famously hidden during World War Two. And here, too, was the long-awaited demon monster's head of which Mariano had talked so animatedly back in Pizza Express; terrifying when described by the vibrantly ebullient Baino, but oddly unimpressive when viewed in the harsh light of a grey Odessa dawn.

This was no surprise – almost *all* horror movie monsters look tacky when seen in the raw, and before the application of sexual lubricants. Ask any SFX guy and they'll tell you that the only way to make monsters look good on screen is to smear them with K-Y Jelly and get a good cameraman to backlight them in a manner which catches the oozing sheen of slime in evocative close-up – very much like porn in fact. And it's not just low-budget shockers whose creatures lack the X-factor in the flesh. I once interviewed Italian special-effects whiz Carlo Rambaldi who did the extending mandible head effects for Ridley Scott on *Alien*, and the models he showed me (which looked so terrifying on screen) all looked laughably Tony Hart-like in the flesh. At one point the great Rambaldi disappeared off into his workshop and came back lugging a rotting lump of brown Styrofoam with what looked like a load of battery-operated Meccano hanging out of its insides. Two rotating poles were attached to big bulgy eyeballs which seemed oddly familiar, but I couldn't quite place where I'd seen them before.

'Look!' said Rambaldi sadly, swinging the sack of bolts around by its arm. 'Look what 'as 'appen to ET!'

I gasped in recognition as the ragbag collection of rubber and metal suddenly took shape in my head and I recognised it as the most famous screen alien of all time, albeit in somewhat decrepit condition. 'They want me to fix it for twenty-first anniversary celebrations. For his birthday! I must make him look new again. And walk again. Ha!'

'Can I touch it?' I asked, aghast.

'Touch it? Yes, touch it. Is just rubber foam.'

I reached out and touched ET's finger – a symbolic gesture of species reaching out across eternal intergalactic divides.

It fell off.

'Ah, yes, I must fix it more, always more,' muttered Rambaldi and dragged the bedraggled but uncomplaining movie star back into his workshop. If only A-list actors were as malleably compliant.

Back in Odessa, I was starting to wonder whether we were *ever* going to meet up with Mariano, or whether this whole 'first feature film' thing was simply a massive hoax. There had been rumblings that the *Dark Waters* shoot was not an entirely happy one, and the few stragglers we met in Odessa hinted that relations between the Russians, the Ukrainians, the Brits and the Italians were taking on a Babel-esque quality. I started to feel like Martin Sheen in Coppola's *Apocalypse Now*, travelling endlessly and inexorably upriver in search of Mariano's Colonel Kurtz, arriving at each new station only to discover that he had already moved on, presumably descending ever further into madness. I half imagined that when we finally caught up with Baino he would be bald-headed and covered in warpaint, quoting lines from Eliot's 'Hollow Men' while lopping the heads off babies to the amusement of Dennis Hopper …

As ever, the reality was more mundane. Far from being a jungle, Feodosiya is described in the travel literature as 'a popular resort city with a population of about 85,000 people with beaches, mineral springs and mudbaths' on the edge of the Black Sea – which sounded quite nice. It was here that Mariano had made his new base camp, striking out for the beach-bound location shoots which were currently happening at night. We were hot on his trail. Our goal was in sight.

'So,' I said with a sense of oddly familiar dread. 'This Feodosiya place. Is it … near?'

'Um … not really,' said the helpful British crewman who had been showing us around the deserted swimming pool.

'Not really?'

'No, not really "near". At all.'

'How "not really near at all" is it?'

'Well it's quite a long drive.'

'So we're going to drive there?'

'Yes. Well, yes and no. I'm going to drive. You're going to go in the back.'

'In the back of what?'

'In the back of the van. I've got the rest of the equipment in there and they've asked me if I can stick you three in the back and take you on down with me. I'm leaving in an hour.'

'I see. So we're going to go in the back of the van …'

'Yes.'

'To Feodosiya …'

'That's right.'

'Which is "quite a long drive" away.'

'Yup.'

'Right. And how far *exactly* is "quite a long drive"?'

'Well, it's hard to be precise because the roads around here are a bit dicky.'

'Then I'll settle for vaguely. How far *vaguely* is "quite a long drive"?'

'Well … we'll definitely get there today.'

'Today?'

'Yeah. If we leave soon.'

'But it is still early morning now. And you are talking about driving until the end of "today". Which would in effect mean driving *all day*.'

'Yes, but I don't mind. I'm fed up with being here. I want to get out to Feodosiya. It's meant to be good there.'

'Well, that's as maybe, but you're still talking about driving *all day* with us in the back of the van.'

'It doesn't bother me,' he repeated amiably.

There was a long pause. Nige and I were both clearly in a similar 'emotional space' and both waiting for the other to speak first. In the end, it was Nigel who finally broke the silence.

'No,' he said simply, but firmly.

'No what?'

'No, we are not going to travel in the back of a van for a day.'

'But there isn't any other way of getting there.'

'Look,' said Nige, 'this is clearly not your fault, and I appreciate that you are doing everything you can to help us. Thank you. But we have just travelled on a train for *twenty-seven hours* in order to get here, and we are not about to spend the rest of the day in the back of a van. We are going to travel to Feodosiya in a car, which Victor is going to sort out for us.'

'Oh, right. Has he done that then? Organised a car?'

'No,' said Nigel. 'He has not. But he will do.'

And with that he turned politely and went off to find someone who could translate his declaration about the car from fantasy into fact.

Amazingly, it worked. Whether through charisma or sheer force of will, Nigel effectively magicked a car into existence, complete with a driver, who would transport us forthwith from Odessa to Feodosiya. It was a miracle.

It was also a trap. Because, as it turned out, we would have been happier in the back of the van – *much* happier. If I die and go to hell, I am pretty certain that I will be transported there in the car in which we travelled from Odessa to Feodosiya. And when we arrive at the gates of Hades, and it is time to throw myself into the pit of eternal fire thence to be roasted and tortured for evermore, I shall slip gladly out of that post-mortal vehicle, safe in the knowledge that whatever unearthly tortures the Devil has in store for me cannot possibly be any worse than spending another minute in that bloody car.

It was a Lada – of course. In Russia, where they're built, by the AvtoVAZ corporation, they call them Zhigulis – the word 'Lada' being officially used only for the export market, apparently. In the West, particularly in the nineties, everyone made jokes about Ladas (What do you call a moving Lada? On tow; What do you call a Lada with a sunroof? A skip; What do you do when your Lada bursts a tyre? Change the Lada; and so on). Their Czechoslovakian counterpart, the Skoda, came in for the same humorous treatment. Yet in my experience there's really nothing wrong with a Lada that a good motorway pile-up wouldn't fix. I used to be in a band with a washboard player who had acquired one on the cheap and we prided ourselves on being 'the band that fits snugly into a Lada – including the double bass!' Admittedly, they're not built for comfort, or indeed style. But if you're involved in a low-speed collision with a cow, or some spunky young tractor driver challenges you to a burn-up at the next lights, you won't find a more reliable and sturdy vehicle for the price.

This particular Lada (or Zhiguli) was the standard issue colour of curdling milk – somewhere between off-white and sickly cream. It arrived outside the Odessa studios about an hour after the van with the equipment and space 'in the back' had shipped out. We looked very pleased with ourselves for having achieved this small victory. The van would have been miserably uncomfortable, but a Lada was a modestly spacious vehicle which could fit one in the front and two in the back without overly compromising anyone's personal space. Nige and I had already decided (in a rare moment of benevolence) that Yolena should have the more roomy front passenger seat; after everything she'd been through thus far, she surely didn't deserve to be squished up against one of us for an entire day's travel. Also, she could converse in Russian with our driver, which would make a nice change from having to translate everything for the two short-tempered British nitwits. All in all, things were looking up. Or at least, they *seemed* to be …

The first problem came when it transpired that our driver already had a passenger on board. She was a young and rather unhappy-looking woman who had taken root in the front passenger seat and wasn't going anywhere, thank you very much. It turned out that she was the driver's 'girlfriend' and was coming along 'for the ride'. Judging by her demeanour I suspect that she wasn't too thrilled about the prospect of travelling for hours on Ukrainian roads with only Feodosiya at the other end of this long day's journey into night. But still, she was doing this 'for fun' – which tells you a lot about just how little 'fun' there was to be had in Ukraine in those days. I had nothing against her, other than my knees which were to be crammed up against the small of her back for the next fourteen hours as she proceeded to enjoy a level of spacious comfort in the front passenger seat of which the *three* of us now sardined together in the back could only dream.

And then there was our driver, who shall be referred to henceforth as Mr Nyet. As you have probably surmised, Mr Nyet was not his real name. It was a sarcastic sobriquet earned by his fondness for the Russian word meaning 'no'. He said it a lot, and to the exclusion of any other utterance. Indeed in all the time I was with him (which turned out to be a *very long time indeed*) I swear by all things unholy that I never heard him say any word to me other than '*nyet*'. Here was a standard exchange with Mr Nyet:

'Hello. All well?'

'*Nyet*.'

'Oh, you don't speak English?'

'*Nyet*.'

'But you can understand me?'

'*Nyet*.'

'Right. So you can't give me any idea how long the journey will take?'

'*Nyet*.'

'Do you know where we're going?'

'*Nyet*.'

'Any chance of stopping for a pee?'

'*Nyet*.'

'You don't really care what I say, do you?'

'*Nyet*.' And so on.

Mr Nyet and I took against each other almost immediately and during the course of the ensuing journey our initial linguistic uneasiness settled down into a deep and lasting international animosity. As you will remember, I have decided to cast the wild-eyed German actor Udo Kier to play Mr Nyet in my version of this story, not because of any physical similarity between the two but because Udo has just the right edge of barely suppressed on-screen craziness to give the role real dramatic *oomph* (he also has a comedy accent, and I'd love to hear him 'doing' Ukranian just for the hell of it).

If, on the other hand, this were 'Un Film de Mr Nyet' you would doubtless find Omar Sharif behind the wheel of the car while the role of 'spoiled whingeing Western brat' (i.e. me) would be filled not by handsome Jason Isaacs (nor Jesse Birdsall, nor even Nick Faldo) but by a Gollum-like CGI special effect with pasty skin, twisted disposition, and a snivellingly creepy voice, all expertly provided by 'Kermode Award' winner Andy Serkis in a mo-cap suit. In *that* movie, the audience would be encouraged to sympathise with Mr Nyet who had been called upon at short notice to drive a staggeringly long way across country simply because a couple of molly-coddled Brits (nicknamed Mr Moan and Mr Whine) were too prissy and uptight to do the damned journey in the back of a perfectly good van.

But this is *my* movie, and in *my version* you're going to be sitting in the back with Jason Isaacs and generally sharing his/my pain while Udo Kier cackles away in the driver's seat, navigating his tank-like vehicle toward every pothole and obstacle between Odessa and Feodosiya, psychotically chanting his one-word script. ('Excuse me, are we lost?' '*Nyet.*' 'So you know where we are?' '*Nyet.*' 'It's just that I'm pretty sure we hit that exact same pothole about an half an hour ago.' 'A ha ha ha ...*Nyet! Nyet! Nyet!*')

Even allowing for my capacity for overstatement, that journey was a gruelling experience. For the most part Nigel, Yolena and I sat in stunned silent terror as Mr Nyet gaily reinvented the rules of the road for his own amusement, blithely navigating the veritable playing field of uneven concrete eruptions which resembled nothing so much as the heavily cratered surface of the moon. If you thought the roads were a bit rough and ready in the furthest reaches of

Cornwall, you should try hitching a ride in Ukraine, an experience that will shake you out of your over-privileged travelling expectations and give your bowels a good clear-out to boot.

On the subject of which – things were not going well … *downstairs*. For a while I'd been thinking that I was suffering from some sort of low-level intestinal complaint. But as anyone who has ever endured major spinal surgery will know, back problems and bowel problems are closely intertwined and often hard to distinguish. All you really know is that everything down there *hurts*, and the prospect of 'evacuation' is at once pressing and terrifying.

So there I was, crushed and crumpled, racked with pain in my lower abdomen, tormented by worry about Linda's ongoing funeral arrangements, increasingly convinced that we were *never ever* going to meet up with Mariano, and imagining my career going down the toilet, when something went *bang*!

The car lurched, slewed to the side, stalled, rallied, slewed some more, and then came crunchingly to rest on the side of the road at what TV cameramen humorously refer to as a 'Dutch angle' (everything's flat in Holland, thus squiffy camera angles are called 'Dutch' in the same way that 'Little John' wasn't – hilarious). Had we been travelling at any speed at all it would probably have been excitingly scary, but since we were doing the entire journey at a petrol-saving 27 mph, the adrenaline factor was somewhat diminished. But hey, at least lolloping lopsidedly off the road made a change from driving down the middle of it into oncoming traffic, so it wasn't all bad.

Mr Nyet sat in the driver's seat, saying nothing, gripping the steering wheel, staring unflinchingly ahead. No one said anything. There really wasn't much point. Still, I thought, why break the habit of a lifetime?

'Have we broken down?'

'*Nyet*.'

'Oh, that's good. So, are we stopping for a rest?'

'*Nyet*.'

'Right. But we have stopped, haven't we?'

Silence. This was new. No negative response, so clearly the fucker *did* understand me.

'Has something happened to the car?'

More silence.

'Did we burst a tyre?'

Even more silence. On a conversational level, this was a sensational breakthrough.

'Shall we have a look?'

'*Nyet*.'

Back to normal then.

'Right, well I *need* to get out anyway, so I'm going to take a look. OK?'

Silence. Another glimmer of hope!

Nige and I got out of the car together, and after a brief bout of torturous stretching we wandered round to observe the rear driver's side tyre which was, indeed, flat. Obviously. Under other circumstances we might have been mildly mythered about the time we'd lose changing the wheel, but by now we'd been travelling for so long that further delays couldn't make things any worse. The sky was already starting to darken and by the time we got going again it would be early evening. But at least a flat tyre was fixable – it wasn't like we'd broken down and were in need of a mechanic. Any idiot could change a tyre, couldn't they?

Worryingly, we appeared to be the only idiots showing any signs of actually getting out of the car. Mr Nyet just sat there in the driver's seat, staring straight ahead, apparently waiting impatiently for these slow-poke Brits to get on with whatever they were doing and get *back* into the car so we could all get going again. Maybe he hadn't realised what had happened. Was that possible?

I limped round to the driver's window and waited for Mr Nyet to roll it down. He didn't. I waited some more. He didn't some more. Finally, feeling like some comedy policeman from a naff sixties movie, I tapped on the window and made the hand-rolling gesture that is the international symbol of 'please roll down your window so that I may take down your particulars'. Mr Nyet sighed gruffly, mouthed some indecipherable obscenity, and then made the international symbol which means 'I'm sorry officer, I'd love to co-operate with your request but sadly the window-winding mechanism on this fine vehicle is currently out of order.' Either that or 'I fart in your general direction, you English poof' – it was hard to tell.

I looked at Nige, exasperated. He looked back, similarly unimpressed. Clearly Mr Nyet wasn't going to help. Presumably he blamed us for bursting his tyre. After all, we *were* in the back, weren't we? And it was the overburdened *back* tyre which had gone bang, was it not, rather than the correctly weighted front tyre?

With a sense of terrible inevitability we both trudged back round to other side of the vehicle, opened the back door, and got in.

'Hi Yolena. Could you possibly tell our driver that the rear driver's side tyre is burst and we need to change it?'

Yolena did just that. Mr Nyet failed to respond. She tried again. Again, nothing.

'What's his problem?' I asked with a sense of mounting annoyance. 'Are we going to change the bloody tyre or not?'

Yolena asked him something else in Russian, and this time got the standard response.

'*Nyet*.'

'*Nyet?!*' I burst out. '*Nyet* what? "*Nyet*" we haven't got a busted tyre? Or "*Nyet*" I'm not going to change it? In which case, *we'll* change it.'

I got out of the car again and stomped round to the boot which should have been locked but (surprise surprise) was merely held shut with a piece of string. I started scrabbling at the fastening, wondering whether the engine in a Lada wasn't actually buried in the boot like a Hillman Imp, which would make me look pretty stupid and presumably give Mr Nyet a big laugh ha ha ha. But not to worry – the boot opened up and engine was there none.

Nor was there a spare tyre.

'Where's the spare wheel?' I shouted round the side of the car, although even as the question left my lips I already knew the answer.

'*Nyet!*'

And Mr Nyet was right. There was indeed *nyet* spare tyre.

Nada.

Nil.

Nothing.

Nederland nul points.

Nige came round and looked into the open, empty boot.

'There's no spare tyre, is there?'

'Nope.'

We both stared into the boot, as if hoping that doing so would make a spanking new tyre materialise out of thin air. I got down on the ground to see if there was a spare wheel sneakily strapped to the undercarriage of the car as is the case with some models. But not this one. No sir. No matter which way we looked at it, the answer was the same. We had no tyre. We'd have to call the breakdown service. What was Russian for AA? Presumably 'азь азь'.

Yolena joined us, and performed the same strange looking and scowling routine that we had just perfected.

'There is no spare tyre,' she said, correctly.

'No, there isn't. And I imagine our driver already knows this, which is why he is not getting out of the car. So what do we do? Call for a breakdown truck?'

Yolena looked fore and aft along the chaotic road on which we were now stranded, trying to get her bearings, troubled but – as always – uncomplaining. The look on her face suggested that this was not a brilliant place to break down and also strongly implied that professional help would be hard to come by in such a remote area (she had a very expressive face). The road was major, but the region was minor in the extreme. Worse, the sun was threatening to set soon and none of us fancied being stuck here after nightfall. But in this pre-mobile age, with neither a phone box nor a village in sight, there was simply no way of calling for assistance other than flagging down a passing car. As we stood there on the side of road, sucking our teeth, a couple of cars cruised past, one of them stuffed with thick-necked young men who seemed worryingly interested in our plight. Being of paranoid disposition I wasn't certain whether these burly brutes wanted to help us or rob and kill us. Probably the latter. Yolena walked back to the driver's door where Mr Nyet was still resolutely refusing to leave his seat. She exchanged a few words with him through the closed window, then came back and explained the situation to us.

'He says we must get back in the car and drive on.'

'With a flat tyre?'

'Yes, I suppose so.'

'But it will ruin the wheel …'

'He says no.'

'… and it will probably ruin us too.'

Yolena shrugged. Clearly she had expected nothing else, and she wasn't about to get agitated about circumstances she couldn't change. Unlike me.

Then, in a flash of inspiration, it occurred to me that there was a simple solution to our problem. We needed a spare wheel which would fit on to a Lada, and every single car that was passing us on the road was indeed a Lada. I could just flag one down and *buy* their spare wheel. Secreted in my shoe I had one hundred American dollars, an invaluable insurance policy against just such an inevitable disaster. Back in England, the only advice anyone who'd been to Russia would give me was 'take hard currency – and hang on to it'. A friend who had travelled from Ukraine into Russia by coach remembered that packets of Western cigarettes were pretty useful for bribing corrupt border guards (the only kind, apparently) but dollars were like kryptonite. If you had dollars, you could do *anything*.

Emboldened by my ingenuity, I whipped a twenty-dollar bill out of my left sock and waved it at the first Lada coming down the road. The result was impressive – the approaching vehicle performed such a note-perfect emergency stop that the car behind nearly piled into its rear end. American Express? That'll do nicely sir.

The driver of the car got out, all smiles, and despite the language barrier seemed to comprehend almost immediately that I wanted to buy his spare tyre in return for this twenty-dollar bill with which he could quite probably buy a new car. He was happy, I was happy, *everyone* was happy with this transaction. Everyone except Mr Nyet. For just as handshakes were exchanged and our new knight in shining Lada hoiked open the boot of his car, Mr Nyet came storming round the side of the vehicle, gesturing wildly, muttering strange imprecations, and generally giving the impression that he wasn't happy with any of this *at all*. I had no idea what he said, but the next thing I knew our potential spare-wheel supplier was back in his car and off down the road and we were all back where we started.

'What the hell was all that about?' I asked Yolena in dismay.

'I think that maybe he feels insulted,' she said, with infinite sympathy and patience.

'*Insulted?*'

'Yes, I think so.'

'*How?*'

'He has a lot of pride.'

'But he has *no* spare tyre.'

'No, that is true …'

We stood dejectedly by the roadside, listening to the inevitable decline of capitalism.

'Come on,' said Yolena eventually, in that reliably reassuring manner of hers. 'We should go.'

And so we did. The three of us shambled back into the rear seat of the car and no sooner were we suitably squished than Mr Nyet hit the gas and the Lada lurched forward and back out into the oncoming traffic.

The next few miles are something of a blur. I remember the bumping, the groaning, the grinding of metal on tarmac as our trusty Lada discovered life in the pre-pneumatic age. I remember the previously creeping bud of pain and discomfort which had taken root just above my pelvis blossoming into a blood-red rose of raging, burning misery and anguish, making me think that my insides were actually on fire. I remember Nige and Yolena stoically saying nothing while the woman in the front passenger seat yelped and gargled in jostled distress as the car smashed around the concrete assault course that passed for a road in this godforsaken region. And I remember the particularly violent jolt which finally pushed me over the edge – a savage thrust from the underside of the car which seemed to have been kicked by some dormant giant awakened from its slumbers by the screams of Mr Nyet's Lada. At which point, I felt something *move* in my back – something which, by all rights, needed to remain *stationary*, firmly wedged in place. The spasm which gripped me in the aftermath of this jolt was almost religious in its intensity – I felt as though every atom of my body was on the brink of sneezing, and if I relaxed my whole body would disintegrate and be exploded out through my own nose, voiding into the darkening Ukrainian night. It was very unusual – and not in a good way.

I squealed like a freshly stuck pig (or like Ned Beatty in *Deliverance*), shrieking with such vigour that the normally unresponsive Mr Nyet promptly slammed his foot on the brakes, throwing my head forward so that it snapped sharply off the back of his girlfriend's headrest, making a satisfying cracking sound in the process. The car slopped to a halt and I yanked open the door, stepping out into the centre of the road with little care for the passing traffic. I put my hand out to steady myself on the side of the car, bending at the waist as if genuflecting toward the gods of lost travellers and lost causes. Thusly folded, I walked gingerly round to the back of the car, still apparently studying the road with the intensity of a pervy asphalt fancier.

Here was my problem: I could not stand up. I was stuck.

And that was when I lost it.

Suddenly, and with little or no dignity, I started screaming and swearing and shouting and raging, calling for hellfire to rage down upon this pestilential piss-hole and flatten everything and everybody from here to Minsk. I was rude, abusive, aggressive, unreasonable, and my tone could quite possibly have been seen as threatening were it not for the fact that I was bent double and therefore all my insults were directed straight down into the ground. If you'd driven by and seen me you would have thought that I was having a heated row with the road, which in a way I was. At some point in this avalanche of anger, Nigel came out of the car, stood beside me, and attempted to put his arm round me in a comforting brotherly fashion. It was a sweet gesture, spoiled only by the fact that my absurdly twisted position meant that the best he could do was to rest his hand on my back, making me look like a human coffee table.

And that was how we stayed for quite some time.

I could go on (and on, and on, and on). I could tell you how I was gingerly jackknifed *back* into the car, and how that three-legged warhorse smashed on another few miles before arriving at a village where some very friendly, helpful locals came out of their houses with spare wheels that sadly wouldn't fit Mr Nyet's Lada. I could tell you how we *did* eventually flag down another passing vehicle and buy their spare wheel for twenty dollars, our driver (who was by then as defeated as the rest of us) helpfully putting aside his pride, and how we proceeded on to our ultimate destination, getting further lost on the way.

Suffice to say that we finally staggered into Feodosiya

at some ungodly hour, and considering how hard it had been to get there, it was all a bit of a let-down frankly. To my eyes, it looked like a dump – although the sight of the most beautiful city on earth would probably have failed to lift my all but broken spirits by then. If I go to the internet now and call up images of the Feodosiya 'resort' it looks perfectly nice – pretty buildings, lovely sunshine, picturesque beach blah blah blah. Shame about the unsightly shipping and mechanical plant just next to the main bathing spot but, hey, you can't have everything, and if we'd been there for any length of time I'm sure it would have started to seem quite relaxing. Certainly there were plenty of holidaymakers apparently having a good time in Feodosiya, and the *Dark Waters* production members we spoke to were in good spirits about their surroundings. As for the actual 'location reports' which Nige and I were meant to file from there ... well, they'll have to wait for the moment. Because it had taken us so long to get to Feodosiya that almost as soon as we'd arrived it was time to turn round and start heading back again.

And so we did.

Having refused point-blank to get back into a Lada (*any* Lada) or travel cross-country on that stinking toilet of a train, it was agreed that the *Dark Waters* production team would arrange to *fly* us from Kiev to Moscow. Hooray. We could have flown more directly from Kiev to Heathrow, but for reasons which none of us understood we had return tickets from Moscow and there was nothing anyone could do about that. So, rather than suffer the indignities of land travel on the former USSR's terminally depressed road and rail networks, we would take to the skies.

A few words about flying in the former Soviet Union. Back in the dark days of the early nineties there were many hair-raising tales of air-related 'incidents' which gave the impression that these were not the safest skies in the world. Most notoriously, on 23 March 1994 (a year after our *Dark Waters* adventure) Flight 593 flew out of Moscow and promptly crashed near Mezhdurechensk after the pilot allowed his fifteen-year-old son to 'have a go' sitting at the controls, accidentally overriding the autopilot and killing all seventy-five people on board. Such was the notoriety of Flight 593's demise that the popular Canadian TV series *Mayday* (better known as *Air Crash Investigation* here in the UK) dedicated an episode to it self-explanatorily dubbed 'Kid in the Cockpit'. Catchy title, huh?

Along with the apparent element of danger, there was the equally pressing issue of customer care. In 2003, BBC News reported that the Russian airline Aeroflot had employed a British public-relations team to improve their standing as one of the least inviting airlines in the world and help them shed their 'long-time reputation for service with a scowl'. 'Their stewardesses used to be very austere and authoritarian,' admitted Tom Austin, deputy chairman of Identica, 'and they certainly weren't very friendly.' Which, as understatements go, is on a par with saying that the heroine of *Ilsa: She Wolf of the SS* wasn't exactly the sort of girl you'd want to take home to meet your mother. But what was most disturbing about the BBC's report was that it contained confirmation of something which I had been wondering whether I had actually *imagined* for almost a decade: the fact that as recently as the early nineties flight operators within the former Soviet Union 'regularly took on extra passengers for cash, resulting in dangerously overcrowded planes'.

It is oddly reassuring to see the phrase 'dangerously overcrowded' used by a news agency as solidly reliable as the BBC because it means that what I'm about to tell you is very probably *true*, despite the fact that it sounds like I'm *making it up*. Here's my experience of flying from Kiev to Moscow in the days before modernisation made the phrase 'I'm Olga, Fly Me,' something other than a very bad joke.

First up, we tried to book the tickets by phone, with a credit card, only to discover that neither phone *nor* credit-card bookings were acceptable. This was to be a cash-only transaction, and it had to be done *in person* at the airport in Kiev. So, less than forty-eight hours after arriving at Feodosiya, Nige and I found ourselves standing at a sales-kiosk window attempting to effect safe passage out of the place in the following Kafkaesque manner.

Firstly, I proceeded to the sales window, where a list of flight times and prices was prominently displayed. Having checked which flight we wanted, and counted out exactly the right amount of Russian currency, I attempted to purchase a ticket for myself.

'Hello,' I said brightly to the sour-faced wonk behind the window. 'Do you speak English?'

'*Da*.'

'Great. Then I'd like to buy a ticket for the next plane to Moscow, please.'

'*Nyet*.'

'I have my passport, and the correct money in roubles.'

'*Nyet*.'

'Pardon?'

'*Nyet*.'

I had the horrible feeling that I'd been here before.

'*Nyet?*' I said, pathetically.

'*Nyet*,' he replied, firmly.

'I see. So is the next plane full?'

'*Nyet*.'

'It's *not* full?'

'*Nyet*.'

'Then I *can* buy a ticket?'

'*Nyet*.'

'I *can't* buy a ticket?'

'*Nyet*.'

'Why not?'

Silence.

I turned to the *Dark Waters* production assistant who had accompanied us to the airport, having being ordered to make sure that Nige and I got safely on to the plane. 'What am I doing wrong?' I asked him. 'I have money. I have my passport. I can *see* that there's a plane to Moscow in two hours and he says it's not full. But he won't sell me a ticket. Why not?'

'Let *me* ask,' he said encouragingly. So he asked, and got some terse reply which included words other than '*nyet*'. Clearly he had the knack.

'You have to bribe him,' he said, briskly.

'What?'

'You have to bribe him. To sell you the ticket. He knows you're English and he wants a bribe.'

'Oh, OK, fine. How much?'

'Hang on, I'll ask.'

So he did. Then he reported back.

'Ten dollars, apparently. Each.'

'So that's twenty dollars? Plus the ticket price – in roubles?'

'That sounds right.'

'OK, great. Thanks.'

I took ten dollars out of my wallet, and placed it on the counter in front of the teller. He took it. I tried again.

'Hello,' I said. 'I'd like to buy a ticket to Moscow. I have my passport and—'

I didn't even finish the sentence. He took the money, didn't glance at the passport, and slapped a white and blue ticket on the counter. Interestingly, it was almost entirely blank, with a series of unfilled-in spaces where all the usual relevant information would be. Airline? Blank. Flight number? Blank. Seat number? Blank. Departure time? Blank. Destination? Blank. I looked at it, unimpressed.

'So this is the ticket is it?

'*Da*.'

'Shouldn't it be filled in?'

'*Nyet*.'

'So I can get on the plane with it like this? All not filled in?'

'*Da*.'

'You're quite sure?'

'*Da*.'

'You can't fill it in just to humour me?'

'*Nyet*.'

This was clearly all I was going to get. I stepped away from the counter and turned to Nige. 'Your turn …'

Nige stepped up to the window, put down his ten dollars, watched it disappear under the counter, then went through the same ritual involving roubles, tickets, and an utter lack of flight-specific information. Simple.

'There's just one thing,' said Nige, turning back towards the sales window with a look in his eye that I had come to recognise as a sign that his buttons had been pushed. 'I don't mind bribing you,' he said to the stony-faced stooge, who gazed back unblinking. 'It's just that it would be a lot more efficient if you put the price of the bribe on the price list. Right next to where it says how much the ticket costs in roubles, you just add "plus bribe of ten dollars". That way, we would *know* how much to bribe you so that we could buy a ticket and the whole procedure would take less time. And be a lot less irritating.'

With which he strolled off toward the departure gates, with me scurrying along in his wake.

When we got to the gate, it became clear exactly *why* there was no information on the ticket. There was a plane on the tarmac which was allegedly bound for Moscow, and a ragtag group of people in the departure lounge (or 'holding pen') all of whom had similarly unmarked tickets, and whose total number seemed surprisingly large for such a comparatively *small* vehicle. After waiting for an indeterminate period of time, the plane was declared ready for boarding, at which point an official opened a glass door facing the tarmac and the entire assembled crowd *ran* like a pack of rampaging hyenas out on to the runway and up the shuddering gantry in a desperate attempt to snag a seat – *any* seat. I was pretty sure that there were more people on the plane than was customary, but the doors weren't closed until we were crammed to busting and the last few stragglers were left waiting on the tarmac before being herded back into the cattle-yard to wait for the next plane.

If there were any safety announcements I missed them, as presumably did the people who were still standing in the aisle and therefore unable to fasten their seatbelts. Instead, the plane lurched off down the runway and up into the air with its human cargo merrily rattling around like the milk bottles in Ernie's ghostly crate. Interestingly, although most aeroplanes tend to level out after completing their ascent, our flight seemed to be somewhat rear-end heavy and flew the entire distance from Kiev to Moscow at an angle which meant that if you dropped anything on the floor it would roll all the way back to the inevitably out-of-order toilets. As for our landing – we flew in a straight line until we were directly above Moscow airport at which point the plane simply dropped like a stone out of the sky, heading downwards in an almost vertical descent which caused your brain to attempt to crawl out through your eardrums, and making young children and adults alike scream in agony at the vomit-inducing pressure drop. When we were about a hundred feet above ground, the plane levelled out before smashing on to the Moscow tarmac, the doors popping open almost instantly to allow the suffering hordes to stagger shell-shocked out on to the runway and scurry for the safety of the arrivals hall.

Blimey.

From Moscow we flew to Vienna, a gleaming capitalist paradise where Nige and I celebrated our escape from Russia by smothering ourselves in consumer durables purchased with infinitely flexible credit cards (I bought a Rick Astley CD, because I *could*!) and making long-distance phone calls without the handicap of a two-day wait. Another sixteen hours later and we were home, back in the arms of our respective loved ones, neither of whom had much sympathy for the ordeal we claimed to have endured. They had both been busy with *real* jobs while we had been arsing around in the former USSR, and neither of them were in the mood to feel very sorry for us. Within hours of returning home, the Russian jaunt had effectively ceased to have any 'real' meaning whatsoever, morphing swiftly into a near-mythical amusing anecdote which Nige and I would roll out at dinner parties for years to come, a story which people would listen to and laugh at (if we were lucky), without experiencing any of the pain, the pain, the *pain* ...

But ah, I hear you say, what about the set report, the *raison d'être* of the whole trip? What about the fabulously newsworthy coverage of 'the first Western feature film to be shot in Ukraine after the collapse of the Soviet Union'? What happened when we finally got to Feodosiya?

The short answer is ... nothing.

Nada.

*Niente.*

Nul points.

*Nyet.*

Oh, we did interviews – loads of them, with the cast, the crew, and the director Mariano himself. And the interviews were pretty good. But you can do interviews *anywhere*. The key thing about set reports is that the journalist is meant to report *from the set*, observing and recording the actual filming *actually happening*. This is what makes set reports special. Moreover, it is what makes them 'set reports'.

The night that Nige and I finally arrived in Feodosiya, Mariano had been out filming, shooting into the early hours of the morning on the beach, returning back to base camp about the same time that we shipped up, ready for action. Unfortunately, this was also the exact same moment that Mariano and his team ran out of film – literally. Apparently, most of the film stock available in Russia and Ukraine had the perforations on the wrong side, and thus it had been necessary to purchase vast quantities of Western-compatible stock in advance and import it. However, once inside the former Soviet Union the Western stock commanded a high market value, which had inevitably led to someone selling it off at a handsome profit, thus leaving the *Dark Waters* production team temporarily stranded, with nothing to run through the camera other than the cold Ukranian air.

And so the awful truth is that, after having travelled for four days to get to Feodosiya, Nige and I didn't see *one single frame* of film exposed. Not *one*. Hell, we never even got to the location – what would have been the point? There was nothing happening out there because *nobody had any film*. It was a film *without film*. It was, in effect, an *anti-film*, at least for the forty-eight hours that we were there. In this respect, the slog to Feodosiya to file a 'location report' on *Dark Waters* had been the single most pointless journey I have ever made.

There – I've said it. I feel better now.

*Dark Waters* did finally get finished – a miracle of which Mariano should be rightly proud. And despite its hideous production history, the movie turned out to be a pretty decent calling card which won several international awards, and garnered solidly appreciative reviews from the mainstream and genre press. At the Fantasia Film Festival in Montreal, *Dark Waters* won the Prix du Public, while at the Fantafestival in Rome it was awarded the Special Vincent Price Award for 'outstanding contribution to Fantastic Cinema'. In 1995 it played at the Fantasporto Film Festival in Portugal where it was nominated for the Best Film Award, losing out (very respectably) to Danny Boyle's debut feature *Shallow Grave*. At some point a version of the film seems to have become available in the US under the somewhat more gaudy title *Dead Waters* – although Mariano apparently had no role in either the retitling or the frankly scruffy packaging of this release. As recently as 2006, a company called No Shame issued a digitally restored director's cut of *Dark Waters* on DVD, solving many of the technical problems of the original cut, and tightening up the running time by around seven minutes to produce what Mariano proudly calls 'the best-looking version of the film I've ever seen'.

Over the years *Dark Waters*' reputation has grown, drawing praise for its moody atmosphere, haunting visuals, and lack of on-screen gore (which of course annoyed the *Fangoria* readers no end). All in all, it was an arresting first feature for Mariano who is still making movies, and from whom I confidently expect great things in the future.

As for me, I filed an encouragingly upbeat report for *Fango* and did some follow-up interviews for the BBC. I even got Mariano on Radio One where he was interviewed by Emma Freud who said that she had found *Dark Waters* 'absolutely terrifying'. Mariano was speechless.

A year or so later, I collapsed and was hospitalised in Southampton where I was diagnosed as having two ruptured discs in the lower part of my spine. At first I was told that I would have to have titanium rods inserted into my back which would prevent any movement in the lower lumber area and make me walk upright like a man with a chair leg up his arse. Later, I was lucky to have extensive microsurgery which simply picked the insides out of the ruptured discs and left me with two 'flat tyres' as they are known in the trade. The official diagnosis was that the discs had probably been deformed from birth and I had no one to blame but my ancestors and their genetic imperfections.

That's the official version.

But I know the truth. I know what *really* happened to my back. I know why I spent six weeks off work, two of them in hospital, staring at the ceiling and cursing the day that I decided there could be nothing worse than travelling across Ukraine in the back of a van.

I know what was to blame.

But I'm saying nothing.

Nada.

Nul points.

*Nyet*.

# Chapter 6

## RADIO RADIO

'What is my role in all of this?' Simon Mayo asked me recently, as well he might. After all, we're into the sixth reel of this damned movie and so far my illustrious radio mentor has been notable by his absence. If things carry on this way much longer it'll be like Marlon Brando only showing up (fat and unrehearsed) for the last twenty minutes of *Apocalypse Now*, or Dame Judi Dench bagging an Oscar for *Shakespeare in Love* after having been on screen for less than nine minutes. In fact I'm sure there's plenty of you out there who are only reading this because you know that I'm Mayo's irritating 5 Live sidekick and you were secretly hoping this book would really be about *him* rather than me me *me* in the same way that everyone really wanted that movie *Factory Girl* to be about exciting art innovator Andy Warhol rather than self-obsessed clothes horse Edie Sedgwick (a role for which Sienna Miller was, incidentally, perfectly cast). So ladies and gentlemen, for your viewing pleasure, please welcome to the screen SIMON MAYO, who will be played neither by Mr Brando nor Dame Judi, but rather by Charles Hawtrey.

As I mentioned briefly in the Prologue, Mayo has no one to blame for this apparently unkind piece of casting but himself. In the early summer of 2009, Simon and I were interviewed by the *Independent* newspaper for a regular feature entitled 'How We Met' and the piece was accompanied by a photograph of us standing back to back in which (as Simon correctly pointed out) we did not look at our best. 'You look like an Orc!' he told me with his customary frankness when the paper showed up on the news-stands. 'And I look like *Charles Hawtrey*.' He was right on both counts, although luckily for me an Orc is a fictional character rather than a real-life actor and anyway Jason Isaacs was already in rehearsal (in my head) for the role which he was surely born to play. As for Hawtrey, he may be dead but nowadays that's no impediment – Oliver Reed posthumously completed his scenes for *Gladiator* thanks to whizzo CGI trickery, and Brando even turned up in *Superman Returns* several years after shuffling off his ever-expanding mortal coil. Plus I've seen *loads* of movies starring people who *appear* to be dead – think of anything Val Kilmer made between dying on his feet in *The Saint* and experiencing an unlikely career resurrection in *Kiss Kiss Bang Bang*. Or any of the Mickey Rourke 'wilderness years' movies (*Another 9½ Weeks*, *Harley Davidson and the Marlboro Man*) in which he even *looked* like a reanimated corpse.

So, can Jason Isaacs and the late Charles Hawtrey make their collective way to the set, please, and Charles let's take it from your line: 'What is my role in all of this?'

The scene we are shooting here (which features this timeless line) is an interview for yet another popular London newspaper of which I had never heard. (Mayo claims that this is because I have only heard of *two* publications – the *Guardian* and *Fangoria* – which is *clearly* untrue because I have also heard of *Sight & Sound*. And *Hair Products Monthly*. So there.)

In the wake of my absurd Russian escapade I had concluded definitively that travel in general and set reports in particular were not for me and had concentrated instead on carving a much more comfortable career niche for myself as a stay-at-home radio film critic. In this endeavour I had been aided incalculably by Mayo with whom I had been bickering about movies from the comfort and safety of various BBC studios for well over a decade. Now we were branching out into television, on which we would continue to bicker like cinema's answer to Hinge and Bracket, only with pictures. Progress!

'Your role is essential,' I replied, 'crucial, inexplicable, and indefinable. Or, to put it another way, easy. I do all the hard work and you take all the glory. Just like on the radio, except that now everyone will be able to see how much better dressed than you I am, and how much nicer my hair looks.'

Sadly, the paper opted not to run the interview on the grounds that my answers were too short (a first!) and also that we didn't really say anything about the programme which we were meant to be promoting. Instead (they claimed) we just descended into petty insults and personal sniping which didn't really give the reader much of an insight into how we worked. On the contrary, I think that shelved interview said it *all*, neatly summing up our on-air relationship which has remained essentially unchanged since we first met at Radio One back in the mid-nineties. Simon is polite if somewhat irritable with me, and I am rude and opinionated with him – together, we sound increasingly as though we are going to strangle each other. Several people (some of them quite intelligent) have concluded that Mayo and I *really* don't like each other, and that our on-air animosity is too 'real' to be faked. Indeed, there are endless internet discussions about the 'barely suppressed' tensions between us. Here's a typical thread from the always engaging and entertaining forums of the Internet Movie Database.

'I wonder if Simon and Mark *really* hate each other' wrote 'Fork Q' on 15 February 2009 after hearing an altercation between us on 5 Live which ended in an ominous 'dead silence'.

'I don't think they *hate* each other' replied 'Tweekums' the next day 'though that certainly was an "uncomfortable silence".'

'No no no!' chipped in 'HF Fan' on 23 February. 'They clearly *like* each other very much … In fact I think they *love* each other in that non-yucky, non-Brokebacky "we're both married to women and happy with that thank you very much" kind of way.'

'They absolutely *loathe* each other' concluded 'thunderroad90', as was 'confirmed on the radio show today'.

And so on ...

For me, the phrase 'old married couple' gets closer to the truth of our radio relationship than the 'do they/don't they' debate which seems set to rattle on forever. I do believe that in the same way everyone has a soulmate in 'real life' there is also a professional partner for everyone who, in the words of Jerry Maguire, 'completes me' (or 'you', as the case may be).

In broadcasting terms, Simon 'had me at "Hello"'. Being clearly the best broadcaster in the country (and having the awards to prove it) he plays the knowledgeably open-minded Everyman with ease, a voice with whom audiences can identify and in whose company they feel interested, entertained and informed. If the trick of radio broadcasting is to make it sound as though you are talking to one single listener (so that each individual listener feels that you are talking directly to *them*) then Simon must have the biggest audience of 'single listeners' in the country. Everyone warms to him, listeners and interviewees alike, and for this reason he manages to get the best out of both. If you put a donkey in a radio studio with Simon Mayo he could make it sound good.

Which, in my case, is exactly what they've done. Within the protective cage of Simon's unforced professionalism (and believe me, you have to work *really hard* on your research and preparation to sound that relaxed and carefree in the studio) I am able to behave like an un-house-trained animal. I don't need to worry about whether what I say sounds reasonable, or even *sensible*, to the audience; that's *his* job. *My* job (as far as I can tell) is to talk about films in the only manner I know how – as if my life depended on them. Which isn't very hard, because sitting through crap like *Pirates of the Caribbean: At World's End* (a 'family' film which opens with an entertaining scene of child hanging – oh ha ha ha) I have seriously started to wonder whether suicide really is painless (and whether it really does 'bring on many changes' as the theme from *M*A*S*H* so awkwardly informed us). Indeed, in the case of *POTC3* (as I believe the fans call it) I was still *furious* about having to sit through the damn thing by the time I got on-air with Mayo to review it. The resulting transnational tirade (I was in Cannes, Simon was at some sporting event in the UK, a satellite feed linking the two of us) was videoed by the BBC so that everyone could *see* Simon nonchalantly looking at his watch, yawning, and theatrically reading a newspaper while I blathered on hysterically about Johnny Depp's performance resembling a drunk karaoke singer showing off in a crowded room. I went further, demanding that director Gore Verbinski be given a custodial sentence for crimes against narrative cinema, and inviting the audience to see whether they really could distinguish between the supporting cast and a range of handsomely polished MDF furniture. 'Is that a nest of tables?' I screamed. '*No*, it's Ikea Knightley and Orloondo Bland locked in a passionate embrace that is positively teaky!' To date, 107,000 people have watched this meltdown on YouTube, and as usual many of the comments ('I f**king LOVE how much Simon Mayo HATES Mark

Kermode' – AnEyeOut) flag up the deep-seated negative energy that apparently arcs between Mayo and me even when separated by the English Channel.

It seems pointless to claim that quite the opposite is true (at least from my end) because whenever I do so it just comes out *wrong*. For example, during that *Independent* interview I made a point of repeating my mantra that Simon is a broadcasting genius and if our show worked on-air at all then it was down to his skill rather than my inane ramblings. Yet when the article appeared, Simon was quoted as talking warmly, affectionately, and generously about me, while I was quoted as talking warmly, affectionately, and generously … about *me*. Honestly, I don't know why he puts up with it.

I started doing film reviews with Simon when he was presenting Radio One's morning show. The station, which had earned an easily mockable 'Fab FM' Smashy and Nicey reputation over the preceding decade, was in the process of being revitalised by an influx of new talent including Mark Radcliffe, Steve Lamacq, Trevor Nelson, Tim Westwood and Mark Tonderai, the latter of whom has recently resurfaced as a successful film-maker with his impressive debut horror feature *Hush*. It was an exciting time, although there was a lot of spilled blood on the carpets as the old-school dinosaurs (Dave Lee Travis, Simon Bates, Gary Davies et al.) either resigned or were culled. The changes were not immediately popular, and for a few years the station haemorrhaged listeners. But somehow Mayo rose above all the storms, sailing gently from a very successful run on the breakfast show to an even more accomplished stint in mid-mornings, and thence (some years later) to his multi-award-winning afternoon slot on 5 Live. By early 2010 he had moved to drivetime on Radio Two, and sharp-eyed readers will notice an inexorable progress though the hours of the day, with each new slot offering Mayo an ever more forgiving wake-up call. Presumably, this drift will culminate in an eventual late-night spot sometime around 2029, which the semi-retired Simon will doubtless be able to present from the comfort of his own bath chair. Personally, I likes the sound of them hours and my plan (such as it has been since we started working together) is to hitch my wagon to his star and hang on for as long as possible.

To me, Simon is so much more than a friend and colleague. He is also a pension plan – in a very real and legally binding way.

In our early days, Mayo and I used to condense a review of the weeks' movies *and* video releases into two three-and-half-minute segments, with a record in between. The rules on speech-to-music ratios at Radio One were strict, and if the movie talk overran, the underlying 'music bed' would simply stop and a current popular chart hit would duly grind into gear – and there were few more sackable offences on Radio One than 'crashing Sting's vocals'. By the time we got to 5 Live, we had an entire *hour* of talk-time to fill, with news, sport and travel our only interruptions. Yet in keeping with the law that states that work expands to fill the time allotted to it Mayo and I still found ourselves struggling to cram everything into that massively expanded space, the amount of blather having multiplied like mould upon rotting cheese – which, as Barry Humphries once pointed out, is essentially the definition of 'culture'. By the time you read this, our Friday afternoon show on 5 Live will have expanded to *two* hours and I bet you we are still running out of time before adequately addressing the Movie of the Week. You call it two old men wittering, we call it 'wittertainment – at its most wittertaining'.

Quite why things have worked out so well between Simon and me is anyone's guess. After all, it's not as if we're each other's first radio wives. In fact, when we picked up our prestigious (have I mentioned this already?) Sony Award for Speech Radio in May 2009, Mayo celebrated the moment by embracing his former Radio One cohort Jakki Brambles on stage and telling everyone how lovely she was and how much he missed working with her.

Thanks for that.

But hey, two can play at that game, so let me detain you a while with tales of *my* former radio partners and all the good times *we* had together before I settled down to become one half of medium wave's very own George and Mildred. If you cast your mind back to Chapter Three, you'll recall my incompetent spell at LBC during which I learned that the sound of me 'pretending I didn't know what I was doing' was somehow preferable to the sound of me reviewing the new releases in a timely and orderly fashion. Well, as luck would have it (and I have been *very* lucky over the years) my path would cross again with that of one-time LBC presenter Sarah Ward, who called me out of the blue a few years later.

'Hi Mark,' said Sarah, in her distinctively sultry jazz-club voice, a cross between Julie London and Whispering Bob. 'I've got a new job on a new radio station and I was wondering whether you'd like to be my film critic.'

This sounded too good to be true, but it turned out she wasn't kidding. For reasons which I never fully understood, the BBC had conjured up an entirely new station – something called 'Radio Five' – which would broadcast a bizarre mixture of sports, schools, and Open University programmes with anything else anyone could come up with jammed uncomfortably in between. Sarah had been asked to co-host the breakfast show along with Jon Briggs, the owner of a golden larynx who would later achieve fame as the voice of TV's *The Weakest Link*. And now they needed a film critic.

'Great!' I said at once. 'What day do you want to do the film reviews on?'

'Um, Friday would make sense,' replied Sarah, offhandedly.

'You mean "Fridays",' I said. 'The day that new movies open – always a good day for film reviews, Fridays.'

'Well, yes, "Fridays" in general would be good,' said Sarah, now sounding like a caller in *Play Misty For Me*. 'But actually I did mean "Friday".'

There was a silence – as ever.

'Friday? As in "*this* Friday".'

'Yup.'

'As in "the day after tomorrow", it being Wednesday now.'

'That's right.'

'So let me get this straight – you want me to be the film critic for an entirely new radio station of which I hadn't heard anything until two minutes ago when you told me about it, and you want me to start in less than forty-eight hours and then carry on until…?'

'Until *indefinitely*,' replied Sarah.

This *had* to be a hoax. Didn't it?

'This is a hoax, right?' I asked.

'*What?*' said Sarah, sounding genuinely perplexed. 'Why would it be a hoax? If you don't believe me, tune your radio into 909 or 693 and you'll hear a strange kids' serial called *Wiggly Park* being broadcast right now. And believe me, if I *was* making this up, that *isn't* something that I'd make up.'

And it wasn't. And *she* wasn't. But I was.

Made up, that is.

If memory serves correctly (and it almost certainly doesn't) I did a little dance of joy around the living room, *thrilled* at being invited into the bosom of the BBC – albeit a bosom protruding from a strange tumour-like growth which would have to be cauterised and cut off in due course, to be replaced with something altogether more sleek and aesthetically attractive. That something would be Radio 5 Live, which would be born in March 1994 and would go on to be the natural home I never knew I had. But in that interim period, in which lowly 'Radio Five' seemed to be merely holding the fort until something better came along – oh what lovely times we had.

Sarah and Jon's Radio Five breakfast show was great fun, and was the first proper radio training I received. It was here that I learned to wear headphones like a professional (one ear on, one ear off, in the manner of the Bee Gees in all those faked studio pop videos, or the assembled cast of Band Aid's 'Feed the World' which still makes me cry every time), to cut movie clips from quarter-inch reel-to-reel tape (razor blades and Sellotape – who knew?), and to say important-sounding things like 'I need a little more cue in my cans' (whatever the hell *that* meant). In fact, looking back I probably have that show in general (and Sarah in particular) to thank for the fact that I have continued to have a career in this most magical of mediums.

After a year or so things started to change and the breakfast show (dubbed *Morning Edition*) found itself under the incoming care of the self-proclaimed 'New Sheriff in Town' – Danny Baker. I'd never actually met Danny before he got the job at Five, but as a teenager I'd stuck to my bedroom wall a review he wrote for the *NME* of the abysmal post-Sex Pistols cash-in LP *Sid Sings* which began with the timeless phrase: 'If rock 'n' roll had any backbone it would close Virgin Records down.' That review was music to my ears, as were two other famous stories about Danny: firstly, that he had forcefully remonstrated with a London shopkeeper for selling swastika T-shirts, a gesture which Julie Burchill had found to be 'really sweet'; and secondly that on the night of Elvis' death he had taken to the stage in a jeering punk club and told the assembled masses that there was more rebellion in Elvis' little finger than in all their dyed mohicans and safety-pinned bondage trousers.

On-air, Danny was every bit as electrifying as he was in print. Walking into his studio was like walking out on to the bridge of ship in a force-ten gale, and if you weren't sure of your footing you would get unceremoniously swept overboard. We met for the first time on-air, and had a blazing row about Martin Scorsese's remake of *Cape Fear* which I insisted was no good at all despite Danny's insistence that I was a know-nothing bozo who wouldn't know a good movie from a hole in the ground. I thought our first encounter had gone terribly badly and I assumed that I was fired, but after the show Danny was boisterously upbeat and continued to insult me in a manner which seemed more affectionate than annoyed. It transpired that confrontation was *exactly* what he wanted and thus I held on to my job and learned an important lesson – namely that there is *nothing* to be gained from moderating your opinions because you think it will please those around you. It won't. In a world in which every lazy hack falls back on the old 'if you liked *that*, then you'll love *this*' cliché, the only thing a critic has to justify their essentially parasitic existence is the belief that they are right and everybody else is *wrong*. Sod cultural studies and all that non-judgemental aesthetic relativity claptrap – the Leavisites were right! There really *is* such a thing as good and bad art. And if you don't believe me, try watching *Taxi Driver* and *Cape Fear* back to back and then telling me that they're both 'equally valid'. No they're not, and you know it. One of them is really good, and the other is really rubbish. End of story.

Anyway, back to Radio Five. After being OK'd by Danny I was promoted to 'co-presenter' of the afternoon show, a very strange mix of music, sport, quizzes, and phone-in hooey which I helmed on Mondays, Wednesdays and Fridays with former *Blue Peter* presenter Caron Keating – who was the very dictionary definition of 'lovely'. Stylistically Caron and I were all over the shop, and on any given day, our show (which was charitably entitled *A Game of Two Halves*) could feature any or all of the following: an interview with Todd Haynes talking frankly about sadomasochistic sex practices in film; an instalment of a peculiar American radio soap entitled *Milford Haven* which seemed to have been picked up by the BBC simply because it had the same name as a place in Wales; a live performance by Paul Da Vinci, the uncredited lead vocalist of the Rubettes' falsetto seventies hit 'Sugar Baby Love' with skiffle accompaniment; a pub-style phone quiz played between rival newspaper offices (*Fangoria* vs the *Guardian*, obviously) and featuring sound effects from *Dougal and the Blue Cat*; a romp through the news and music of a random 'Vintage Year' as chosen by Mr Humphries from *Are You Being Served?* ('I'm free!'); and sport. Heaven knows what it sounded like to the listeners, but as long as we kept broadcasting and didn't swear or defame the Royal Family the bosses just let us get on with it. After all, they had bigger plans in the shape of the emergent 5 Live, with ramshackle old Radio Five being later described by a BBC boss as 'a network with no audience focus, born out of expediency'. Our days were always numbered, but for a couple of years we experienced freedom on a level unparalleled since the heyday of the pirates back in the late sixties. You know that Richard Curtis film *The Boat that Rocked* which everyone agreed was too long and rambling for its own good? Well, that movie had a better script and generally made much more sense than anything we ever broadcast at Radio Five.

But it wasn't as much fun.

Happy days.

It was newly ensconced station boss Matthew Bannister who suggested to Mayo that he should get me in to do movie reviews when Simon started his mid-morning stint at Radio One in 1993. Simon and I seemed to hit it off immediately, but back then our relationship was far from monogamous. In fact, in those early days I was involved in a racy *ménage à trois* with Mark Radcliffe and Marc Riley whose Manchester-based 'graveyard shift' show (10 p.m. till midnight) on Radio One blended an eclectic mix of non-playlist music with live performance, poetry readings, comedy and more, developing a cult following among listeners whose devotion bordered upon the religious. My job was to present 'Cult Movie Corner' – a long-running feature in which I rambled on incoherently about a favourite film (everything from *Mary Poppins* to *The Wicker Man*) whilst 'Mark and Lard' attempted to put me off with pointedly ill-judged asides ('Fancy a brew, our kid?') and off-colour comments about Elvis. The latter resulted in my storming out of the Manchester studios after Mark repeatedly insisted that Elvis had died on the toilet (he collapsed in his bathroom, which is rather different) although looking back I'm fairly certain that it was a prearranged stunt designed to cover a planned absence over the next couple of weeks. I say I'm *fairly sure* that that's what happened, although knowing me (which, as we have learned, I don't) it wouldn't be beyond the bounds of possibility that my upset was real. In general, I consider the commandment 'Thou Shalt Not Be Disrespectful About Elvis' to be up there with 'Thou Shalt Not Kill' and 'Nor Shalt Thou Review Movies Which Thou Hast Not Seen'.

When I wasn't storming out of the Radcliffe show I was *passing* out *on* it. Somewhere in the vaults of the BBC (and also doubtless out there on the internet) is a recording of me stopping mid-sentence one rainy Manchester evening and then making a strange croaking noise like the victims in *The Boston Strangler* (Tony Curtis in split screen!) before slipping semi-conscious off one of the studio's plush orange plastic chairs. Ever the professional, Mark leaped to my aid with that time-honoured trick of playing a record and hoping that no one would notice. Meanwhile, Lard dragged me outside, resuscitated me with his Ventolin inhaler, and then steered me back into the studio to carry on where I had left off when the music stopped. At the time I lamely attributed this incident to an asthma attack although there was (and *is*) no evidence that I have ever suffered from asthma. The more awful truth is that it was probably a panic attack, the broadcasting equivalent of stage fright, provoked by who knows what. One minute I could breathe, the next I could do nothing but listen to the sound of blood rushing in my ears and wait for the floor to come up and hit me in the face, which it did with some alacrity. It was, frankly, not pleasant, and in the wake of this incident I seriously wondered whether my broadcasting career was over. Let's face it, if people employ you to speak on the radio, it's safe to assume that they'll probably expect you to be able to do just that without apparently falling asleep (or falling over) on-air.

Incidentally, in case you're starting to think that there's anything confessional about me admitting that it was stage fright rather than asthma that floored me all those years ago, let me be clear that I'm not telling you anything that hasn't appeared in print before. In a 2009 profile piece for the *Guardian*'s G2, Mark Lawson outed my on-air collapse as a thinking (rather than a breathing) problem. And he was almost certainly right, although in that same piece Mark also insisted that I was a Sunday school teacher, a badge of honour which I would clearly be sorely ill-equipped to wear.

I loved doing the graveyard shift, not least because I got to haul my sorry arse up to Manchester which was about 180 miles nearer to Linda (who lived in Liverpool) than London. I recently bumped into Radcliffe at the Sony Awards (did I mention this already?) where we both commiserated with each other about the fact that we would surely go home empty-handed, and then both went on to win our respective awards (no, really, stop me if you've heard this one ...), making us look like self-serving *faux*-modest tossers who had *expected* to win all along.

When Radcliffe departed from the Radio One arts programme *The Guest List* to host the graveyard shift, I took over as the programme's presenter and it became one of a string of formerly successful programmes that have been killed by the 'curse of Kermode'. Other victims of this uniquely paralysing power have included *The Antique Records Roadshow* (which ran for years under Andy Kershaw's steady hand but which I killed in two short series), *Clingfilm* (the horribly entitled Radio One film programme which I both spawned and sank, though at least I wasn't responsible for that godawful name); the *Movie Update* (ditto, with a little help from James King); and Danny Baker's short-lived BBC TV show *After All* on which I was musical director and which similarly withered on the vine. I have also sunk not one but two movie magazines (*Fear* and *Flicks*, the latter of which had been going for donkeys' ages till I came along), an entire radio station (the aforementioned Radio Five) and of course the Film4 Extreme Cinema strand which briefly flourished before going the way of all things in which I have had a hand. Last year the *Observer* newspaper (for whom I am a regular writer) pluckily bucked the accursed trend by weathering doom-laden reports about its 'uncertain future' for which I hold myself cosmically accountable. By the time you read this book, it is very probable that its publishers Random House will have gone bust, in which case let me take this opportunity to say how nice it was to work with them and how sorry I am to have put them all out of a job.

At the height of my tenure hosting *The Guest List* most of my time seemed to be spent on trains to and from Manchester. On Mondays and Tuesdays I'd watch films in London before heading up North to do the show with Mark and Lard on Wednesdays, finishing at midnight after which we'd decamp to an uninviting club around the corner from the BBC whose sole allure was the fact that it sold tuna sandwiches and chips until 2 a.m. On Thursdays I'd present *The Guest List* which would include a film-review slot in which someone other than me would tell me what they thought of the new releases while I kept quiet as if I hadn't seen them yet. Then I'd plod back to the hotel where I'd watch German-dubbed reruns of *Kojak* ('das ist eine troublesome murder case, Saperstein') on the only twenty-four-hour channel in town before getting the 5.20 a.m. train back to London to do my own movie slot on the Mayo show wherein I would babblingly evaluate the new releases about which I'd been so ignorant the night before. Anyone listening from 9 p.m. to 11 a.m. would presumably have got the impression that I'd somehow watched all those films in the wee small hours of Friday morning, and if asked I would tell people that that's *exactly* what I did. Why spoil the magic?

So all this stuff was going on simultaneously with the Mayo show, and if Simon is reading this now (which he won't be, obviously) I hope he realises just how popular I was back then and just how many other offers and suitors I had to beat off in order to plight my radio troth to him and how much better I could have done if I had wanted to which I didn't but that was my choice and *don't you forget it* thank you very much no don't mind me I just work here incidentally here's your coffee, oh don't mention it, not that you've ever got coffee for me oh no far too busy being famous on the radio while I do all the hard work ...

Am I hamming this up?

If so, it's only because that's how it feels sometimes – hammy, with a side order of cheese.

At the time of writing, Mayo and I have been 'together'

for around sixteen years, give or take a two-year break between me leaving Radio One and him taking up residence at 5 Live whereupon we picked up pretty much where we had left off – which, basically, was bickering. I'm fairly sure that my first words on his 5 Live show were 'And another thing …' and it all just continued from there.

The odd thing, of course, is that despite being professionally joined at the hip we've never really socialised together, probably because we have very little in common. He's intelligent, interested in current affairs, and keen on football. And I'm not. In fact the only thing that genuinely bonds us is the fact that we both have families in whose company we'd much rather spend our spare time.

In the summer of 2009, entirely by coincidence, the pair of us ended up in an East Anglian village and for three consecutive nights Simon, his wife Hilary, Linda and I went to the pub together and experienced something akin to normal human interaction. We sat, we drank, we laughed, we moaned, we ordered more drinks, ate too many crisps, and we all developed pleasantly low-level headaches. At some point Hilary and I discovered that we had been in Manchester at around the same time and we swapped enthusiastic reminiscences about the old haunts until Simon got the hump and banned any further talk of Manchester on the grounds that he hadn't been there and couldn't join in. Through the haze of a few pints of Johnny-Knock-Me-Down I argued that Linda hadn't been in Manchester either, but then she pointed out that she *had* been there and it was bloody typical of me to forget that that was where we *met*, so I slunk off to get more drinks and crisps and by the time I got back to the table Simon was drawing up his plans for world domination on the back of a scrappy table napkin in between bouts of earnest tweeting.

At this point, our future together seemed worryingly uncertain. Despite Simon's conversational ban, the subject of Manchester just wouldn't go away because 5 Live was moving there en masse and Simon had made it clear that he wasn't going with it. There were rumours of a new job for him at Radio Two, and even though he'd assured me that nothing was going to break up the old team I was going through all the usual paroxysms of thinking that I was about to be dumped – or 'chucked', as I believe the teenagers still have it. Simon's career was clearly going from strength to strength, and the possibility of being left behind seemed very real – like Cynthia Lennon missing the train at Euston station because a policeman didn't believe that she was the superstar's wife.

So when no one was looking I slipped Simon's scrap of paper off to one side, huddled into a corner, unwrapped it furtively, and scanned it to make sure that *my name* was on it.

Somewhere.

Anywhere.

To be honest, there wasn't much of anything on that napkin scrap. Circles and triangles, some numbers underlined, an ink splodge here and a beer stain there. It looked unimpressive, but if you've ever seen Nelson's hastily drawn plan of action for the Battle of Trafalgar you'll know that it wasn't much better; some crosses, an arrow, a couple of squiggly lines, and the rest is 'Kiss me Hardy …'.

Eventually my sore eyes settled on something amidst the crisp crumbs and doodles which, if you turned the paper a certain way in the half-light, looked like it might *just* be a pair of initials.

*My* initials.

'MK'.

Followed by a question mark …

# Chapter 7

# NOW THAT'S WHAT I CALL QUITE FUNNY

I have a rule about walking out of movies – I don't do it, unless they involve scenes of *actual* cruelty to animals or the abuse of children. Or they feature Julian Sands. (Only kidding. Sorry Julian. Old habits.) The reasons are obvious, and are to do with consent. Whereas grown-ups can *agree* to be filmed while hammering nails through their genitals (as the late 'supermasochist' Bob Flanagan did in Kirby Dick's terrific documentary *Sick*), animals and children need to be protected from the whims of film-makers who are often less than kind in their attitude to the on-screen talent (Hitchcock famously said that actors should be treated like cattle, and he's generally regarded to be a genius).

To me this issue of consent seems inarguable, but you'd be amazed by how many problems it causes for our censors who are forever attempting to balance concepts of freedom of expression with the harsh realities of the law. Let me offer two examples which seem to crystallise the madness around these issues.

Firstly, take as typical the case of acclaimed European director Emir Kusturica's 2004 film *Life is a Miracle* which offered the director's usual mix of politics, fantasy, war, and loud brass bands. Having played to muted but reverential applause in Cannes the film was submitted to the BBFC who noted that it contained a brief shot of a cat mangling a live pigeon, an image which appeared to be unsimulated and which could therefore fall foul of the 1937 Cinematograph Films (Animals) Act which outlaws the mistreatment of animals on film. The BBFC duly presented the distributors with two options: provide credible evidence that the scene was simulated; or make a cut of slightly less than two seconds. After some consideration, the distributors plumped for the second option, apparently considering the issue unworthy of a protracted verification process.

Sadly, no one asked Emir about this, and when he got wind of the decision, he hit the roof. Outraged at the censoring of his fine work, Kusturica told the British media that he would rather see *Life is a Miracle* shelved indefinitely than 'butchered' by the BBFC. Asked to reconsider their decision, the Board pointed out politely that they were simply complying with a statutory regulation which was not theirs to overturn – the film *seemed* to depict a live animal being mistreated, and it was therefore incumbent upon the film-makers to prove that such was not the case before they could grant a certificate. Quick as a flash, Kusturica shot back that the pigeon was already *dead*, and that he had found it lying by the side of the road. The BBFC pointed out that since the pigeon was still *moving* (its wings are demonstrably flapping in the scene) it seemed probable that (unlike Monty Python's infamous parrot) Kusturica's pigeon had yet to join the choir invisible. Unless, of course, Emir could provide evidence to the contrary.

Having backed himself into a corner with his own threats of pulling the movie, and apparently realising that both common sense and UK law were against him, Kusturica admitted that, yes OK the pigeon was moving, but *only because he had cleverly wired it up with bits of string*, in order to *simulate* the writhings of a live creature. When asked to verify this assertion, the director promptly produced a letter attesting that no pigeons were harmed during the making of *Life is a Miracle* – honest. Displaying the patience of Job, the BBFC duly looked at the scene *again* and conceded that, yes, unlikely as it sounded, it was *just about possible* that the bird in question was part of some Gerry Anderson-esque puppet show. Since they were unable to *prove* that Kusturica wasn't telling the truth, and since (contrary to popular belief) they don't like cutting movies unless they absolutely have to, the Board agreed to reverse their initial decision, and allowed *Life is a Miracle* to be passed uncut.

Personally, I would have tied Kusturica up with a piece of string and thrown him to the pigeons.

Which, incidentally, reminds me of a related incident also involving our feathered friends: the case of John Waters' seventies cult classic *Pink Flamingos*. The film, which has become a milestone of self-aware trash cinema famously climaxes in transvestite icon Divine eating dog shit – for *real*. This is fine by me – after all, in my younger years I ate at McDonald's. But there's also a sequence in which a live chicken is used as an unwilling sexual aid, and that's where I draw the line – from the chicken angle, rather than the sex angle, obviously.

I was in Cannes in the late nineties when *Pink Flamingos* was getting a twenty-fifth anniversary re-release and John Waters (whose work I generally like) was doing the rounds of press interviews. Inevitably the subject of chicken sex reared its ugly head and I felt compelled to tell Waters that I still thought that scene was unforgivable.

'Oh for heaven's sake,' said Waters with a flamboyant flounce. '*Everyone* still goes on about that damn chicken scene. I honestly don't know what all the fuss is about. People *eat* chicken all the time. With *Pink Flamingos*, the chicken got fucked, got to be in a movie, and *then* the cast *ate* it that evening. And I bet you all those people who complain about that scene went straight out and ate a chicken sandwich.'

I pointed out that, as a vegetarian, I did no such thing.

'OK,' he conceded, 'but it's not like you keep chickens as pets, right?'

I pointed out that this was *exactly* what I did, and that Elvis, Priscilla, Clarrie and Shula were very much a part of my extended family.

He thought about this for a moment.

'Fine,' he said after a while. 'To *you*, the keeper of the chickens, I apologise. Everyone else can kiss my ass.'

See how much fun I can be in interviews?

You'd think the situation would be more clear-cut in relation to the protection of children, but inevitably it is not so. The most bizarre case of which I have had personal experience was that of *Baadasssss!*, a docudrama by actor-director Mario Van Peebles celebrating the work of his father Melvin who made the seventies blaxploitation classic *Sweet Sweetback's Baad Asssss Song*. In the late nineties, in my role as host of Film4's Extreme Cinema strand (which, as previously noted, fell foul of the 'curse of Kermode') I had introduced a screening of *Sweetback* which tells the story of a young man's journey from wide-eyed innocent to militant outlaw. The film, in which Melvin plays the adult Sweetback, opens with the hero's younger self (played by someone who looks an awful lot like a fourteen-year-old Mario) losing his virginity to a prostitute. Despite being simulated, the scene is somewhat explicit, and I was surprised that it hadn't been cut under the Protection of Children Act. So I rang the BBFC who told me that they had on file a letter from Melvin Van Peebles attesting that the actor in that scene was *not* in fact his son Mario, but Hubert Scales (who was over eighteen), an assurance the Board were inclined to accept since Melvin was hardly likely to have placed his own son in a potentially compromising situation.

So far, so good. Until, that is, the now grown-up Mario came to make *Baadasssss!* in 2003, wherein he restaged the filming of the infamous scene from *Sweetback* with his younger self in the starring role. Rather than merely skirting the issue, *Baadasssss!* went into great detail about how Melvin (here played by Mario) insisted that his own son perform the scene because it wouldn't be right to ask someone else's kid to do it – a version of events which hardly tallied with Melvin's letter to the BBFC.

When I first saw *Baadasssss!*, I wondered whether this retrospective admission would have any effect upon the BBFC's previous decision. Surely if Mario was now telling the world that he *had* performed the scene in question, then Melvin's assurances to the contrary were, to say the least, suspect. Sure enough, in the wake of *Baadasssss!* the BBFC took another look at *Sweet Sweetback*, taking into account 'information that has come to light since 1998 [that] has cast considerable doubt on those assurances' formerly offered by Melvin. 'It now appears', the BBFC concluded, 'that the actor in the scene in question was in fact the director's son Mario Van Peebles, who cannot have been older than fourteen years at the time of filming.'

This 'new information' presented the Board with a very grave problem for, unlike issues of taste or potential offensiveness, the Protection of Children Act offers no room for manoeuvre. If a scene of a sexual nature features an underage performer, it runs the risk of indecency, regardless of dramatic or artistic intent. Despite appreciating the historical and cultural significance of the movie the Board had no choice but to show the sequence first to their own specialist advisor, and then to 'one of the leading QCs in this area', to determine whether the scene fell foul of the law. 'The legal advice was unequivocal' they discovered. 'The sequence was likely to be considered indecent under current UK law.'

The ramifications of this conclusion were far-reaching, and included the BBFC having to contact the distributors of previously uncut editions of the *Sweetback* video to warn them that the '18' certificate had been rescinded, and further distribution could incur prosecution. Despite much woolly liberal rhubarbing about the retrospective 'desecration' of an accepted classic, I think the BBFC were right and were left with no option but to enforce cuts. The only people the Van Peebles have to blame for the cutting of *Sweetback* is themselves.

For the record, I'd also like to state that since a major regime change at the end of the nineties the BBFC have been doing a sterling job of allowing adults to decide what they watch whilst still policing legally unacceptable images with discretion, insight and patience. This is good news for UK filmgoers, but has a downside for me because the Board's thoughtful vigilance means that there are now precious few occasions on which I find it legitimate or justifiable to walk out of a movie. Which is a shame, because there are few things quite as satisfying as being able to storm indignantly out of a really terrible film. At the Cannes Film Festival (of which yet more later) the seats in some screening rooms are of the flip-down variety which make a pleasing banging sound when swiftly vacated. During particularly 'problematic' screenings one can thrill to an increasing crescendo of percussive clatters which invariably starts with a random single beat before advancing toward a free-form jazz drum solo of thumping disgust. That sound is one of the few things I actually *like* about Cannes.

So, to answer a question I get asked all the time, yes I really do watch all those movies from beginning to end, even the ones I really *hate*. Even *Transformers: Revenge of the Fallen*. Very occasionally, I confess, I have succumbed to *sleep*, which I suppose is the psychological equivalent of walking out – your body's still there, but your mind has left the building. A recent example would be the really very boring 'comedy' *Year One* which failed to raise a titter despite the presence of Jack Black and Michael Cera, both of whom I generally find innately humorous. But the film was a stiff – such a bore, in fact, that when Radio One film critic James King lost all patience and decided to take a toilet break (another variation on the 'walkout', offering only temporary escape) he had to wake me from my slumbers in the seat next to him to let him out. Film executive Jack Warner used to judge movies by how often he had to go to the bathroom, famously calling *Bonnie and Clyde* 'a three-piss picture'. Now that's what I call constructive criticism.

Sadly, my rule about never walking out of movies is not always reciprocated by the film-makers. While I will sit through any movie from beginning to end on the basis that if you walk out you're bound to miss the *one* thing that would have made the viewing worthwhile, film-makers seem to feel less concerned about getting to the end of *me*.

I received my first proper lesson in film-maker walkouts from Ken Russell (who now ranks as one of the very few film directors whom I consider a *friend*) in Southampton in the mid-nineties. Having written umpteen laudatory pieces about Russell's outrageously outré work for magazines like

*Sight & Sound*, I was asked to chair an onstage discussion with Ken at the newly gleaming Harbour Lights cinema down by Southampton waterfront. The talk would accompany a screening of Russell's fiery 1971 masterpiece *The Devils* which had famously proved unpalatable to censors and studio executives alike and had accordingly suffered extensive cuts. Inspired by Aldous Huxley's 'real life' account of alleged demonic possession in seventeenth-century France, *The Devils* was a profoundly political work which raged against the unholy marriage of church and state (Russell called it 'my most – indeed my *only* – political film'). Oliver Reed delivered his finest performance as unruly priest Urbain Grandier who was burned at the stake after rallying the citizens of Loudun to stand firm against the destruction of their city walls. The film's most flamboyant sequences depicted theatrically blasphemous orgies staged by the Ursuline nuns who claimed that Grandier had possessed their bodies, spurred on by the twisted passions of Sister Jeanne of the Angels – a shrieking tour de force performance from theatrical stalwart Vanessa Redgrave.

According to Russell, chief censor John Trevelyan told him early on that he would have to lose his most prized sequence in which the nuns tore down and ravished a huge effigy of the crucified Christ. But Trevelyan's reservations were nothing compared to the anger of the film's American backers who considered even the depiction of pubic hair beyond the pale, and demanded that the film be further butchered for American release. Russell recalls the reaction of the stateside studio suits to their first viewing as being one of 'utter outrage. They called me to their suite in the hotel, and they just let me have it,' he told me. 'One of them, who looked like a gangster, got up and said, "I have chased every broad from here to Chicago and I have *never* seen the likes of this disgusting shit!" They really *hated* the movie.'

When I asked Ken what had happened to the treasured 'rape of Christ' sequence which he insisted contained 'some of my best work' he told me dejectedly that it was 'gone, lost, forever probably'. In a moment of rash bravado I told him that I would *find* that missing sequence and restore it to its rightful place in the film. And eventually I did just that, prodding Warner Brothers into producing a tin of film which contained several censored sequences including the 'rape' which was duly reinserted into the movie by ace editor Michael Bradsell. The restored director's cut of *The Devils* was premiered at the National Film Theatre in London in 2004 as part of a 'History of Horror' season which I co-curated with Linda. It got a standing ovation and was duly earmarked for future DVD release. But then the Americans got wind of what we were up to and, in an uncanny echo of their actions back in the early seventies, effectively banned the intact movie all over again. At the time of writing, Ken's cut of *The Devils* is still gathering dust on a shelf in Hollywood, despite having long since been given a clean bill of health by the UK censors. All of which means that the only thing preventing *you* from watching one of the greatest British movies of the past fifty years is the peevishness of an American studio. So much for the First Amendment.

Anyway, let me climb down from my soapbox and return

to the mid-nineties when my friendship with Ken was still in its very early stages, and the idea of a director's cut of the *The Devils* seemed even more remote than the possibility of an Austrian body-building sci-fi movie star someday becoming 'The Governator'.

So there I was at the Harbour Lights cinema, on stage with Ken Russell, a packed audience hanging on his *every word* as he laid the groundwork for the screening which was to follow. He was in ebullient mood, a glass of red wine in one hand, the other making grandiose gestures as he conjured riveting anecdotes from thin air like the master storyteller he is. Inevitably the conversation turned to the restriction of artistic freedom at which point I naïvely invited Ken to hold forth on the evils of censorship. But, ever the contrarian, Ken decided to do just the opposite.

'The thing is,' he told the attendant throng, 'that people *assume* that I must be anti-censorship, but I'm *not*. Far from it. I really *believe* in censorship.'

There was an awkward silence in which the audience and I tried to figure out whether this was a joke, whether Ken was pulling our collective legs.

He wasn't.

'Censorship is *essential*,' he went on, warming to his theme. 'You *have* to have it.'

'Um, *why* do you "have to have it"?' I asked tentatively, my woolly liberal sensibilities somewhat befuddled by this turn of events.

'Well, because otherwise people will just do whatever they want,' declared Ken, sounding slightly impatient.

'And that would be bad because …?' I ventured pathetically.

'Because we *know* what happens when people do exactly what they want,' he replied firmly.

At which point I did the very thing that lawyers are always told *never* to do in court: i.e. to ask a question to which you do not already know the answer.

'And what is it that we "*know*" happens?' I blundered.

'Well, for example, we "know" that people have died as a result of *Natural Born Killers* …'

Ken was referring to a series of frankly scandalous news stories which had appeared in the preceding months alleging that Oliver Stone's controversial rehash of *Badlands*, *Bonnie and Clyde* et al. had inspired copycat crimes in America and France. These stories would later be roundly debunked, and today Ken insists that he *never* said such a thing anyway, and even if he *did* (which he is sure he *didn't*) he only did so to get a reaction out of me because I was becoming boring.

In fact, I was becoming rattled – enough to take my eye off the ball and to misread Ken's mischievous mood spectacularly.

'Oh you don't believe that,' I scoffed in an entirely inappropriate and dismissively offhand manner.

'Don't I?' replied Ken.

And with that he put down his glass of wine, got up out of his chair, and walked off down the aisle and out of the cinema, leaving me there on stage like the proverbial spare dick at a wedding, with all eyes upon me waiting to see what we did now.

There was a horrible silence. I had no idea what to do.

I still wasn't sure whether this was actually a joke. Was Ken suddenly going to reappear, laughing at his madcap pranks?

I waited.

The audience waited.

We all waited together.

We all waited together some more.

Apparently he *wasn't* coming back.

'Er, right …' I said, with a mixture of fear and embarrassment. 'Well, I think that perhaps we'd better just start the movie. Roll the film!' And with that I scuttled up the aisle, out through the exit, and into the nearest toilet where I hid, awash with shame and self-loathing.

After a few moments, and several splashes of cold water to the face, I ventured out into the foyer where Ken was sitting, smiling happily, apparently without a care in the world.

'Ken!' I almost screamed, 'What the *hell* was all that about?'

'All *what* about?' he replied with bemused amusement.

'All that walking out in the middle of the interview!' I gasped, as if it somehow needed explaining. 'What was all *that* about?'

'Oh, that? I just thought they'd all heard enough and they wanted to watch the film.'

'But Ken,' I pleaded helplessly, 'we were in the middle of an interview. They've *paid* to see you talk about the film. And you just *walked off and left me there on stage*.'

'Did I?' mused Ken, clearly failing to grasp the severity of the situation.

'Yes you did!'

'Ah,' he chortled. 'Well, never mind.'

'*Never mind!* How can I *not mind*? We need to go back on after the film and do some more, otherwise it's going to look *terrible* and people will be ... well, they'll be cross. Or disgruntled. Or worse.'

'Worse than "disgruntled"?' said Ken in quietly mocking tones. 'Well I thought it was funny.'

'*Funny?*'

'Yes. Quite funny.'

'*Quite funny?*'

'Yes, quite funny. I thought so. But if you insist, we'll go on again after the film.'

Which we did. And guess what happened? Ken answered a few more questions, then got bored and walked off stage *again*.

Which presumably was also 'quite funny'.

Looking back, I can only conclude that Ken was testing me – albeit playfully – and I presume that our subsequent friendship has somehow been built upon this trial by fire. In which case, it was all worth it.

Other hostile encounters have not yielded such positive rewards. Take the Nick Broomfield incident which made the pages of *Private Eye* and sparked a really petty feud that would fester away for the best part of a decade – at least from my side (in the words of St Moz, 'Beware, I bear more grudges, than lonely High Court judges ...').

Here's what happened.

Back in 1998, alongside doing reviews on Simon Mayo's show on Radio One, I also presented the station's weekly film programme, and functioned as an all-round low-rent 'movie-tsar'. In an attempt to stave off any suggestions that I had 'sold out' by working for the nation's number one pop station, I had made a point of being 'honest' with film-makers about their work – an honesty which frequently bordered upon rudeness. In the case of Broomfield, who was a very successful documentary maker, I had enjoyed many of his previous films, particularly *The Leader, His Driver and the Driver's Wife* in which he efficiently mocked white supremacist Eugene Terre'Blanche simply by documenting his lengthy attempts to interview the creep. This laid the template for a series of films (*Tracking Down Maggie*; *Aileen Wuornos: The Selling of a Serial Killer*; *Fetishes*) in which Broomfield effectively took centre stage, his bumbling *faux naïf* shtick providing a comic narrative backbone which prefigured the work of Michael Moore in the US, helping to popularise documentaries, for which we should all be grateful.

With *Kurt & Courtney*, however, that joke wasn't funny any more. One theme of the film was an investigation into (clearly spurious) allegations that various persons – including Courtney Love – had somehow colluded in the demise of Kurt Cobain, the Nirvana frontman who famously blew his own head off with a shotgun. The film concluded that such allegations were probably bunk, but en route offered a platform for a menagerie of unreliable assholes to make outrageous and unsubstantiated claims about Love.

Unsurprisingly, Love had declined to co-operate with Broomfield, a refusal which (it seemed to me) the film-maker had taken as a licence to throw metaphorical mud at her. Watching *Kurt & Courtney*, I got the strong impression that this 'rockumentary' was less about the question of who killed Kurt Cobain (I think it was Kurt, in the garden house, with the shotgun – I win!) than about how cross Broomfield was with Courtney Love for not cooperating with his film.

Since Broomfield had become known for pursuing recalcitrant interviewees with headphones and boom mike in hand (a persona he later mocked in a series of TV adverts) I figured he must be pretty tough-skinned, and therefore resolved at the outset to tell him just how much I didn't like *Kurt & Courtney*. I thought he would appreciate such refreshing straight talk, and over the years I've found this policy to be fairly productive. For example, when interviewing pop-video maestro turned feature-film-maker Garth Jennings for *The Culture Show* I felt morally obliged to tell him that he had made 'a complete Horlicks' of *The Hitchhiker's Guide to the Galaxy*, to which he responded politely, 'I see. Am I allowed to tell you to fuck off?'

'Of course,' I replied.

'Right then, fuck off.'

After which we proceeded with the interview on exceptionally genial terms.

I also told Leonardo DiCaprio that I forgave him for *Titanic* which he seemed to take well, if you interpret his silence as comedic rather than stroppy.

Broomfield, however, simply took the hump, becoming more and more irate about being taken to task by some grubby oik from a pop radio station who should presumably have been giving him an easy ride and lots of free publicity. After about seven minutes of mildly confrontational badinage, he rolled his eyes and declared that my entire problem with his movie was that I simply didn't have a sense of humour.

At which point I said, in what I believed to be extremely measured tones, 'I just don't see what's funny about accusing a woman of being complicit in the death of the father of her child.'

And that was it.

The next moment Broomfield, who had just made a movie about a star who wouldn't speak to him, got up out of his chair and stormed out of the room, followed in Keystone Cops comedy fashion by a bumbling radio reporter with a microphone to whom he was now refusing to speak. 'I can't *believe* you're walking out!' I yelped as he stomped through the corridors of his PR's offices and out into the street. 'I can't believe you're *walking out of an interview* ...'

But he was. And in a moment he was gone.

As was my career, probably.

In the embarrassed silence that followed Broomfield's departure I was struck by a clawing sense of terror that the whole thing was my fault and I had *failed* to do my job – which was to interview a famous film-maker and get him to say interesting things about his work. Looking at the counter on the tape machine I realised that I had recorded less than eight minutes of material, one or two of which would have been taken up by the unbroadcastable sounds of doors banging and feet scuttling.

This was not good. This was not good *at all*.

I started to pack my bags.

Broomfield's PR appeared at the door.

'What *happened*?'

'I don't know,' I said shaking my head. 'I told him I didn't think the film was funny and he stormed out.'

'Oh bloody hell,' she sighed in exasperation – whether at me or him I wasn't sure. More likely me.

I trudged back up Portland Street, past Broadcasting House, and into the warren-like surroundings of Yalding House from whose stuffy basements Radio One kept the nation's pop pulse pounding. With a growing sense of doom and despondency I handed the tape over to my producer. 'You listen to it,' I said. 'You tell me whether I cocked up. If you think I did, I'll quit. Sorry.'

And with that I went off to hide in the toilet – something which had helped the last time a film-maker walked out on me.

After about ten minutes (plenty of time for my producer to listen to the *whole* tape) I slunk sheepishly back into the studio wondering whether it was too late in life to take up teacher training or explore some similarly worthy character-building career outside of radio broadcasting.

I looked like death. My producer just looked nonplussed.

'Bit of an overreaction,' she said, non-committally.

'By who? Me?'

'No, *him*, the director.'

'So you don't think it was my fault.'

'What, that he overreacted?'

'That he *stormed out of the interview*. You don't think it was *my* fault?'

'Well, you were spiky and petulant and you weren't very nice about his movie.'

'But I didn't *like* his movie. I was only telling him the truth. I can't *lie* about it.'

'Why not?'

'*Why not?* Because I *can't*. And he's going to find out what I think of the movie when I review it anyway. I can't just sit there and let him think I liked it and then slag it off on the radio.'

'Why not?'

'Because that would be *awful*.'

'More awful than having him storm out of the interview?'

'*What?* Yes of *course* "more awful" than that! More awful than *anything*.'

'Well, there you go then – what are you worrying about?'

'Pardon?'

'You've just told me that letting him think you liked the movie would be "more awful" than him storming out of the interview. And having listened to the tape I'm pretty sure he now *knows* you didn't like it. So what's the problem?'

'The problem is that I made him *storm out*.'

'Which was quite funny.'

This hadn't occurred to me.

'Was it?'

'Yes. Quite funny.'

'Hmmm. Let me hear it.'

And so we sat there and listened to the tape together.

There was the sound of me setting up the microphone and testing the levels; there was Broomfield being suave and nonchalant when he came into the room, there was me telling him I didn't like his film; there was him getting irritated and telling me I had no sense of humour, there was me being sanctimonious and self-righteous (there's no denying that's how it sounded); and finally there was him throwing all his toys out of the cot and refusing to play any more.

It was, indeed, 'quite funny'.

'My advice,' said my producer, 'is to just play the whole thing. Put in a few clips, add some music – it'll be fine. And funny.'

And so we did.

And it was.

Funny enough, in fact, that John Peel (who once referred to me as his 'favourite film critic' – a thrill tempered only by his admission that he couldn't actually think of any others) wrote a column about it in the *Radio Times*, which was then the biggest-selling weekly magazine in the country. Peel, who had met and *liked* Courtney Love, wrote entertainingly about Broomfield being 'the biter, bit', and made much of his inability to deal with having the tables turned on him, a line also taken by *Private Eye*, albeit in rather more sarcastic tones. Overall, the general opinion seemed to be that Broomfield had indeed overreacted which was good because it meant that I probably wouldn't get fired. At least not yet.

Several years later, Broomfield was on 5 Live talking about his career which had gone from strength to strength in the wake of our brief on-air altercation. I wasn't in the studio that day, but Simon Mayo inevitably brought up the subject of the *Kurt & Courtney* walkout and asked the director if he had anything to say about it. Broomfield replied that the reason he had walked out was nothing to do with my line of questioning but was entirely due to the fact that I smelled really bad. Apparently he had found it intolerable being in the same room with my stinky breath and simply had to dash out to get some fresh air.

In his defence, I have to concede that there may be some truth in this. I have never considered a Mary Archer-like fragrance to be an essential part of film criticism, and have probably spent too little time worrying about personal hygiene, partly on the advice of Wreckless Eric who once memorably complained in song about people who 'partially stifle [their] natural odour with underarm spray' (ahh, they don't write songs like that any more). So perhaps when people tell me that my opinions stink (as they frequently do) they are speaking literally rather than metaphorically. Perhaps I really am the world's most offensive critic in every sense, the film hack equivalent of John Waters' scratch 'n' sniff masterpiece *Polyester*. Coming soon to a cinema near you '*The Mark Kermode Story*... In glorious Odorama!'

(Hang on, I think that's Jason Isaac's agent on the phone telling me his client is pulling out ...)

More importantly, Broomfield's comment reassured me that our long-standing run-in was indeed nothing more than a childish spat, something which pleased me since I have been a fan of much of his work since. I particularly liked his docudrama *Ghosts*, a very moving piece ('inspired by real events') about the tragic deaths of Chinese cockle pickers at Morecambe Bay. In fact, I met Broomfield last year for the first time since 1998 in a toilet at a swanky London venue where I was co-presenting the *Index on Censorship* Awards. We shook hands, smiled politely, and made friendly small talk, the bad blood between us apparently forgotten.

Or maybe he just thought I was Jesse Birdsall.

Despite this détente, there has been plenty of 'comeback' from other film-makers about whose movies I have been unkind, along with journalists and filmgoers who feel that my opinions are on a par with the plague. Many people think that all critics do is slag off other people's work without any sense of how hurtful this can be, but I'm proud to say that I've been on the receiving end of much vituperative spleen-venting and know *exactly* what it's like to be enthusiastically badmouthed in public. If you're in any doubt about this, just Google the words 'Mark Kermode' and 'Wanker' and see what fun awaits you out there on the internet. Best of all was a site entitled 'Fifty People More Annoying than Mick Hucknall' on which I featured for years, with visitors leaving a string of anatomically impossible suggestions for things I should attempt to do with myself. Sadly, the fabulous exclusivity of this club has since diminished, and it now seems to exist as the altogether less impressive '1,000 People More Annoying than Mick Hucknall', a clear indication of declining standards.

Indeed, such is my status as a figure of contempt amongst the film-making fraternity that I have even featured as a deeply unflattering 'fictional' character in a novel entitled *The Golden Age of Censorship* by an industry insider of whom I have never heard. I have been forced to the not unreasonable conclusion that this character is based on me because a) he is called 'Mark Carmody'; b) he uses phrases which are pretty much direct quotations from things I have said in print and in public; and c) he is a totally obnoxious arse whom everyone else in the novel (as much as I read of it) hates.

After a while, you get to pick up on these subtle signs.

I'm not complaining about this – on the contrary, I actively encourage it. In fact, I think it's good to be regularly reminded just how crap some people think you are. It's healthy. And if you're not annoying half your audience at least half of the time, then frankly you're just not trying.

So I took it as a compliment when recently I was 'playfully' punched on the arm live on-air by Benedict Cumberbatch on behalf of his *Atonement* co-star Keira Knightley as punishment for calling her 'Ikea' and referring to her acting style as 'flat-packed'. It was an oddly nostalgic experience which took me back to my youth in Manchester and getting thumped in the Cornerhouse bar for being rude about *Blue Velvet* – happy days!

And it's not just individuals whom I have managed to offend – apparently I can get on the wrong side of entire film festivals (or they can get on the wrong side of me). For example, despite its status as the world's premier celluloid knees-up I was for many years a Cannes Conscientious Objector who once impolitely suggested that if North Korea wanted to test their nuclear weapons, the Croisette would be a good place to start. My problems with Cannes were born out of a five-year stint reporting on the festival for Radio One who (like almost everyone else at that godforsaken place) were more interested in celebrity interviews than film reviews. When I look back on my Cannes coverage in the nineties, I remember not a carefully selected smorgasbord of international cinema but a Kafkaesque round of bizarre confrontations with befuddled famous faces. I remember chasing – or perhaps '*stalking*' – Sly Stallone for thirteen hours before finally cornering him in his hotel lobby after being effectively told that if I didn't get Stallone I needn't come back to England. In the ensuing three minutes of monosyllabic grunting, Sly told me that he was now a serious actor; that he had put action roles like Rocky and Rambo behind him, and that doing any more sequels would be 'stoopid' – comments that came back to haunt me as I sat through screenings of his recent *Rocky* and *Rambo* sequels, which were very 'stoopid' indeed.

And then there's the 'round-table interviews', which were clearly invented by people who *hate* film critics. I can still vividly remember being herded into a spacious cupboard (literally) with six other international hacks at the Hotel du Cap and being told to '*Attendez en silence!*' until the previous group's four-minute encounter with Johnny Depp had wound to a close. Then being rudely dispatched to ask a single piercing question ('So Johnny ... how are you enjoying yourself here at Cannes?') before some guy from the Netherlands started rambling on about an eighties TV programme which, it turned out, Depp wasn't actually in.

By which time, of course, we were '*Finis!*' and it was back into the cupboard to wait for Benicio Del Toro. As it happened, I really liked *Fear And Loathing in Las Vegas*, which Depp and Del Toro were nominally in town to promote. But somehow the subject of the film itself never really came up.

Other memories of Cannes are no better. I recall struggling to maintain a veneer of enthusiasm while Queen's guitarist Brian May talked earnestly about scoring a new film version of *Pinocchio* ('totally different to Disney') and Eric Clapton fretted about whether *Trainspotting* glamourised heroin. Worst of all, I remember weeping tears of relief when Robin Williams imitated my 'hilarious' British accent at a press conference for his after-life epic *What Dreams May Come*, thereby giving me a genuine 'scoop' – a personal, public mocking from a real-life celebrity!

My low point came during a screening of Lars von Trier's massively self-indulgent Dogme epic *Idioterne* about a group of annoying Danish arseholes who go around pretending to be handicapped. Hilarious. Having sat reverentially through an hour or so of hand-held Euro-twaddle, the assembled Cannes cognoscenti were duly rewarded with a few fleeting seconds of hard-core porno action for which von Trier (in clear contravention of Dogme's fastidious 'vow of chastity') employed a 'stunt-knob' since his main actors apparently weren't up to the task. The sequence was utterly pathetic but prompted fawning applause and murmurs of 'Bravo!' from the assembled hacks who love nothing more than to praise the kind of 'groundbreaking' fare which has become old hat to the honest hand-shandy brigade.

Rattled by the heat, exasperated by the festival, and appalled by the dual standards which apparently rendered this dreary spectacle 'art' rather than 'exploitation', I cracked. Rising from my seat and summoning up whatever remained of my long-failed O-level French, I began to growl: '*Il est* merde*! Il est le plus grande merde*… dans le monde*!*' OK, so the grammar was lousy, and the delivery shambolic, but the sentiment was clear enough to ensure that I was escorted swiftly through the doors and out on to the Croisette.

Later, I would queue for an hour to see an incomplete print of Michael Bay's preposterous *Armageddon* (not in competition, obviously) only to discover that the ticket I held was not a ticket for the unfinished film but for some promotional fairground ride which had been erected specially for this non-event. It was a moment which seemed to define the exquisite negativity of my entire experience of Cannes: not being allowed to see a film that was neither good, nor finished, nor indeed part of the actual festival. Oddly enough, our old friend Nigel Floyd, with whom I habitually shared lodgings in Cannes, had an absolutely spiffing time at that very same festival – catching up with Liv Tyler, spending 'quality time' with Steve Buscemi, and making entirely sound judgements about the wide variety of films it had been his pleasure to watch. A BBC documentary crew followed the pair of us around that year, and captured on camera our last day on the Croisette – Nigel a picture of smart festival chic; me, a man barely alive.

Not unlike Russia, really. But at least (according to the programme makers) it was 'quite funny'.

In the wake of my Cannes meltdown I gave the festival a miss for several years, returning only on condition that I didn't have to speak to any stars, attend any parties, go to any red-carpets, hide in any cupboards, or chase after Sylvester Stallone and his Planet Hollywood cronies. That arrangement has served me pretty well in recent years, but I still get a headache the minute I set foot in France which lasts right through until I arrive back in Southampton and wash away the pain with a pint at the Mayflower.

And there are still plenty of people to annoy back here in Blighty. My most recent triumph was being publicly handbagged by Her Majesty Helen Mirren after declaring that *The Queen* was little more than a TV film and wasn't best served by being screened in cinemas. As you'll probably know, *The Queen* went on to win umpteen major awards all around the world, with Dame Helen picking up deserved Best Actress gongs at the Globes, the BAFTAs, the Oscars, and more. By the time she got her hands on the coveted statuette at the Academy Awards, Mirren had effectively ascended to the status of royalty, her public appearances provoking the kind of awestruck admiration usually reserved for Brenda herself. In fact I'm pretty certain that if shown a photograph of Helen Mirren most Americans would identify her as 'the Queen of England'. And in a way they'd be right.

The Oscars were still in the future, however, when Dame Helen decided it was high time to send me to the Tower. The occasion for our meeting was the British Academy Film Awards (or BAFTAs, as they're more commonly known) which I had been proudly attending for a few years, despite being told rather pointedly by one A-list film-maker that 'It must be difficult being in a room with all these people who you've slagged off …'.

On this particular occasion Linda and I were in the upstairs foyer of the Royal Opera House, an extremely grand building filled with film-makers in their finery. We were dressed up too: Linda looked lovely, I looked like an undertaker – so, business as usual. As is my wont I was keeping my head down and generally staring at my shoes when a hand tapped Linda on the shoulder.

'Excuse me,' said an oddly familiar voice, 'but I want a word with your partner.'

Linda looked around and was greeted by the sight of an extremely imposing figure upon whom all eyes in the room were turned.

'Blimey,' said the voice inside Linda's head, 'that's Helen Mirren.'

The voice *outside* her head, however, said, 'He's all yours,' in an appropriately awestruck fashion.

Meanwhile, the voice inside *my* head was saying something along the lines of, 'Hey, I just had a moderately pally conversation with Ricky Gervais who was nice to me and knew who I was, I must be doing *really well* …' because, with my usual flair for social networking and top-flight celebrity reportage, I was looking the other way when the most famous person in the building decided to doorstep my wife. Consequently the first I knew of Dame Helen's designs upon my person was when a regal voice appeared as if from out of the heavens and sayeth clearly unto me: 'Oi, what do you mean "It's not a *real* film"?'

I looked around, wrong-footed, and was greeted by a shimmering vision of magisterial wonderment, clad from head to foot in radiant white (at least, that's how it looked to my momentarily blinded eyes), bedecked with handsomely appointed jewels (again, my memory *may* be embellishing this bit), glowing iridescently with radioactive presence (poetic licence) and clocking in at about six foot seven in her heels (OK, I'm *definitely* exaggerating here – she's five foot four – but I'm aiming for 'emotional truth' rather than hard facts, and the truth is that Helen Mirren seems quite tall).

By a peculiar coincidence, the voice inside my head said *exactly the same thing* that the voice inside Linda's head had said just moments earlier, i.e. 'Blimey, that's Helen Mirren!' I take this as a sign that Linda and I are soulmates who were *meant* to be together in much the same way that I place great significance on the fact that she *hated* Lars von Trier's wanky *Breaking the Waves* every bit as much as I did. The latter was a defining moment in our relationship because we went to see it together at the Harbour Lights cinema in Southampton after I'd dismissed the film on first viewing as a piece of misogynist claptrap. Others disagreed, and despite my negative response Linda was intrigued by the positive reactions of those whose opinions she trusted – which was basically anyone but me.

In an attempt to be open-minded (not a quality for which I am renowned) I'd agreed to give the film a second look, but after the first five minutes it was clear to me that my contempt for the movie was going to increase rather than abate. I spent the next two hours in utter torment worrying about how I was going to cope if Linda actually *liked* the film, which seemed to be getting a reverential response from everyone else in the cinema. Would we be able to carry on together with such a massive chasm between us? Or would we simply fall apart, citing 'irreconcilable cinematic differences' in the ensuing divorce-court showdown which would surely follow?

Was this the end of everything?

When the lights went up, we filed out together in silence, the sombre adulation of others ('a masterpiece, so artful, so *true* …') ringing in our ears. Finally I could stand it no more and blurted out: 'So, what did you *think* …?'

'Of the movie?' asked Linda, as if I could possibly be asking about *anything else*, such as the quality of the seating, the crispness of the popcorn, or the behaviour of the audience.

'Yes *the movie*,' I cried in despair. 'What did you *think of the movie*?'

She paused, briefly, and then said simply: 'Utter bollocks.'

And that was that.

I love Linda very much. Very *very* much indeed.

Anyway, back to the Royal Opera House.

So there I was, face to face with Helen Mirren, being unexpectedly confronted with a perfectly accurate precis of my complaints about *The Queen* (I had indeed suggested that it wasn't a 'real film' at all) and quite legitimately being asked to explain myself, young man.

Unfortunately, all I could think of at first was *Caligula*, which frankly didn't help matters. In fact, my gut reaction was to leap into a heated defence of director Tinto Brass (of whom Mirren has spoken fondly) and thence to an earnest attack upon producer Bob Guccione for cut-and-pasting all that hard-core sleaze into the movie. But somehow, this did not seem like the right time or place to speak of such things.

What *was* required was a polite but well-argued defence of my line about *The Queen* being an essentially televisual enterprise (it *did* start life as a TV movie) mingled with a willingness to accept that the tide of public opinion was against me, and topped off with a fulsome appreciation of Dame Helen's flawless performance and a fence-building complaint about Michael Sheen being overlooked in the Oscar nominations. Flattering, then, but also firm on the issue of small-screen versus big-screen on which point I would remain immovable. Claiming that I 'hadn't really meant it' was out of the question, because clearly if I was going to say that *The Queen* 'wasn't a real movie' on the radio and in the newspapers then I damn well ought to be able to say it to Dame Helen's face. And the fact remained that I wasn't having a go at *her*, but at the film – or rather the 'not film', as the case may be.

Whatever happened, I knew that this was an 'important' moment and if I wasn't up to the challenge then frankly I should get out of film criticism forthwith. As I had discovered with the Broomfield episode, you can't *lie* about your opinions just to avoid a potentially awkward encounter, although that's exactly what every atom of my being wanted to do right there and then.

But I didn't. Instead I took a deep breath, gathered myself (think Kate Winslet, minus the posh head-girl charm), tried to expel all thoughts of *Caligula* from my mind, failed, tried again, failed again, tried a third time, did rather better, took another deep breath, and began to speak – slowly, calmly, clearly.

If you'd been there with a tape recorder, you would have been proud of me. Because despite the temple-crushing pressures of the moment I did *not* deny having said that *The Queen* was not 'a real film', but rather offered an explanation of my opinion which was at once firm but fair, critical yet kind. I conceded that other opinions were available, and that my complaint was clearly a minority view. I praised the cast of *The Queen* for their sterling work, and congratulated Dame Helen for the awards which she had already won and for those which were undoubtedly to follow. I finished by conceding that 'not all films need look like *Pan's Labyrinth*' (a phrase which Dame Helen had whipped out of thin air – she'd clearly done her homework) but that many very fine screen stories were perhaps best enjoyed from the comfort of one's armchair. I even suggested that this might be a blessing, and that 'televisuality' may simply be another word for the 'intimacy' we share with films which we would wish to invite into our homes, like old friends.

Like I said, if you'd brought a tape recorder you would have been impressed.

A video camera, however, would have told a very different story. Because even as my mouth said one thing ('these are my opinions and I am proud to stand by them') my body – traitor that is – began to say something altogether different. As I concentrated all my energies on making my lips move (harder than it sounds) my knees took the opportunity to mount a royalist revolt and, without telling my head, started to buckle and bend beneath me. Like the mutinous crew of a ship, the rest of my body swiftly followed suit – my neck bent, my head started to droop, and I began to sink in slow motion toward the floor, virtually genuflecting as I went. By the time I'd finished saying whatever it was I had to say I was pretty much down on bended knee, head bowed in supplicant reverence, presumably awaiting prompt separation from my body.

If I'd had a forelock, I would surely have tugged it. I think I may have tried doffing my quiff. I'm really not sure – I was looking at the floor at the time.

It was pathetic.

After a few moments, I regained my composure and struggled to my feet just in time to hear Linda leaping to my defence by telling Dame Helen, 'Well I'm a film professor and I really loved *The Queen*!'

Oh great. Thanks for that.

'Really?' said Dame Helen, wryly. 'I'd love to be party to the arguments that must go on in your house.'

'Ha ha ha,' said Linda, sounding a bit mental.

'Ha ha ha,' said I, wondering how much more of this I could manage without descending into screaming panic. 'Please God,' I thought, 'please make this end. Please let me crawl away with at least *some* of my dignity still intact.'

In the end I pulled the conversational equivalent of a handbrake turn by shaking Dame Helen firmly by the hand and announcing incoherently that 'I'm sure you have much more famous matters to attend to …' before grabbing Linda by the arm and heading straight for the nearest door.

I didn't get very far. Roger Alton, then editor of the *Observer*, bounded up to me and said excitedly, 'Hey Mark, did you just get handbagged by Helen Mirren?'

Oh great. So *everyone* saw it, and everyone *knew*. Now it would probably be in the papers. I was going to go down in history as the man who went down on one knee to beg forgiveness for his critical indulgences from Dame Helen Mirren. Terrific.

I decided not to say anything.

'Yes he did,' chirruped Linda breezily. 'She asked him what he meant by saying that *The Queen* wasn't a "real movie".'

Thanks again.

'God,' said Roger. 'Was it scary?'

'Oh yes!' declared Linda again. 'Yes, he was definitely scared. He pretty much went down on one knee. It was funny.'

'It wasn't *that* funny,' I mumbled, disgruntledly.

'Oh yes it was,' retorted Linda, clearly enjoying the moment. 'It really was *quite funny* ...'

And from somewhere in the back of my mind I heard the spectre of every film-maker whose work I have ever insulted cackling heartily, enjoying the joke, delighting in my public comeuppance, smirking at my humiliation.

Ha bloody ha.

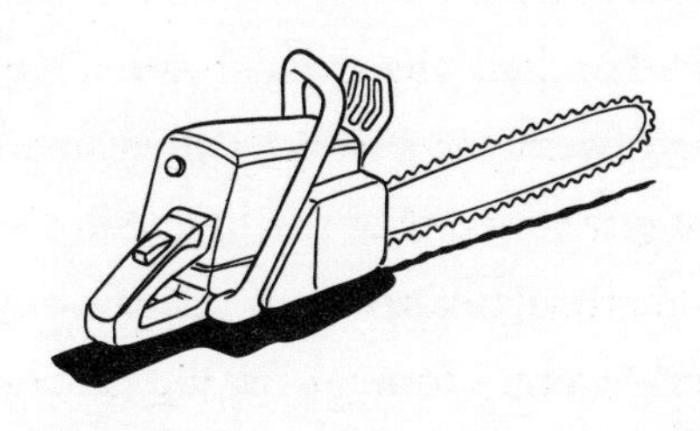

# Chapter 8

# I SHOT WERNER HERZOG

So there we were, up by Lookout Mountain, on the outskirts of LA, when Werner Herzog's trousers exploded.

It was, as I mentioned before, a small explosion, as if a firecracker had gone off in his pocket – a phrase which would later come back to haunt me thanks to the sinister miracle of the internet. But it was an explosion nonetheless, followed by silence broken only by Herzog's morosely Bavarian observation that 'Someone is shooting at us. We should leave …'.

Exactly what happened next is something of a blur – although unflattering video footage of myself hanging off a wire fence whilst attempting to scramble ungainly round a precipitous overhang suggests that I did not proceed in an orderly fashion toward the nearest exit whilst taking care to remove any sharp objects or high heels. I *do* remember experiencing a profound sense of urgency which seemed strangely absent from Herzog's own response. I put this down to deeply ingrained cultural differences: Herzog grew up in exciting Germany, whereas I grew up in Barnet – a place so dull that a decapitated chicken once made the front page of the local press. In short, I had no frame of reference for the seriousness (or otherwise) of the drama now unfolding less than a mile from the site of that infamous eighties drugs-and-porn bloodbath the 'Wonderland Massacre'. All that was clear was that Herzog had been shot (in the pantular region) and befuddled panic was top of my list of possible responses.

For Herzog, however, this was business as usual. As the maker of such rugged classics as *Fitzcarraldo* and *Aguirre: Wrath of God* Herzog had long held a reputation as modern cinema's most fearless foot soldier. Popular folklore had it that working on Herzog's movies was all but indistinguishable from being *in* them, an idea crystallised in Les Blank's brilliant documentary *Burden of Dreams* which found Herzog literally dragging a steamboat over a mountain in pursuit of his elusive cinematic vision. Whereas Lucas or Spielberg would have used models or blue-screen special effects, Herzog simply went upriver into Peru where he introduced a *real* boat to a *real* mountain and filmed the resulting grudge match for *real*.

'It was a necessity because of the story,' he told me by way of explanation. 'I have to accept it and I subject myself to the story. I had no one to learn from because *never* had an object of that magnitude – *never* in *technical history* – been moved over a mountain. Now, I was aware that with a pulley system it was theoretically *possible* to move a ship over a mountain. And yes, the pyramids have been built. But if you give me 300,000 disciplined men and give me thirty years, I could build a *bigger* one!'

Go Werner!

A central motif of Herzog's movies is the image of an obsessed (and often deranged) anti-hero going to extremes to achieve an impossible goal, and it doesn't take a critical genius to find a powerful autobiographical bond between the man and his work. Time and again the madness of Herzog's on-screen adventures has been matched by perilous off-screen antics as the director searches for those rare moments of 'ecstatic truth' which have become his signature. 'I live my life, I *end* my life with this project,' he famously said of *Fitzcarraldo*, and he wasn't kidding. Among the life-threatening on-set adventures which haunted the movie is the story of the extra who got hit in the neck by an arrow which Herzog had to help remove on a kitchen table. Other key Herzog legends involve a crew member hacking his own foot off with a chainsaw after being bitten by a poisonous Peruvian snake. 'It was very wise,' Herzog dead-panned. 'The man survived ...'

Nor has Herzog himself escaped the wrath of the movie gods. In Africa he was thrown into jail after being suspected of organising a military coup ('it was another man they wanted whose name was Hertz – like the hire car') and more recently he was handcuffed at an airport after the producers of *Rescue Dawn* pissed off the famously inflexible Thailand authorities. 'Two of the producers are actually in jail right now,' Herzog admitted. 'But that's fine; what was wrestled away from that situation was a film. And the film is good!'

The zenith of Herzog's life-or-death approach to film-making came when he legendarily used a gun to prevent leading man and 'best fiend' Klaus Kinski from walking out on the odd couple's greatest movie. According to Herzog, the story (which has entered the annals of extreme moviemaking history) has been blown out of all proportion because 'the gun wasn't ever actually pointing at Kinski. I just explained to him, very quietly, as he was packing his things, that if he tried to leave he would have eight bullets through his head before he reached the next bend of the river. Which was probably an exaggeration – I would have missed at least three or four.'

Was he joking? Would he really have shot Kinski?

'I said it very quietly so he understood that it was not a joke. But the story then took on a life of its own, until today you can read that I directed him only at gunpoint from behind the camera! That's baloney. It never happened like that. When I talked to him, I did not have a gun in my hands. However, I *did* have a gun ...'

All of which puts a rather more intense spin on every actor's favourite question: 'What's my motivation?'

Despite such wild tales, Herzog insists that 'I'm cautious about taking risks – I prefer to be alive. And contrary to what rumours say and what the media report about me, I'm a very circumspect and prudent person. I eliminate danger as far as it can be done. And as proof, I can say that in fifty-eight films, not one of my actors got injured! Not one!' Yet when I suggested to Herzog on stage at the BFI Southbank that 'Most film-makers would not go to the lengths you went to make *Fitzcarraldo*' he replied assertively, 'That's not correct. It's not "most". It's "no one"!'

Most moviemakers are indeed boringly well behaved, but Herzog is one of those rare few who seem to treat cinema as a genuinely spiritual art form, and he is more than willing to suffer for his art if his celluloid vision demands it. Like the wounded heroes of his epic movies, he is a man on a mission which draws him ever closer to the abyss. At the time of our meeting in LA, he had just completed work on *Grizzly Man*, a documentary about gung-ho animal lover Timothy Treadwell who went native with the bears up in Alaska's remote 'grizzly maze'. Treadwell spent thirteen summers communing with these bears, living, sleeping and eating with them until (inevitably?) one of them ate him. Treadwell was amiably nuts, giving these mammoth beasts cuddly names like 'Rowdy' and 'Mister Chocolate' which suggested a wild underestimation of their capacity for casual slaughter. Tellingly, Herzog described Treadwell as having 'something missing' before embracing him as 'definitely one of the family. He had something volatile. Something broken, something dark, something inexplicably wild in him. He had something in his nature which reminds me of some of my leading characters, like Kinski.'

In his commentary for *Grizzly Man* (which recalls the writings of Joseph Conrad) Herzog talks of Treadwell's misjudgement of nature as essentially benign in contrast to the quiet dark-hearted horror which underwrites his own cosmic philosophy. 'Once in a while Treadwell came face to face with the harsh reality of nature,' he intones over footage of Timothy examining the severed paw of a young bear – torn off not by hunters, but by an adult male bear seeking food, fighting, and sex, and with no time for kids. 'This did not fit into his sentimentalised view that everything out there was good, and the universe in balance and in harmony.' Where Treadwell saw growing friendship in the faces of the bears, Herzog found only 'a bored interest in food', culminating in his deadpan declaration that 'I believe the common denominator of the universe is not harmony, but chaos, hostility, and murder.' Considering the fact that Treadwell's blindingly naïve optimism led to the violent death of not only him but also his long-suffering girlfriend Amie Huguenard it's hard not to conclude that Herzog was probably right. No wonder he viewed getting shot at as so utterly unremarkable – something to be expected in a uniformly hostile and chaotic world.

In fact, the reason we were up on that wretched promontory by Lookout Mountain in the first place was Herzog's declared expectation that he would probably get shot at if we stayed at his house. Upon our arrival chez Werner, our BBC director David Shulman had asked if we could get an establishing shot of me arriving at the house and meeting Herzog in his front garden – the fearless Bavarian legend now ensconced on the leafy borders of Hollywood. Herzog shook his head gravely and explained, 'This is not a good idea. I do not want the outside of my house to be shown on television because I attract crazy people.' By way of example, Herzog recounted being in his office back in Munich when a woman arrived demanding to see him.

The woman had rung several times insisting that she was close to Herzog and forcefully requesting his assistance in her current (non-specific) travails. Somehow she had managed to inveigle her way into Herzog's office where she declared that the director was in league with 20th Century Fox to destroy her life. 'She had a bag with her,' Herzog remembered, 'and she began to reach inside it. I don't know what it was, some kind of *intuition* – but as she reached into her bag I *lunged* across the table and grabbed it, and in the bag was a gun. Loaded. It was somewhat upsetting.'

And that's not all. Other attacks upon Werner's person included someone 'diving through my kitchen window at night, flying through it like Batman, a car jack in their hand', the context and gravity of which I was frankly unable to comprehend. What was clear was that we probably *didn't* want to be advertising Werner's home address to any wandering whackos. Instead we decided to take a drive uphill, up toward Lookout Mountain Avenue where the road arches majestically along the edge of the hill and the entire vista of smog-bound LA is laid out below. The sun was hanging low in the late-afternoon sky, and the light as 'magic hour' approaches always looks good on camera. David had earned a reputation as one of *The Culture Show*'s most visually ambitious directors, and it was no secret that he took little pleasure in simply filming two people in a room talking to each other, so the possibility of getting something that actually looked vaguely cinematic was an attractive one.

So off we went, two cars pootling quietly up into the hills, cicadas buzzing gently in the hedgerow – an idyllic evening.

When we reached the appointed place it was impressive indeed, although annoyingly someone had fenced off the particular slice of roadside headland from which the best view of the city was available. Herzog insisted that the fence wasn't there a couple of days ago, and since it didn't seem to be *doing* anything we decided to just scoot round it; after all, who was going to object to us walking on a bit of old scrubland? As it turned out, a resident up the hill started barking at our cameraman that this particular bit of scrubland was 'about to be developed'. We asked if he owned it, or if indeed he *knew* who owned it. He didn't. So, what the hell. We thought: 'We'll get the shot, it'll only take a couple of minutes, and we'll be gone.' We were very polite; we said please and thank you. The neighbour wasn't, and didn't. He just muttered something about us having inappropriate relations with our mothers and stormed back inside his house across the street. We all got on with the job in hand – after all, what's the worst that could happen?

'In Germany,' intoned Werner sombrely as the cameras started to roll, 'I've somehow left a paved road. Nobody cares about my films.' It was a bleak assessment of his legacy in Europe, the continent from which Herzog had effectively fled seeking artistic sanctuary in America. Having spent a lifetime refusing to play the mainstream movie game, it seemed both poignant and bizarre to find him here in the very heart of the beast, lurking on the outskirts of Hollywood, an industry town in which art is endlessly (and unashamedly – even *proudly*) devoured and regurgitated by commerce. A land of agents, percentages and power lunches.

Hardly a place where you'd expect to find 'ecstatic truth'.

Yet Herzog, ever the contrarian, had seen something here that fitted his fractured world view. A few months later he would amaze interviewer Henry Rollins by telling him that Los Angeles was the most 'substantial' city in America. Certainly it made sense for anyone attempting to finance their films to make occasional forays into the wilds of Hollywood like military platoons performing operational raids into hostile enemy territory – get in, take what you need, and get *out*, hopefully unscathed. But Herzog seemed to actually *like* it here, or at least to like it *more* than Europe, which is perhaps not quite the same thing.

And then he got shot – or as Herzog himself later termed it, 'unsuccessfully shot'. Looking back on it now, the entire episode seems so bizarre that I'm inclined to think I must have made it all up. As we've seen, I've spent so much time telling wildly exaggerated stories about my past that I can no longer tell a real-life falling cymbal from a fictional perambulating drummer. More often than not I just end up believing the myths I created for entertainment (and, let's be honest, self-aggrandisement), abiding by that timeless maxim from *The Man Who Shot Liberty Valance* that 'When the legend becomes fact, print the legend'.

So long as the legend is 'inspired by real events'.

But poetic licence aside I'm pretty sure that the Herzog shooting did *really* happen. So I go to YouTube and put 'Herzog/Kermode/Shot' into the search engine, and there it is: Werner and me, together in LA, providing target practice for some nut-job with a BB gun. There's Werner in his dark brown leather jacket, quietly complaining about his outsider status in Germany; there's the weird cracking noise that was the only aural indication that anything untoward had happened; there's the brief moment of confusion as Werner lifts his arm, looks down at his waist and wonders quietly 'What was that?' And then there's the footage of me hanging off the fence trying to get back up on to the roadside, captured by David on his DV cam after the main camera stopped rolling at the first sound of gunfire. The effect is not dignified – although my hair seems to be standing up well. So not a complete disaster.

Back in the car, David kept his video camera rolling as Werner strapped himself in, remarking with a frown that 'Los Angeles is not really very friendly toward film-makers.' No kidding! We wanted to call the police and get Werner to a hospital, but Herzog was having none of it. 'It is not a significant bullet,' he kept repeating, adding that 'in Los Angeles if you report a shooting they overreact. They send out a SWAT team with helicopters and squad cars. We don't need that.'

It was clear that Herzog wasn't going to change his mind ('I have been shot at in the jungles of Peru – *that* is being shot at') and so eventually we headed back down the hill toward his house, Werner trudging woundedly up the garden path, apparently resigned to the fact that he really did attract crazy people wherever he went.

Inside the house, David and the crew began to assemble the barrage of lights, cameras and dolly tracks that make any television interview look like a small-scale military intervention. In a matter of moments we had successfully rendered Herzog's house unfit for human habitation, a criss-crossing maze of power leads and camera cables making every step a potentially electrifying experience. (People who work in television – myself included – complain endlessly about all the health and safety red tape we have to deal with but honestly it's surprising that more people don't die while attempting to tell Richard and Judy about their fifteen-year battle with IBS.) Herzog eyed the expanding chaos with mild amusement before falling into conversation with our cameraman about some innovation in the field of digital photography. Meanwhile I lurked in the background, trying to figure out how to approach the forthcoming interview in the wake of all that weirdness up on Lookout Mountain. Eventually we were ready, and Herzog eased himself gingerly into his chair, ready and willing to be probed, if not actively penetrated.

Herzog was engrossing, and his company effervescent. He spoke eloquently about *Wrestlemania* as a modern form of Greek theatre and explained why it had been important to keep abreast of Anna Nicole Smith's reality TV show. He talked about being a 'good soldier for cinema' and of the poet's responsibility to look the world in the eye and to have 'no fear'. And he spoke movingly of Treadwell's grisly death, the sounds of which had been captured on Timothy's own camera but which Herzog refused to include in his documentary because 'there is such a thing as privacy'. Yet all the time we were talking a voice in the back of my head kept saying: 'He just got shot. He just got *shot*! Jeeze Louise, he *really* did *really* just get *really* shot. *Really*. Surely he's hurt. What if he's *bleeding*? What if he's hurt *and* bleeding and I'm just sitting here talking to him about *movies* and ecstatic truth and *Wrestlemania* and Anna Nicole Smith and all the while his insides are gradually becoming his *outsides*? What if the bullet's still inside him? Isn't that *bad*? Isn't that *very bad indeed*? Won't it go septic? Doesn't someone have to suck it out? Oh no, that's snakes, isn't it. Westerns. Sorry, wrong genre. OK, what do they do in cop movies? Should we pour whiskey on the wound and then get Herzog to bite down on a stick while I remove the bits with a red-hot blade? No, that's Westerns again. Damn, I can't think straight. But that's because I'm talking to a man who *just got shot and has now probably got a bullet lodged in his abdomen*. Why isn't he weeping in pain? Why isn't he giving me a letter and demanding that I promise to take it to his sweetheart in Bavaria? Did any of this really happen? What the hell *is* happening …?'

Eventually I could contain it no more. 'Look Werner,' I blurted as the crew stopped to change tapes. 'I can't just go on not mentioning this. We have to talk about this whole getting shot thing.'

'It is not signif — '

'I *know* it's "not significant" to you, but that's because you're Werner Herzog, the fearless Bavarian film-maker who has faced down death in the jungles of Peru. But I am Mark Kermode the much less fearless film critic who once had fifty pence stolen from him by a tough-looking teenager on Whetstone High Street and thought that was pretty *Mean Streets* so it is *not insignificant to me*! OK? And about half an hour ago I was standing next to you in gun-toting Los Angeles when smoke started to emerge from the waistband of your trousers. And to me that seems *very significant indeed*. And I *need* to talk about it. If that's OK with you.'

'It is OK,' Werner shrugged.

'On camera!' said David in a not very sotto voce stage-whisper.

'What?' we both replied in unison.

'You need to talk about it *on camera* ...'

It transpired that David had no idea whether or not the shooting, which we'd all witnessed and which was now proving so preoccupying, had actually been captured on film. If it *hadn't*, and if we were going to make reference to it in the finished piece, then we needed something – *anything* – to prove that we weren't *making this all up*.

'It happened,' said Werner. 'And I am happy to prove it ... as long as you don't sensationalise what happened.'

Presumably it wasn't sensational enough already.

'Great. Then when you're ready, we'll talk about it. On camera ...'

The tapes started rolling again. I took a deep breath and tried to look casual.

'So Werner, during the course of your career you've been shot at a couple of times. And in fact when we started this interview somebody took a shot at you, and they *hit* you.'

'Yes, yes,' Herzog demurred, beaming, apparently now finding this hilarious. 'Yes, it hit me. I *heard* it. And it hurts a little bit.'

'And I was standing right next to you ...' I interjected.

'Yes, but it is not a significant bullet.'

'So have you got a wound?'

'Yes. I think so.'

'Well *show* me. Let me *see*.'

Unperturbed, Werner got up and started to loosen the leather belt around his waist and undo the top of his trousers. 'I'm sorry,' he intoned drolly, with just a hint of sauciness. 'I shouldn't do this on camera …'

The belt was lengthy, the buttons fiddly, and the overall effect like some bizarrely clumsy striptease. Come Inside! Bavarian Film-Makers – All Nude! But with a degree of fumbling Herzog got his trousers open and lifted up his jumper to reveal blood seeping through into his white woollen vest. Another layer was peeled back to reveal a pair of purple paisley boxer shorts now emblazoned with a darkening red patch. The surreal burlesque continued as the elasticated waistband of his boxers came down to reveal a palpable hole in Herzog's abdomen where (as Billy Bragg once poetically put it) no hole should be. The wound was about the size of a dime, with an angry red bruise spreading out from its enticing epicentre. For a second Herzog teasingly fingered the surrounding flesh, causing the wound to gape briefly like the mouth of a tiny sea anemone. Then after this quick illicit flash the boxers came back up like the feathers of one of Mrs Henderson's racy dancers, and Werner was back – intacto.

'But Werner you're bleeding!' I protested. 'Someone has shot at you and created a wound in your abdomen.'

'It is not significant,' Werner repeated.

'But to *you* it's like this is some sort of everyday thing. "Hello I'm Werner Herzog, the film-maker who gets shot at!"'

'It's not an everyday thing,' laughed Herzog, still retying his belt, 'but it does not *surprise* me to be shot at.'

The cameras stopped rolling, and Werner walked to the sink to get a drink of water, limping very slightly but otherwise apparently unharmed. David was fiddling with something technical in the corner, and called me over for a discreet word.

'We need to get him to a hospital,' he said quietly.

'He won't go,' I replied.

'I know, but for heaven's sake, you *saw* it. He's wounded. OK, it's probably a *small* wound, but do any of us have any idea what a *big* wound is meant to look like? I don't. What if that *is* a "big wound"? What if there's something stuck inside him?'

'I know, I *know*,' I whispered. 'I've been thinking exactly the same thing. What if he gets septicaemia? Isn't that what happens in movies? Someone gets wounded and no one does anything about it and the next thing someone else is having to saw their leg off without anaesthetic because gangrene's set in. Or is that only in Westerns?'

Werner was wandering back from the sink, admiring the mini-DV cams, utterly at ease.

'Look, Werner ...' David and I said in unison. 'We need to get you to a hospital.'

'No!' he said firmly. 'No hospital!'

'But why not? You're hurt. What if you've been ...damaged?'

'Because,' said Werner, 'if I go to hospital with what looks like a gunshot wound then they call the police. And it doesn't matter if you did the shooting or the getting shot *at* – you are *part* of the shooting. It is a lot of trouble. And anyway, I am fine.'

David had a brief go at pulling rank with some 'BBC health and safety' regulations shtick but Werner was having none of it, so eventually we gave up.

Defeated, we packed the gear into the vehicles, the cameras going into a van while David and I piled into his pokey little rental car. We said goodbye to Werner, and pulled away from the house, watching him waving from his garden looking exactly as he had looked when we arrived – only without the bullet hole, obviously.

We trundled down through Laurel Canyon in silence, the oddly pastoral sound effects of the Hollywood Hills warbling away in the background. Finally, I spoke.

'I need alcohol,' I said firmly. 'And food. Although I could probably live without the food.'

'Right,' said David. 'Where do we go to get alcohol? Or maybe food?'

Neither of us had any idea. To be honest, we weren't entirely sure what day of the week it was. I'd only arrived at the airport a couple of hours earlier and my head was still going round and round the baggage carousel.

'Let's go back to the hotel and regroup,' said David.

'Good idea,' I replied. 'As long as we go straight out again and get alcohol. And maybe food. But with the emphasis on the alcohol.'

So we drove down toward Sunset, toward the thrumming

metropolitan area around the Chateau Marmont and the Standard and the Hyatt, just round the corner from the Magic Castle, and all the other reassuringly familiar hotels in which I habitually stayed (along with every other passing media type) whenever I was filming in Hollywood. For some reason, however, David seemed to be going the wrong way, heading *down* Sunset toward the less salubrious end of town, past the 'Sunset Strip' club (Girls! Girls! Girls!) and the In-N-Out burger joint (Burger and Fries $1.99!) and the 'Cheques Cashed' minimart, drifting inexorably toward that end of town where people tend to congregate in search of assistance – financial, sexual and chemical.

'David, where are we going?' I asked.

'We're here!' he announced, pulling into a side street and stopping outside a shabby hotel which seemed to have been specifically positioned for ease of access to pushers and pimps. And burgers.

'Here? Where is "*here*"?'

'At the hotel.'

'Sorry, what do you mean "at the hotel?"'

'I mean "at the hotel" as in "we are at the hotel in which we are staying".'

I peered out into the gloom. Two hours ago I was getting shot at on some alien LA hillside. But that was a walk in the park compared to this.

'David, you're not serious. You're not really staying in *this* hotel.'

'No,' said David. '*We* are staying in this hotel. What's the problem? It's fine. I've been here two nights already.'

The hotel, it transpired, was not David's choice, but had been booked by a production co-ordinator in London who was apparently mad keen on saving licence-payers' money. David understood this admirable intention and was clearly making do. But he was made of sterner (and less pampered) stuff than me.

'But *David*,' I bleated, 'we are in the "wrong part of town", the part of town where people come seeking the kind of "refreshment" for which you and I are not in the market. This is the part of town where anyone who is not a hooker, a pimp, a junkie, a pusher or a john, is clearly *lost*. You could probably get picked up by the police just for being here *without* intent to purchase hard drugs and be beaten up by a large and heavily tattooed transvestite. I wouldn't even park here let alone *stay* here. So please tell me that this is an example of your darkly ironic New York wit, and I will laugh indulgently, and then we can head back *up* Sunset to the nice part where the wanky media types like you and me stay and we can pretend that this never happened.'

'Don't be silly,' said David. 'It's fine. Grab the bag. And the camera.'

'"*Grab the camera*"? Are you *mad*? You want me to parade around the streets with a *big expensive camera*? Why don't I just pin a hundred-dollar bill to my forehead and stand on the street corner shouting, "Hey, I'm from out of town and I'm clearly lost so please mug me!"'

'You're being ridiculous,' said David. 'How bad can it be? Look, we just got shot at in Laurel Canyon and that's meant to be "safe".'

'Oh right. And somehow that's meant to make me feel better is it? The reassurance that *everywhere* is just as dangerous as *everywhere else*?'

But David had gone on inside, and I had no choice but to follow, camera in one hand, kitbag in the other, a look of petulant self-indulgent misery and loathing stamped across my middle-class British face. How bad could it be?

As it turned out, very bad indeed. Having conducted my usual anally retentive room-disinfecting routine (take a towel from the bathroom, place it on the bedspread – the one part of the bed that *never* gets changed or cleaned – grab the bedpsread *through* the towel thereby avoiding physical contact with the vast bacterial ecosystem now thriving thereon, and throw the resulting bundle into the furthest corner of the room before covering it with a *second* towel), I set about investigating the regular thumping sound coming from the wall by the head of the bed. Depressingly, it did indeed turn out to be the soul-destroying sound of the bedstead on the *other* side of the wall (which appeared to have been made of Kleenex and spit) rhythmically shifting back and forth as a couple trudged their slow but sure way toward some form of quasi-congressional climax. Every now and then you could hear some gasping ecstatic yelp the gender of which seemed curiously non-specific. Over the course of the subsequent evening, the neighbours made two further explorational sorties into the world of fleshy fun, each louder and more laborious than the last. Despite the fact that I never laid eyes on them, by morning I felt that I knew them both quite well.

'Alcohol,' I said out loud. Again. 'I *need* alcohol,' and I slammed the door shut and trudged down the corridor toward David's room. When I say 'corridor', of course, I mean no such thing. The connecting passage between David's room and mine was an open walkway which fronted straight on to Sunset, so that anyone who felt the need to do so could actually walk off the pavement and into the room without effort, thus giving the hotel an alarmingly earthy street-side ambiance. (This was also presumably the sort of street-facing window through which the car-jack wielding Batman clone came hurtling in search of Herzog.) More alarming still was the fact that David had *opened his curtains* – a wildly impetuous act as far as I was concerned.

'For heaven's sake David,' I bleated, sounding increasingly like Little Lord Fauntleroy. 'You can't *open the curtains*! You'll be killed in your sleep. And you *can't* put the camera there. Hide it in the wardrobe. Or in the bathroom. Or, better still, move the wardrobe *into* the bathroom and then hide it in *both* of them. Just to be safe.'

David rolled his eyes upward, grabbed his jacket and keys, and strode out into the night.

'Come on,' he said, 'let's go and get some food.'

'And alcohol?'

'Yes, Mark – "and alcohol".'

And off we went.

The next morning we rang Werner to see if he was still OK. Unsurprisingly his abdomen had stiffened up overnight, and the wound itself had become rather more painful. But he insisted that he'd dressed it and it was still 'not significant', so after a few minutes of pleading for him to allow us to take him to hospital we said our goodbyes.

Back in London, we struggled to figure out how to put the piece together. David had checked the tapes and confirmed that the cameras had indeed been rolling when the shot was fired, and everything was captured – both sound and vision. But could we actually *use* any of that footage? Since Herzog had been so determined to downplay the entire event, wouldn't we be exploiting him if we showed the shooting on TV? There also remained the issue of who was to blame for the whole weird affair – not in terms of who fired the shot, but who was responsible for Herzog's safety when the shooting happened. Had we somehow inadvertently placed him in danger?

This latter question particularly troubled David, who is both a brilliant director and an Olympic-level worrier. If David can find a way to take the responsibility (or more precisely the blame) for something then he will do so. That's what makes him such a terrific person to work with – if it all goes well, I get the glory; if things screw up (which they never do with David), it's all *his* fault. Perfect!

We swiftly resolved that we wouldn't do anything with the footage without Herzog's permission. Nor would we talk to anyone about what had happened – although word was already leaking out that 'something really weird' had happened during the interview. After all, if Herzog wanted the issue to remain private, then that was his right.

As it turned out, we needn't have worried. A few days after our return to the UK I started getting emails from people in LA who had heard all about Herzog and the 'crazed sniper' – from Herzog himself. One particular contact sent me a digital photo of Herzog on the set of Harmony Korine's new film (in which he played a small role) proudly displaying the wound to all and sundry. By now the bruise surrounding the hole had started to go a bit manky, and looked a lot larger and angrier than when I had last set eyes on it. But Werner seemed happy and otherwise unharmed, and was clearly enjoying regaling the assembled masses with tales of his fearlessness in the face of adversity.

As the weeks went on the story grew, appearing first in the *Hollywood Reporter*, and then in newspapers back here in the UK. A couple of journalists rang me to check the details, and I confirmed that yes, Herzog had indeed been utterly unflapped by this sudden unexpected violation of his person. And as the story grew, two interesting things happened. Firstly, an 'axis of terror' began to emerge, growing in stature and imbalance with each subsequent retelling of the tale. Within this economy of fear, Herzog's own stoical response to the shooting became increasingly matched and even outdone by a growing hysterical cowardliness on the part of the BBC crew. The braver he got, the more whimpering we became. By the time Herzog recounted the story to Henry Rollins on American TV a few months later, the assembled Brits had been reduced to the status of mere quivering wrecks, fleeing at the first sign of danger while the Bavarian legend impassively took incoming fire.

'Oh yes,' announced Werner proudly when questioned about the press reports. 'I *was* shot on camera while being interviewed by the BBC. It was up near Lookout Mountain … But it was not such a serious bullet anyway. It was probably only a small-calibre rifle. Or a high-powered air rifle. So I was only slightly wounded. I didn't even realise what had happened. I thought that the camera had exploded and something had hit and burned me. And I only realised when I saw the soundman ducking and hitting the ground and then part of the crew fled …!'

'Was anyone ever apprehended?' asked Rollins.

'No, I didn't want to have police called because they would have overreacted and I thought this was not a serious bullet, this is part of the folklore of out here. This is something we can laugh about later on. And we laughed a lot.'

So at least he found it funny.

Quite funny.

Rollins put his head in his hands.

'But I've been shot at with much more serious bullets before in my life,' continued Werner. 'And what I'm trying to say is that it is something very … *exhilarating* … for a man to be shot at with little success!'

The second result of all this press interest was a perhaps inevitable conspiracy theory which grew up on the internet (where else?) suggesting that the whole thing was a stunt designed to make Werner look brave, and orchestrated by

David Shulman and myself. Key to this interpretation was the offhand phrase which I had used to describe the effect of the bullet hitting Herzog's trousers – that it looked as though a firecracker had gone off in his pocket. I had evidently repeated this phrase a few times on my return to England and through the usual process of half-heard Chinese whispers it had transmogrified into a private confession that I had planted a firecracker in Herzog's trousers to make it *look* like he'd been shot. I had, in effect, blown up Werner's boxers.

This latter development came as no surprise. When faced with any random irrational event, conspiracy theorists will invariably seek to replace ludicrous chaos with reassuring order, convincing themselves that all the nutso things that happen in the world are actually carefully planned and calculated. Personally I think this helps them feel safer, more secure. Hey, I used to take solace in Gail Brewer-Giorgio's bonkers books *Is Elvis Alive?* and *The Elvis Files* which argued that a fit and healthy Presley had carefully planned and faked his death in 1977, fled Graceland in a helicopter and then restarted his life in privacy and seclusion. Why? Simply because it was less depressing than believing that my hero had got too tired, sloppy and drug-addled to live. And as the King himself said, 'If I can dream, then why can't my dream come true?'

And in some perverse and twisted way it *did* come true in the wake of the Herzog shooting – sort of. After years of being on the outside looking in I suddenly found myself at the centre of my very own conspiracy theory, an all-access pass to a richly cinematic fantasy world in which Nixon killed

JFK, Bush blew up the Twin Towers, Elvis was alive, and I shot Werner Herzog. I could go on the internet and read thrilling accounts of how I had secreted explosives in the region of Werner's crown jewels. One astute viewer noted that if you look closely at the footage of the interview you can clearly see that Werner's head turns the *wrong way* in response to the alleged angle of the 'shooting', adding a Zapruder-style 'back and to the left' analysis to the events.

In the end I thought I might as well join in the madness and recorded a video blog on the BBC's *Kermode Uncut* site in which I confessed to having set up the whole Herzog shooting.

If everyone *says* I did it – maybe I *did*.

Maybe 'real life' is only a movie after all …

Since then, my path has continued to cross with Herzog's, and every time we are together the story of the Lookout Mountain sniper and the 'insignificant bullet' comes up. In 2009 I hosted an onstage Q&A with Herzog to celebrate him receiving the BBC4 World Cinema Award for Outstanding Achievement. Backstage he was in his usual dourly ebullient mood, repeating his life-defining mantra that 'the poet must not avert his gaze' no matter how ugly and putrescent the subject matter. At one point he told me in grave tones that a 'respectable' newspaper in the US had recently referred to him as 'certifiably mad'. 'They were writing about the fact that David Lynch's company was involved in producing my film,' he explained. 'And they said "the certifiably mad Werner Herzog and the probably mad David Lynch". Can you believe it? "Certifiably mad"? Me?' He sounded genuinely hurt.

On stage we talked about Herzog's latest documentary film *Encounters at the End of the World* in which he travelled to Antarctica with the specific intention of avoiding 'fluffy penguins' in his search for 'deeper truths'. We touched on his non-remake of *Bad Lieutenant*, the original of which was about the burden of guilt while Herzog enticingly described his version as being about 'the bliss of evil!' It sounded great. Eventually the conversation turned to *Grizzly Man*, and the subject which continues to trouble me most about Herzog's declared world view.

'The thing is,' I said in my most stentorian fashion, 'I have something to say about your theory of the universe being nothing but "chaos, hostility and murder".'

In fact, I had a *lot* to say about this theory which had haunted me ever since our first meeting amid the chaotic, murderous hostility of LA. But in a rare break from tradition I had managed to condense my shambling incoherent thoughts into a single punchy sentence, and I had waited until now to tell Werner (and you, dear reader) what I *really* thought of his films and his philosophy. This was it – all or nothing.

'One of the things that convinces me that that is *not* the case,' I ventured tentatively, 'is the beauty that I see in your films, and I just can't see how "chaos, hostility and murder" could produce something that beautiful.'

Herzog looked up at me with a glint in his eye, smiling slightly with either compassion or despair – I couldn't rightly tell. He'd been to the end of the world and looked death in the face – more than once – and now here he was in the cosy surroundings of London's South Bank being told by some woolly-headed English halfwit that his films were too 'beautiful' to be the product of an essentially godless universe. Still, at least I'd told him what I thought – at least I'd been *honest* with him, which is just about the only thing I think any film critic can be. Stupid, but honest. He could laugh at me if he wanted.

But he didn't. Instead, he put his hands together on his knees, let a smile break over his face, leaned in closer toward the microphone, and very quietly said: 'Well . . . I stem the tide.'

There was a moment's silence before the audience burst into ecstatic applause. Werner was grinning, the crowd was hooting, and the room was filled with a life-affirming vigour which thrummed through the auditorium like the sound of God laughing. And in that one fleeting moment, I experienced something akin to the 'ecstatic truth' which Herzog had made his life's pursuit; we were alive, together, and *conscious*, aware of our own mortality, but thrilled by the fact of our own ridiculous existence.

Afterwards, when the crowds of adoring fans had all shaken hands with the maestro and basked briefly in his oddly radiant presence, I found myself alone in a corner waiting for a car to take me home. Werner wandered over to say how much he'd enjoyed himself (as is traditional) and to ask if I was going to be back in LA anytime soon.

'Yes, I've got to go and interview Coppola next month,' I replied, at which he seemed unimpressed.

'Incidentally Werner,' I added, 'have you still got a scar from where that bullet hit you during our interview?'

'Oh yes,' he replied, although this time he declined to get his trousers off to show me.

'Does it ever hurt?' I asked

'Only when I laugh,' he replied. 'If I laugh really … profoundly … then I suddenly get a searing pain in my abdomen.'

And with that we went our separate ways.

On the journey home I thought about Herzog and that magic bullet and the peculiar way in which it had bonded us together; the visionary secularist Bavarian film-maker and the dewey-eyed God-bothering liberal critic from Barnet. And I thought about the fact that every time Herzog, with all his rigorous anti-sentimentalism, was *really* enjoying himself he would feel an annoying pain in his side.

And, in some poetically appropriate way, that pain would be me.

# EPILOGUE

Angelina Jolie likes my hair. She said so. In those exact words.

'I do like your hair,' she said, looking at my hair.

'Do you?' I replied, pretending not to care, like Pooh Bear.

'Yeah,' she confirmed – just in case there was any doubt.

'Thank you very much,' I replied. 'I like my hair too.'

And then, almost as an afterthought, Ange added, 'I must get Brad to do that …'

'Well of course he already *did*,' I burbled. 'In that film *Johnny Suede*.' This was true. Before becoming officially the Sexiest Man in the World Ever, Brad Pitt had starred somewhat self-deprecatingly in a little New York indie-pic directed by Tom DiCillo who famously shot Jim Jarmusch's black and white cult favourite *Stranger than Paradise*. The titular character was a somewhat dorky fifties throwback who worships Ricky Nelson and sports a bouffant pompadour on which you could balance your hat, coat and shoes and still have space for a compact Wurlitzer jukebox. I really loved that movie, and indeed the British poster consisted of a picture of Brad's hair with the quote 'Quifftastic! – Mark Kermode, *Q Magazine*' emblazoned across it.

'Oh right,' said Angelina, nonplussed. 'I never saw that movie ...'

So that was that.

I still wonder from time to time whether, in between bouts of photogenically physical interaction, Ange ever turned to her beloved and said, 'Hey, I met this weird middle-aged English journalist with really great hair and I think you should try to look more like him ...'

Probably not.

Still, it's something to tell the grandchildren.

My grandchildren, not hers, obviously.

I mention this incident only because I'm pretty much done here, and I realise that I haven't mentioned it before. This is fairly typical – I'll spend ten pages talking about *Krakatoa: East of Java* and then fail to mention one of the very few events in my life that might actually constitute a bona fide 'celebrity anecdote'. I'm rubbish at those, as you've probably noticed.

But having pitched this book to you as the reading equivalent of a TV Movie of the Week I feel I that should attempt to stay true to its generic roots. I could always take a steer from *The Karen Carpenter Story* which starts with our heroine pegging out to the strains of 'Rainy Days and Mondays' but somehow manages to end with her telling her mom that she loves her and then breaking out into a great big cheese-eating grin. So even though Karen died of heart failure at the age of thirty-two, the film still manages to have a happy ending! Brilliant!

As for Ange's comments about my hair, they are perfect 'Chubby? Hmmm…' fodder, providing a neat narrative bookend which I wish I'd thought of when I started writing this, but it's far too late to go back and fix it now.

Picture the scene: we open on a sepia-toned shot of an awkward young kid with stupid unruly hair being mocked at school and called 'Mr Pineapple Head', which was just one of the terms used to deride my upstanding hair when I was young. Other insulting sobriquets included 'Spiny Norman', a reference to the imaginary twelve-foot hedgehog from Monty Python's Piranha Brothers sketch, and 'Bogbrush' which I think is fairly self-explanatory.

The camera follows this scrawny kid home, *alone*, passing en route a cinema (showing a double bill of *The Exorcist* and *Mary Poppins*) and a desolate barber's shop, the window of which showcases a handsome array of male hairdressing products and pomades. Cut from here to the kid at home, spooning wax into his hair, with Elvis playing on an orange plastic Decca Dansette, his mum shouting from downstairs for him to come and have his tea, but his attention entirely gripped by the sleekly handsome quiff which he has skilfully crafted from his previously ragtag spikes.

The camera closes in on said quiff, delving into the hair like David Lynch's extreme lawn close-up at the beginning of *Blue Velvet* which foretells great horrors to come. Then we pull back to reveal that very same hairstyle, utterly unchanged, although now it adorns the head of our adult star (Jason Isaacs to the set, please) whose barnet has remained immovable despite the passage of time and the ageing of his face.

After which we'd get the movie, which would be pretty much what you've just read – or 'skimmed', as is apparently popular. Then, as the end approaches, we'd come to the crucial scene in which La Jolie (played by herself – as a favour to me) compliments Jason's hair in the most fulsome manner. He laughs nonchalantly but then, unexpectedly, seems to retreat into his own inner world. As the crowd of technicians and cameramen scuttle on the outskirts of the frame, we follow Mr Isaacs back to his dressing room where he sits silently in front of a mirror and takes out two old battered tins – one red, one blue – and places them on the table before him.

Slowly, the music starts to swell and as it does so we see Jason staring at his own reflection in the mirror, the distorted sounds of childhood taunts echoing around his head like the creepy kids' nursery rhyme ('One, two, Freddy's coming for you ...') in *A Nightmare on Elm Street*. As we watch, the reflected image of Jason's face dissolves into a nostalgic scene of the previously awkward kid striding boldly through the school corridors, ignoring the jeers of his classmates, safe in the knowledge that his hair is immaculate and they are all just idiots.

He is right, they are wrong. End of story.

At some point the kid looks over his shoulder, straight

into the eyes of his older self, and winks. Then the camera pans down from the mirror on to the tins of pomade, and the credits roll …

'Sponsored by Dax and Sweet Georgia Brown
Fine pomades for a life free from frizz'

THE END

# ACKNOWLEDGEMENTS

Despite its rampagingly egotistical nature, this book has benefited hugely from the input of others so, in the manner of Kate Winslet's Golden Globes speech, I would like to '*gather*' and say thank you to:

Linda Ruth Williams, who lived this movie with me, and then had to live it all over again (and *again*) as my uncredited producer, script-editor, assistant director, sound mixer, and test audience.

Hedda Archbold at Hidden Flack, for her wise guidance and repeated use of the phrase 'don't worry, I'll sort it out' – which she invariably did.

Sophie Lazar at Random House, for being an exemplary editor who endured endless 'tweaks' and demands for 'a bigger chainsaw' with unflappable finesse.

Geoff Andrew, Mariano Baino, Nick Cooper, Nigel Floyd, Ed Glinert, Nick Jones, Simon Mayo, Saul Rosenberg, David Shulman, Andy Spinoza, Sarah Ward, and Tim Worman for reading (and correcting) the parts of the story which they remember far better than I do.

Craig Lapper and Sue Clark at the BBFC for being constantly available to answer 'just a very quick question…'

Kim Newman, for his encyclopaedic film-fact checking; and Alex Archbold Jones for knowing his cannibals.

And Jason Isaacs.

# INDEX